Healthy Anger

Also by Bernard Golden

New Hope for People with Bipolar Disorder
(coauthored with Jan Fawcett and Nancy Rosenfeld)

Healthy Anger

*How to Help Children and Teens
Manage Their Anger*

Bernard Golden, Ph.D.

OXFORD

UNIVERSITY PRESS

2003

OXFORD
UNIVERSITY PRESS

Oxford   New York
Auckland   Bangkok   Buenos Aires
Cape Town   Chennai   Dar es Salaam   Delhi
Hong Kong   Istanbul   Karachi   Kolkata
Kuala Lumpur   Madrid   Melbourne
Mexico City   Mumbai   Nairobi   São Paolo
Shanghai   Taipei   Tokyo   Toronto

Copyright © 2003 by Bernard Golden

Published by Oxford University Press, Inc.
198 Madison Avenue, New York, New York 10016
www.oup.com

Oxford is a registered trademark of Oxford University Press

Library of Congress Cataloging-in-Publication Data
Golden, Bernard
Healthy anger : how to help children and teens
manage their anger / Bernard Golden
p.   cm.   Includes bibliographical references and index.
ISBN 0–19–515657–9
1. Anger in children.
2. Anger in adolescence.
3. Child rearing.
I. Title.
BF723.A4 G65 2002   155.4'1247—dc21   2002022009

Criteria for depression and other disorders described in Chapter 17 are reprinted with
permission from the *Diagnostic and Statistical Manual of Mental Disorders,* Fourth
Edition, Text Revision. Copyright © 2000 American Psychiatric Association.

"Warning Signs of Teen Violence," brochure cited in Chapter 17. Copyright © 1999
by the American Psychological Association. Adapted with permission. For additional
information, visit http://helping.apa.org/warningsigns.

Typeset by Glen R.J. Mules, New Rochelle, NY

1 3 5 7 9 8 6 4 2
Printed in the United States of America
on acid-free paper

𝒞

To Dale

𝒞

Contents

Acknowledgments

Completing this book marks the end of a very long and rewarding journey. It is one I have taken with the personal and professional support of family, friends, and colleagues. Therefore, I would like to express my deepest gratitude to some of the many people who have helped make *Healthy Anger* possible.

First, I am extremely grateful to Nancy Rosenfeld, my friend, my agent, and the source of the idea for *New Hope for People with Bipolar Disorder*, a book she and I coauthored with Dr. Jan Fawcett. The feedback and encouragement she provided on that project and this book helped push me in a direction to make the manuscripts the best they could be. I am again, and still, appreciative of her determination, drive, and commitment to quality.

I want to also thank the many friends and colleagues who over the years have listened to my ideas and offered critical feedback and support. Specifically, I want to thank Drs. Bonnie Holstein, Bonnie Rudolph, Frank Gruber-McCallister, Adrienne Allert, and Robert Marshall.

I am also grateful to Ray Bramble, a friend and colleague who contributed to my doctoral research and for almost three decades listened to my plan to write a book about anger.

I am especially thankful to Dr. Patricia Robbins for her thoughtful consideration and confidence in introducing me to Nancy Rosenfeld.

I am most appreciative of Joan Bossert for her extremely supportive response when we first contacted Oxford. As vice president and associate publisher, she gave this project a most powerful reception that convinced me that Oxford was the best possible publisher for this book. I am also grateful to other members of the Oxford team, including Helen Mules, Sue Warga, and Kim Robinson.

I want to thank my mother for her love, support, and ongoing encouragement, especially in the writing of this book.

Finally, I want to thank the many clients and their families, the workshop participants, and the students I have worked with, all of whom taught me many lessons regarding anger.

January 2002   B.G.

Introduction

Whether observing the annoyance of a two-year-old demanding to have his way or responding to the hostile, rejecting rage of a distraught adolescent seeking greater independence, dealing with a child's anger is one of the most frustrating and challenging tasks a parent faces. Such anger usually arouses in parents a variety of intense emotions, including hurt, guilt, rejection, frustration, confusion, and, yes, even anger. Through words and by their behavior, consciously and unconsciously, parents greatly influence how their child thinks about and handles anger. At the same time, children and teens receive a wide variety of messages about anger from peers, siblings, teachers, others in the community, and the media.

As an outcome of such influence, some children learn constructive ways to manage anger. In contrast, many children learn ineffective ways of managing anger. While the negative impact of mismanaged anger may be minimal, it may also lead to a variety of more severe emotional and behavioral difficulties such as underachievement, social isolation, substance abuse, excessive guilt, depression, and interpersonal conflict. The child who has not developed appropriate strategies for the expression of anger experiences much pain and anguish in his adult life.

In part, my own difficulties with anger as a child prompted my interest in the subject as well as my desire to help children and teens more successfully manage the many challenges of responding to this emotion.

My anger never really resulted in seriously harming anyone. I was never in trouble with the law, and I never became violent like the teens we sometimes hear about in the headlines. Nevertheless, I experienced a host of difficulties related to my anger. Early on I found that I was often quick to anger. As a young child, I was involved in a number of altercations. One of them was with my neighbor Jay.

I was about eight years old at the time. Jay was ten but bragged about being almost eleven. He was four inches taller and ten pounds heavier than me. I really do not recall what started it. We were angrily wrestling, each trying with all his might to pin down the other. He was getting the better of me, making my face meet the dry, powdery dirt that was part of the construction site a block away from where we lived. Jay was a friend of my older brother, another member of the elite group of friends that I wanted so much to join.

As we fought, I scraped my right arm and the knuckles of my left hand. We took turns pinning each other down, once on our backs, again on our bellies. For a moment I was feeling quite proud that I could hold my own against one of the older kids on the block. But very shortly I was feeling quite winded, especially after being forced to inhale some of the dirt and grit that lodged in my nose and throat. I managed to turn over, but he was once again able to pin me down on my back with both arms held in check.

Then it happened. In hindsight, although I do not recall feeling especially threatened, I must have anticipated that I would be seriously hurt if I did not take immediate action. All at once I became overwhelmed by frustration and rage. I forcefully removed my right arm from his grip and impulsively reached over to pick up one of the many rocks that had been pulled up from the ground to make room for the Cross Bronx Expressway. It wasn't huge, but it was big enough that I couldn't fully close my fist around it. Holding it tightly, I arched my arm to the side in order to maximize my swing. Initially aiming for his head, I drew my weapon forward. But then, like a batter who changes his mind in the middle of a swing, it suddenly occurred to me: "This is crazy! I can't really hit him with this rock." I instantly slowed my arm and, with renewed control, tapped him on the shoulder with the rock. It was enough to get his attention without really hurting him, but it was threatening enough to get him off me.

This was just one of many examples in my childhood when I recognized I had a short fuse and had difficulty with anger. It seemed that I rapidly moved from annoyance to rage, with few gradations of anger in between.

Now, you might read this and wonder how, at age eight, I was able to talk myself into gaining control. In actuality, in spite of the physical altercations I had as a child, I was very self-conscious and reflective. Following that incident, I vowed not to let myself become that angry again. However, I still did not know how to manage such anger, and gradually I began to minimize, deny, or stifle it. As a consequence, I often experienced and focused my attention on a range of negative emotions instead of anger. As I will emphasize throughout this book, when we experience anger, we also experience emotional pain in some form, whether disappointment, rejection, frustration, guilt, or shame. These are the negative emotions that precede anger and are associated with it. When I felt uncomfortable with anger, I increasingly became more aware of and focused on these other emotions. But I no longer lost control of my anger.

Messages from family and those around me communicated that I should not be angry—and that when I was, I was making a big deal of what was really a minor issue. My parents, like most parents then and now, dealt with anger and emotions in general in the best way they knew how. Their behaviors and messages, both direct and indirect, communicated that anger was not a good thing. As I tried to avoid anger, I similarly began to second-guess the appropriateness of other emotions. In sum, I developed confused beliefs and self-doubts regarding assertiveness, anger, and conflict.

These early experiences and my work at better understanding and managing them led to my interest in emotional awareness and development in general and anger in particular. Even as a student in elementary school, I was puzzled by the absence of discussions regarding emotions, including anger. Over time I developed my strong belief that we need to prepare children and teens to effectively make sense of and manage anger, from the mild intensity of annoyance through intense rage.

Years later, as an elementary school teacher in the South Bronx during the late 1960s and early 1970s, I purposely chose to work with disruptive children. Many of these children experienced anger for a variety of reasons, including living in one of the most deprived areas in our nation. I quickly found that my passion for teaching was related to seeing these children develop openness to self-reflection and candidly explore their feelings about important issues in their lives. While emotional education was not a core subject of the curriculum, I helped these children explore anger and other emotions in the context of studying current events, history, literature, and composition. I firmly believed then, as I do now, that such reflection frees us to be connected with others and ourselves. Through this process children and teens can be helped to truly value themselves. As a consequence, they can be more empathic with others and with themselves. Such empathy is the foundation for constructively managing anger.

Most significant is that as an outgrowth of my teaching experience, I became further convinced of the need to prepare children and teens to effectively make sense of and manage anger before they resort to more destructive strategies for dealing with this highly charged emotion.

I have personally worked with hundreds of children, teens, and adults whose depression or anxiety was very much related to their difficulties in recognizing, understanding, accepting, and managing anger. These are often individuals who have become fearful of their own anger as well as that expressed by others. Many of them are paralyzed by guilt and shame about their anger and are quick to minimize and suppress anger due to fears of rejection or abandonment. These are children, teens, and adults who have not had the opportunity to learn constructive ways of dealing with anger. For the most part, they were children who learned to handle their anger by chance, without open and clear discussion, guidelines, and support.

I have also worked with children, teens, and adults whose anger was destructive to property, to others, and to themselves—individuals whose anger turned into aggression and who lacked clear and constructive guidelines for channeling anger. Some were victims of physical or emotional abuse. Others, already predisposed to difficulties with anger, were also observing members of an increasingly violent society. These were individuals who experienced little control over managing anger.

Nevertheless, in spite of the significant developmental challenge for children to understand and constructively handle anger, few schools provide parents or children formal classwork and instruction in the management of this complex and charged emotion. Similarly, few books on parenting focus attention on this essential aspect of emotional well-being. And while in recent years there has been an increase in the number of books published about anger, most of these address aggression rather than the full spectrum of anger. The majority of these focus on helping children and teens who already display severe difficulties surrounding anger.

In contrast, *Healthy Anger* focuses on preparing children and teens to make sense of and manage anger long before it escalates to more serious forms of anger, which may include aggression. It reflects the movement of positive psychology, emphasizing and fostering the development of knowledge and skills that are a part of healthy emotional functioning and coping. I have titled this book *Healthy Anger* for this reason. Healthy anger management is based on the following key guiding principles.

1. Anger is a natural human emotion.
2. Anger varies in intensity and duration.
3. Anger is often a reaction to other emotions.
4. Anger is a reaction to emotions and thoughts within us.
5. Anger really tells us more about our own wants and needs than about the person or situation that may lead to our anger.
6. The emotion of anger is distinct from the behavioral expression of anger.
7. As we increase our awareness of thoughts and emotions leading up to anger, we gain increased freedom to choose how we express anger.
8. Healthy anger management is based on specific skills that can be taught.
9. Healthy anger management is based on being able to flexibly choose from a variety of anger management strategies.
10. Real intimacy grows with an increased ability to share anger and other emotions.
11. Healthy anger management involves being able to let go of anger.
12. Learning theory and skills concerning anger management is an essential component for healthy emotional well-being.

In contrast, unhealthy anger management involves attempts to mask, deny, or avoid anger. Children and teens who practice unhealthy anger management experience little control and may be quick to react to anger with hostility or aggression. They may use anger to manipulate others. In addition, they may develop chronic anger that further impairs their judgment and predisposes them to become angry.

This book offers you specific knowledge and practical skills that you can teach your children and teens in order to make sense of and manage anger in everyday life. It is based on the fact that effective anger management involves both understanding the emotion and developing specific skills to manage it. It presents a model of anger that I have developed and used for twenty years. Although originally focused on helping those who have already experienced difficulties with anger, this model has been increasingly applied with a preventive focus. While I began using this approach with clients in inpatient and outpatient settings, I have since presented it in workshops and classes for children, teens, and adults, as well as for parents, teachers, and mental health professionals and in various work settings.

The model of anger presented in this book emphasizes that anger is not an experience that occurs in isolation. Rather, it occurs in the context of an individual's personality. As such, it is influenced by needs, attitudes, perceptions, and emotions. Children confront an anger-provoking event with a personal history that influences how, when, and to what degree they may experience anger. Some of the factors that contribute to this experience include expectations of others and oneself, the ability to be objective, past history with anger, and the ability to "sit with" emotional pain.

Comprehensive education for anger management involves helping children and teens understand that their anger tells them more about themselves than it does about the target of their anger. It involves helping children develop skills in self-reflection to better understand and recognize other emotions related to their anger. Similarly, in-depth anger management involves helping children and teens understand how their thinking impacts their anger. While anger moves us to direct attention outward, self-reflection involves directing our attention inward. This is a fundamental first step in effective anger management.

The constructive expression of anger is also based on the capacity to moderate and manage one's anger. The child who can tolerate the emotional and physical tension stirred up by feelings of anger is a child who develops an internal sense of adequacy, competence, and self-direction based on self-control and self-mastery. Through this experience a child develops a strengthened capacity for self-soothing and dealing with conflict and tension in general. This child becomes an adult who understands that anger can be a rich emotional resource that can motivate someone to right what is wrong, to adaptively respond to adversity, and to strive for success. In a meaningful relationship, healthy self-assertion reflects the constructive expression of anger. Such assertion fosters improved sharing, intimacy, and mutual understanding.

Most important, I focus on addressing anger in the context of a relationship that fosters and reflects connection. Unlike teaching reading, writing, and arithmetic, helping children and teens make sense of and manage anger requires us to focus on our relationship with them. It requires extreme sensitivity, modeling, and a commitment not only to teach but also to learn. It requires a relationship in which we practice empathy, model the strategies presented, and are committed to being open. As parents or caretakers, we have the best opportunity to share this knowledge. Intimacy includes a physical embrace, engaging in activities together, and sharing facts or feelings. However, when we teach our children how to make sense of and manage anger, we form with them a deepened emotional connection as well as give them the gifts of increased awareness and resilience.

I have provided numerous vignettes in an effort to clarify the concepts and skills presented throughout the book. While many of these are based on actual clients, certain details have been changed in order to maintain their confidentiality.

I thank all of those individuals who have provided both knowledge and experience on which I have based my writing. I acknowledge my appreciation to the educators who have provided me formal training, but, more important, I acknowledge my gratitude to the many clients who have taught me about the wide variety of ways in which we express anger. I also thank the many individuals who have attended my workshops and have shared their experiences, concerns, and support.

Finally, I thank you in advance for reading this book, and I wish you patience and success as you respond to the demanding challenge of helping prepare your child to make sense of and manage anger in everyday life.

I

Understanding and Recognizing Anger in Children and Teens

1

The Key Component for Anger Management: Your Relationship with Your Child

In recent years it has become all too common to read newspaper headlines describing the latest incidents of child and adolescent violence. These events are immediately followed by cries for gun control, a reduction of violence in the media and in video games, and an increased emphasis on teaching morality in schools and at home. Addressing these contributing factors may help to prevent some violence. However, while the media highlight violence, only a small percentage of children and teens express anger in this most extreme way. Far more children and teens who have ongoing difficulty with anger exhibit bullying, underachievement, substance abuse, social isolation, truancy, prejudice, gang participation, sexual promiscuity, and suicidal behaviors. At the same time, some children and teens who appear fine on the surface experience depression, excessive guilt or shame, or intense anxiety related to mismanaged anger.

Gun control, the use of metal detectors in schools, reducing violence in the media, and teaching morality may help reduce certain forms of violence and aggression. But in actuality, these remedies may only address secondary contributions to such violence and aggression.[1] Rather, ongoing research continues to support the finding that aggressive and violent children and teens lack a true sense of connection in their relationships—with others and with themselves.

By *connection,* I mean a relationship that actively and openly encourages sharing, discussing, and exploring our internal landscape, including our emotions, thoughts, passions, and fears. It involves a level of intimacy that allows for and is not threatened by expressions of conflict or tension. Children, and especially teens, need these connections with peers, but the strength of the parent-child connection plays a key role in influencing how they manage tension, conflict, and anger.

A relationship with your child that fosters connection is one that can tolerate disagreements, even when you set limits on behaviors that reflect such disagreements. It involves your ability to be empathic with your child's feelings without being overwhelmed by them.

Healthy connection involves a relationship that is nurturing. Specifically, it offers empathy and, in doing so, teaches your child to be empathic. Empathy refers to understanding another person and his thoughts and feelings as if you are that person. Empathic listening involves listening without judgment and letting your child know that you can understand her experience. Being noncritical allows and encourages your child to more freely and fully explore her emotions and thoughts—a major task in making sense of and managing anger. Whether you agree or disagree with your child's perspective is a separate issue from being empathic with her experience and sharing. Most important, being empathic does not imply acceptance of or tolerance for what you deem to be inappropriate behavior.

Such a relationship leads your child to feel loved, and it shows that you are genuinely interested and emotionally invested in her as an individual in her own right. When a child experiences such connection, she does not experience herself as having to live life primarily to satisfy the standards of others. Genuine connection allows a child to learn that her thoughts, emotions, values, and attitudes are respected and have meaning. She does not see her parents as arbitrarily imposing standards and expectations as a reaction to their own needs, hopes, and expectations. Rather, she perceives such standards and expectations as genuinely focused on her overall well-being.

William Pollack, the director of the National Violence Prevention Center, emphasizes, "It is the potency of family connection that guards adolescents from emotional harm and gives them succor from a world that's rough, a niche where they may express their most vulnerable and warm feelings in the open without fear of ridicule. By protecting them from the harm of disconnection, we in turn are protected from being harmed by violence as their desperate last attempt at connection."[2] Your child's connection with himself very much depends on the degree to which he is supported and encouraged to explore his internal life. Specifically, self-reflection allows your child to develop an interest in and understanding of his emotions and thoughts. Healthy connection offers him positive regard and support in getting to know himself. Valuing his internal life gives him permission to self-reflect. Similarly, it frees energy that might otherwise be wasted in minimizing, hiding from, or denying parts of himself.

In contrast, when a child is encouraged to minimize, deny, or suppress her emotions, especially anger, she loses touch with her real feelings, thoughts, and attitudes. As she loses touch she becomes more prone to present a false front to those around her. Once she begins the process of hiding parts of herself, she begins to feel disconnected from herself. This heightens her need to feel connected with others but at the same time makes her feel less secure, more confused, and more tense. When extreme, this level of alienation is accompanied by hurt, disappointment, and a sense of inadequacy that underlies and fosters anger in the form of violence. And it is this same disconnection that leads to difficulties in managing anger even when less intense.

These are children who need connection, not just when they are feeling most alienated but long before they feel so disconnected. These are children who need to be heard. They lack skills in understanding or managing the negative emotions—hurt, rejection, guilt, or disappointment—that can accompany anger and make them feel disconnected. It is through connection and the development of specific skills that your child or teen can be prepared to cope with anger in everyday life. As William Pollack emphasizes in *Real Boys,* boys are raised to mask their real feelings and present an image of strength, bravado, and self-confidence while they hide any evidence of shame regarding vulnerabilities, powerlessness, and loneliness.[3] This idealized image of masculinity, described by Pollack as the "boy code," has been inherited from the days of the pioneers, when men were supposed to show courage. The code is inherited from a time when fathers were minimally involved with their sons and related to them only when they were old enough to help out by doing their share of the work on the farm or ranch.

Boys raised to follow the "boy code" try desperately to conform to our culture's expectations that they not show fear, uncertainty, and feelings of loneliness or neediness. More significant, however, is the fact that they minimize, ignore, deny, or suppress these feelings. Subsequently, they lose touch with themselves—with their emotions, needs, and desires.

While they struggle to avoid exhibiting or experiencing their vulnerabilities, they mismanage their anger. Some may feel their hurt most deeply and attempt to stifle their anger. Others deny their hurt, focusing on and maintaining connection only with their anger. Some children and teens deny their anger in order to avoid admitting to themselves the powerful influence others have had in leading them to feel hurt, disappointment, fear, uncertainty, or neediness.

Mismanaged anger does not just disappear. Anytime we try to ignore our deepest emotions, they develop an increased drive for expression. They act like compressed gases seeking a way out through the slightest opening in a closed container. This is the anger that may lead to bullying, social withdrawal, underachievement, substance abuse, anxiety, depression, excessive guilt and shame, or, in the extreme, devastating violence.

In their comprehensive study *Anger: The Struggle for Emotional Control in America's History,* Carol Stearns and Peter Stearns indicate that, as a nation, we have evolved through periods when anger was acceptable, when it was strongly repressed, and when we experienced much ambivalence toward it.[4] As reflected in the work of Pollack, anger expressed by men has received approval and encouragement—it was seen as a part of healthy aggressiveness and competitiveness and essential for getting ahead in the world.

Girls also seek connection and are often made to feel responsible for maintaining that connection. Similarly, they become angry. However, while boys are supported in accepting anger and even encouraged to aggressively express it, girls are taught to ignore and suppress their anger. As a result, girls grow up to be more focused on their hurt, sadness, and guilt than on anger.[5] When it is expressed, it is often indirect—reflected in critical gossip, teasing, or malicious behavior.[6] A thirteen-year-old may purposely sabotage a peer's party by seeking allies to avoid it. A third grader may tease a neighbor about the style of her dress or the color of her hair. At the other extreme, girls who are more directly aggressive are called tomboys when they are young or "bitches" as they mature. Influenced by recommendations that we turn the other cheek, do unto others as we would have them do unto us, and respond to anger with an eye for an eye, as well as by our shifting views regarding feelings, thoughts, and action, we have developed conflicting views about how to experience and express anger.

Lack of connection with others occurs for a variety of reasons. Even the most caring and well-meaning parent may not be genuinely available to really connect with his or her child. The demands of a career, trying to provide the basics, and trying to "have it all" may greatly interfere with forming a connection. Similarly, the especially difficult challenge of being a single parent can compete with our ability to form a close relationship with our children. In addition, as noted above, we live in a culture that often challenges emotional expression. You are a

product of that culture and have been influenced by the many ambivalent messages regarding the expression of emotions in general and the
handling of anger specifically. For this reason, you may experience personal vulnerabilities that interfere with and challenge your ability to
truly connect with your child. Your personal history with experiencing
empathic connection and with being empathic will greatly influence
the degree to which you foster an authentic connection with your
child. These vulnerabilities need to be addressed if you are to make the
best use of the material presented in this book.

Following are several guidelines that can help you identify key areas
of concern as you use the strategies presented in this book.

Work at Accepting and Feeling Comfortable with the Range of Your Emotions

Many of the strategies identified in this book involve helping children
and teens identify and differentiate the full range of their emotions.
The more you accept and can be comfortable with your own emotions
in addition to anger, the more you will be open to exploring them with
your child. The more you are able to identify your emotions and differentiate them, the more you will be able to help your child sort them out.

We often bring into our adult life the same fears and anxieties about
anger we experienced as children. Addressing these concerns is essential for being able to help your child explore his anger. The approaches
presented in this book are aimed at helping you and your child feel
more comfortable with anger. This includes being able to experience
it, appropriately express it, and even be the target of another's anger.
On the other hand, you may be overly sensitive to anger and overreact
to your child's anger when it does surface.

Your ability to openly discuss emotions will foster your child's emotional growth in several ways. You set an example and give your child
permission to share his emotions when you model these behaviors.
When you share reactions regarding your workplace, incidents that occur between you and others, events that occurred when you were
younger, or emotions regarding your immediate family members, you
communicate that it is permissible to experience such emotions and to
discuss them. Children learn about their own emotions when others
use specific words and describe the impact associated with such emotions. Through your sharing, they learn to value their own emotions
and to take seriously the type of self-reflection that leads to such awareness.

Certainly you should be clear about your motivations to share certain emotions. I am not suggesting you share emotions inappropri-

ately. For example, relating to your child as a confidant or in order to obtain inappropriate support would really be serving your needs rather than helping her feel more comfortable about expressing emotions. Candid sharing of emotions is beneficial, but it is damaging and a burden when it compels children to be "parents" to their parents.

Emphasize That Self-Reflection Is Constructive for Healthy Emotional Development

Self-reflection is a major component of all of the strategies presented in this book. Self-reflection involves being open to exploring our inner thoughts and feelings. It consists of skills that help us become more aware of our thoughts, emotions, and physical states. Through self-reflection, we can develop increased connection with our true emotions and thoughts. It is basic for trust in yourself and acceptance of and trust in others. It is also a building block for making genuine changes in behavior. The more comfortable you are with looking inward, the more your child will value self-reflection.

Just as some people feel uncomfortable with anger, some have negative views or ambivalent attitudes toward self-reflection. Perhaps they believe that self-reflection involves obsessive rumination that may lead to paralysis in taking an action. Similarly, they may believe that self-reflection involves a search to understand what underlies contributions for every emotion, thought, or action. These are examples of unhealthy self-reflection. In contrast, healthy self-reflection encourages us to know ourselves more fully, especially in terms of understanding our motivations, emotions, and thoughts as they impact meaningful decisions and actions we make in life. As such, self-reflection is a building block that helps us to connect not only with our children but with ourselves.

Learn to Feel Comfortable Discussing Conflict with Your Child or Teen

Much of our ability to manage anger depends on how candid and comfortable we are in expressing our own emotions and thoughts, even if they conflict with those of people we care about. Such open communication involves discussions of feelings, thoughts, and attitudes. When conflict is not openly discussed, the frustration or anger surrounding it is often suppressed and seeks expression in different ways. Allowing for open discussion of conflict does not mean you need to agree with your child. Nor does it mean that you should allow your child to freely share his views in ways that you deem inappropriate. Fostering candid sharing should be coupled with genuinely trying to see your child's perspective.

Your sensitivity to disagreement or conflict may interfere with your ability to genuinely listen to him. Similarly, the prospect of disappointing your child or being the target of his anger may interfere with your comfort in hearing his perspective. Being the target of your child's anger may lead you to feel guilt or hurt. You may feel compelled to do anything and everything to help him feel better or to avoid his experiencing anger. In contrast, in reaction to your discomfort, you may feel an intense need to quickly reduce or completely suppress his anger altogether. This discomfort leads some parents to give in to a child's demands. Others become angered and strike out verbally or even physically as a way of managing a child's anger and as a way of managing their own anger.

Fear of a child's anger is often the basis for many of the difficulties surrounding discipline problems with children. Parents who have difficulty setting limits with children often do not want their child to experience disappointment or are seeking approval from the child. At the same time, they try to avoid being the target of anger that is a natural reaction to disappointment.

In recent years, due to shifting views about authority, many parents have allowed their children to be increasingly active in the decision-making processes of the family. They indicate that such involvement helps foster increased independence and maturity. However, at times this can be an attempt to avoid dealing with anger that is a reaction to limit setting.

Work at Being Empathic

Healthy anger management involves empathy—the ability to see another person's perspective and understand that person's thinking and emotions. This is not always easy. It is a challenge to genuinely sit and listen to a child who is expressing emotions or thoughts that may be totally opposed to our own, challenge our values, appear totally unreasonable, or simply make us uncomfortable. When this happens, you may tend to ignore, overlook, or minimize your child's anger.

Observing your child's anger may arouse uncomfortable memories and emotions connected with your own childhood. In addition, you may feel guilty when, in spite of your best attempts to help your child avoid pain, she experiences negative emotions such as disappointment, hurt, shame, or anger. Uncomfortable memories and reactions may cause you to unwittingly stifle your child's expression of anger or any other kind of negative emotion. On the other hand, if you still carry anger about past hurts, you may overemphasize the importance of expressing anger with your child.

You may tend to avoid noticing your child's anger if, during your own childhood, you were embarrassed or made to feel shame or guilt about experiencing anger. For example, you may have difficulty noticing anger aroused by sibling rivalry if, when you were young, you were led to completely deny, minimize, or overlook your anger toward a sibling with whom you felt competitive.

Empathy involves being able to recognize and permit the expression of anger by your child and communicating to her that it is a natural reaction to a variety of situations. In addition, you demonstrate empathy when you recognize and allow your child to discuss hurt and pain associated with her anger. Finally, empathy is reflected in sharing your understanding that it is uncomfortable and challenging to deal with these emotions.

Convey a Genuine Desire to Help Your Child Experience Increased Control

Effectively making sense of and managing anger leads to genuine control. The more this is conveyed in your attitude, whether through teaching or modeling the specific approaches you will learn in this book, the more receptive your child will be to exploring and experimenting with them. In contrast, he may be resistant to them if he believes you are teaching them in order to exert control over him. This is especially true for teens who struggle with wanting increased independence while still being very much dependent. Most important is that with practice, the strategies presented in this book will lead your child to experience satisfaction related to more fully knowing himself, making sense of his emotions and thoughts (especially regarding anger), increasing his sense of assertion and self-control, and constructively managing his anger.

Try to Be Consistent

Consistency will help strengthen your use of the approaches provided in this book. Modeling what you teach will reinforce consistency. Similarly, the more consistent your behaviors and attitudes are with your spouse or other caretakers in the home, the more your child will experience a united message. A lack of consistency can be most problematic when one parent undermines the attempts at constructive anger management by criticizing them or by practicing or teaching strategies that are in conflict with the principles presented in this approach. As caretakers, you will always have some difference of opinion. But these should be discussed and negotiated prior to using this program.

Learning any new habit requires time and practice, and learning habits related to managing emotions is especially challenging. When you or your child is especially stressed, you may fall back on older, less effective anger management strategies. This is less likely to happen if you make an effort to consistently practice the strategies described throughout this book.

Be Open to Learning About Yourself

As already emphasized, the approaches presented in this book are based on increasing our own self-awareness. The more you and your child use the techniques presented in this book, the more both of you will grow in terms of making sense of and managing anger, in your understanding of your emotions in general, and in your interpersonal skills. In addition, you will become increasingly sensitive to the unique needs of your child. Through sharing these exercises you will also develop a deepened bond with your child.

While I focus on helping children and teens, the model of anger is equally applicable to adults. As you use it with your child, you will develop increased understanding and be able to manage anger in every area of your life.

Making Sense of and Managing Anger Requires Commitment, Patience, and Practice

Practicing the guidelines presented in this book take patience and commitment. While the specific skills may be easily learned, your child's ability to make them a part of her life will take much time. Making sense of and managing anger is a lifelong process. However, the more time you spend helping your child work at it, the more it will become a part of her repertoire, and the better prepared she will be to meet the challenges of anger.

The techniques described in this book have been used for over twenty years with parents and teachers, in classrooms, in workshops, and in my practice with adults, adolescents, and children. The model they are based on explains anger and its relationship to other emotions and thoughts. At the same time, it recognizes the interaction of these emotions and thoughts with the physical reactions that both result from anger and further contribute to it.

I strongly urge you to study the model and use the approach I describe to make sense of anger in your own life before you begin using it with your child or teen. Spend time critically reviewing several incidents in which you became angry. Select several incidents that aroused a low level of irritation as well as several that provoked more intense anger. The more familiar you are with the techniques, the better prepared you will be to help your child or teen apply it in his own life. At the same time, you will be developing and enhancing your own powers of self-reflection. Reflection is essential for understanding your own anger. Once you can do this, you will clearly observe how reflection interferes with impulsive action based on anger. Not only does this reflection defuse anger, but it provides you with an opportunity to learn something about yourself.

As you read this book, you will notice that the approach offered here is proactive, offering parents the opportunity to help their children develop the knowledge and skills needed to cope with anger before it becomes a significant problem. It also offers new insights and skills for understanding many aspects of one's emotional life and behavior apart from one's anger.

Once you have become comfortable with the strategies taught in this book, use them to help you better recognize and understand your child's anger or irritation. Before you begin teaching your child specific techniques, spend several weeks observing her and developing hunches about the factors that may be contributing to her anger. Use the approach in your own life as well, to help you improve your connection to your inner self and increase your awareness of your emotions, thoughts, and attitudes toward anger. This will help you be more empathic toward your children, and changes in your own behavior will help to reinforce the lessons you teach your child.

2

Guiding Principles of Healthy Anger

Every adult was once a child who received various messages about anger. These messages, communicated both directly and indirectly, came from parents, teachers, clergy, relatives, and peers. Television, radio, books, magazines, movies, and newspapers also bombarded us with examples of anger and messages about how to manage it. In recent years, video games have added to this barrage of communications regarding anger. Some of these messages are in direct conflict with each other. Some have told us that we should make every effort to control all anger. In contrast, others have emphasized that anger needs to be expressed, but they offer conflicting guidelines for how it should be managed. It's no wonder we have been confused about how anger should be handled, and even more baffled when trying to help children and teens manage theirs. Fortunately, in recent years we have developed a wealth of information to help us better recognize, understand, and manage anger. This knowledge is derived from theory and research in the areas of learning, emotions, cognitive-behavioral therapy, personality, stress, and anger management. From these proven theories, and based on my clinical experience, I have distilled the following twelve principles that can serve as guidelines for the successful management of anger by children, adolescents, and adults. This entire book is based on these principles. They reflect my emphasis on a proactive approach that prepares children and teens to develop the knowledge, skills, and self-awareness needed to cope with anger.

Anger Is a Natural Human Emotion

Anger is *not* a sign of emotional instability. It is a perfectly natural emotion experienced by children, teens, and adults. It is just one of the many emotions that are a part of our daily lives. Anger, like love, guilt, fright, anxiety, sadness, happiness, and other emotions, involves a unique subjective experience. Like many other emotions, it is also accompanied by physical reactions.

Some researchers suggest that anger, like all other emotions, is based on an assessment of the potential of an experience to be harmful or beneficial to us. In this way, our likelihood of becoming angry depends on how we assess others, the environment, and even our own thoughts, behavior, or emotions.

It should also be emphasized that while anger is a natural emotion, it is our discomfort with anger and its potential for aggression that lead to a cultural view that anger is not natural and should be suppressed and minimized. It is this specific view that has contributed to difficulties in both making sense of and managing anger.

Anger Varies in Intensity and Duration

As with other emotions, we may experience anger at various intensities, ranging from a mild level (annoyance) to an intense level (rage).

For example, as a parent, you may feel slightly frustrated when the flu keeps you bedridden and unable to accompany your child to a movie. In contrast, you may experience rage when the car that you have just had repaired breaks down on the way to her graduation ceremony. Children experience a similar range of feelings. A young child may become slightly upset at not getting a certain toy. An adolescent may feel annoyed when her boyfriend won't take her to a certain movie but extremely resentful to find out he is taking someone else to that same movie.

As with other emotions, anger may be a short-lived response to a specific event or it may be chronic, coloring all new experiences and predisposing a person to become angry on a daily basis.

Anger Is Often a Reaction to Other Emotions

Anger can be a primary emotion, an immediate response to feeling threatened. However, very often it is a reaction to other emotions, in which case it is considered a secondary emotion. By secondary, I do not mean less important. Although we are most aware of our anger during or following a given situation, we actually become angry in reaction to and immediately *after* feeling another potent emotion, such as hurt, shame, disappointment, rejection, embarrassment, feeling discounted or devalued, and so on. Another view is that anger may occur in combination with these other emotions, with either anger or another emotion dominating our awareness. At first we may not even be consciously aware of these other emotions. We may only be aware of anger. Often it is only after self-reflection that we are able to recognize and become aware of them. For many adults, the ability to practice such reflection is rarely the focus of formal or informal education. And unless children and teens are helped to recognize these other feelings through modeling or open discussion of similar feelings with parents, the expression of anger is often an easier and more spontaneous response to expectations that are not satisfied.

Anger Is a Reaction to Emotions and Thoughts Within Us

Anger is a reaction to emotions and thoughts within ourselves. It is based on how we perceive events and the conclusions we draw about these events. Such perceptions and conclusions can be realistic and accurate or unrealistic and distorted. In either case, such negative feelings are painful, but they are our own emotions. Certainly we react to people around us, but these reactions are our response to the meaning we give to others and their actions.

Our perceptions of ourselves may be realistic, unrealistic, or a blend of both. Either may lead to negative views about ourselves. Anger is a natural consequence when we develop these unfavorable attitudes about our thoughts, emotions, behaviors, and even bodies. Such anger may then be directed at others or turned inward at ourselves.

I have worked with hundreds of clients who have reported being annoyed, irritated, angered, or enraged in reaction to what other people did or did not do. When explored more closely, it becomes very apparent that the meaning they gave to such actions or lack of actions led to feelings such as rejection, embarrassment, hurt, and shame. These are the uncomfortable emotions within us that are the seeds of anger.

You may be angry with another driver on the road when you are feeling threatened. You may be annoyed with a colleague when you feel inadequate around him. You may feel frustrated when not understood, aggravated when you can't reach an agreement.

The mother who refuses to buy her daughter a popular brand of jeans may be a most devoted mother but also a parent who has a defined budget to follow. Her daughter's experience of her mother's refusal may be "Now I will not be accepted by my friends" or "I will stand out from everyone" or "You really don't care how I feel." These perceptions are based on personal meaning given by her to the experience. The related feelings, such as fear of rejection or hurt, are based on her own reactions to her appraisal of the event. In this way, her anger is a reaction to her own feelings experienced in reaction to the event.

Anger Really Tells Us More About Our Own Wants and Needs than About the Person or Situation That Made Us Angry

When we take the time to reflect on our anger, we can more clearly identify our motivations, which may include our needs, wants, and expectations. When we recognize, listen to, and reflect on our anger, we can clarify what we want, what we think we need, and what expectations we have surrounding both.

On many occasions in couples counseling, a major shift in communication occurs when one partner turns to the other and says, "I guess I feel inadequate around you, and I need to feel adequate, in my eyes and in yours." This is often the first time a partner expresses feelings and motivations underlying the anger, not just the anger. Such a shift in awareness often occurs only after months and years of communication that emphasized anger and lacked a clear recognition and discussion of needs, expectations, or the emotions that precede anger.

It is natural for adolescents to have increased needs to feel accepted, adequate, and competent, while they also want to appear independent. For this reason they are especially prone to mask, even to themselves, the underlying hurt when these needs are not satisfied, instead showing anger. The more troubled adolescent may take things one step further and mask all anger. This is the teen who may be experiencing extreme hurt but tries to convince himself and others that nothing matters. He may become an adult who lacks awareness of many of his needs and wants.

The Emotion of Anger Is Distinct from the Behavioral Expressions of Anger

Anger is an emotion and a subjective experience. It is separate and distinct from the physical reactions that might result from it. Specifically, the emotion of anger may be expressed by behavior that is aggressive, but anger is not equivalent to aggression. Aggression is simply one way to respond to, and express externally, this uncomfortable internal state. The emotion of anger may be expressed through verbal aggression in the form of yelling or cursing. In contrast, anger may be expressed by physical aggression—breaking things or becoming assaultive toward others or ourselves.

In our families, in school, through our religion, and through the mass media, we experience direct and indirect messages that equate a feeling or thought with a deed. We are often told as children that we should not get angry. The important distinction between expressing anger and feeling anger is not emphasized. We may be taught that it is as bad to have angry thoughts as it is to act in an angry way. This attitude is often based on an idealistic view of humans that portrays all anger as a shortcoming, a weakness, or a sign of poor self-control—in spite of the fact that anger is a natural emotion and can be justified. The important distinction between angry feelings and angry actions may have been obscured by the false belief that others can see through us and know our feelings even without our expressing them. Children are sometimes told this directly. This also leads to confusion about differentiating the feeling from the action when it comes to anger.

As We Increase Our Awareness of Thoughts and Emotions Leading up to Anger, We Gain Increased Freedom to Choose How We Express Anger

I emphasize the word *choose* because anger can be expressed or demonstrated by a wide variety of behaviors that are in our control. Although at times we may not feel as if we have or are making a choice, we very much have the capacity to choose how we manage our anger.

Identifying thoughts and emotions that lead to anger helps us to realize what we are really feeling. By taking time to do this we learn more about ourselves and create the time to choose how to address or tend to our feelings of anger.

Bill was an underachieving fourteen-year-old junior high school student whose parents brought him to me for help because he constantly bullied his younger brother, who was a much better student. Hardly a day went by when Bill did not taunt Kevin, order him around, or "accidentally" bump into him. Over time I helped Bill to see that he felt inferior and inadequate when he compared himself to his brother. Bill resented that he could not live up to his own expectations about how he should achieve in school. At the same time, he resented the praise and recognition that Kevin received from his parents. Only with this awareness could he finally drop his anger and examine his disappointment in himself.

A father of an eleventh grader could hardly contain his anger toward his son for not playing well during the high school basketball playoffs. Only after much discussion was he able to recognize that the intensity of his anger related to his own intense competitive drives in every area of his life. While he was very successful, he was a man driven by an underlying fear that if he let up, he would be recognized as a failure—a thought that he harbored without awareness.

By recognizing and understanding the emotions that lead to anger, we can begin to change how we manage our anger, even if our ways of handling anger have been ingrained for many years. Similarly, as a child begins to recognize the emotions that she experiences prior to experiencing anger, she can begin to choose how to manage her anger. When we increase our awareness of our reactions to events, we begin to observe patterns in our behavior. By becoming conscious of these patterns, we gain the self-awareness that is essential for almost all behavioral change.

Healthy Anger Management Is Based on Specific Skills That Can Be Taught

As an adult, you can learn specific skills to better understand and manage anger. Much of understanding and managing anger does not require psychotherapy. Instead, it involves learning and practicing skills that can become a part of your routine. These are skills that you can readily share with children, whether you relate to them as parent, teacher, relative, leader, or friend. Some of these skills are easier to learn than others, and some are more appropriate for certain ages.

And some are more appropriate in certain settings. Some may seem more consistent for individuals in one culture or for individuals of a particular ethnicity. Certain individuals may prefer some anger management strategies to others. The key point to remember is that they can be learned.

Healthy Anger Management Is Based on the Ability to Flexibly Choose from a Variety of Anger Management Strategies

The goal in anger management is to increase the options you have to express anger in a healthy way. By learning a variety of anger management strategies, you develop control, choices, and flexibility in how you respond to angry feelings. A person who has learned a variety of ways to handle anger is more competent and confident. And with competence and confidence comes the resilience needed to cope with situations that arouse frustration and anger. The development of a repertoire of such skills further enhances our sense of optimism that we can effectively handle the challenges that come our way.

In contrast, the individual who responds to anger in the same way every time has little capacity to constructively adapt his responses to different situations. Such individuals are more prone to feel frustrated and to have conflicts with others and themselves.

During one of my workshops, a participant complained, "When it comes to anger, I feel like I am on automatic pilot. I just lose it—I'll hit the wall or throw something. It's like at that moment I don't feel I have a choice. I have no control, and there's nothing in between." Reacting automatically and rigidly, using only one tool for managing anger, can lead to interpersonal difficulties in relationships at work, in school, with peers, and within the family. By helping your child develop a repertoire of anger management strategies, you will enable him to more frequently choose a strategy that best suits the time, place, and persons involved.

Real Intimacy Grows with an Increased Ability to Share Anger and the Emotions Underlying It

Closeness, mutual understanding, acceptance, and freedom to express oneself are all aspects of intimacy that are fostered by the constructive expression of anger in a relationship. This is true for adults as well as for children. A child, adolescent, or adult who feels comfortable enough to constructively express anger with a loved one is an individual who feels confirmed in the experience of his or her emotions. This is a core component of self-acceptance and the development of positive self-esteem. At the same time, I want to emphasize that the two parties do not need to be in total agreement.

The expression of anger can foster real intimacy only when it is accompanied by the sharing of other related feelings. Sharing just anger, or only the emotions that led to our anger, falls short of the difficult challenge to be authentic in an intimate relationship.

Healthy Anger Management Involves Being Able to Let Go of Anger

A fundamental aspect of healthy anger management is being able to let go of anger. This does not mean ignoring or denying our anger. Rather, it entails a commitment to move on once the issues underlying the anger have been addressed, whether or not our needs or concerns are satisfied.

As I have already pointed out, anger tells us more about our own needs and wants than about the person or situation that made us angry in the first place. Identifying our concerns and deciding how to best address them are key elements of healthy anger management. But there will be times when I very appropriately express a desire or need only to be faced with disappointment when it is not be satisfied. This is when the real challenge to let go of anger occurs.

Learning Specific Anger Management Skills Is Essential for Healthy Emotional Well-being

As I emphasized in the introduction, the ability to accept and more comfortably manage anger is a major ingredient in our capacity for comforting ourselves when under stress. This ability to self-soothe helps decrease tension and the adverse feelings related to anger. An individual who can constructively respond to the tension and anxiety of anger is one who can be optimistic about meeting new challenges both within herself and in her environment. This serves as the foundation for a sense of mastery, feelings of competence, and improved self-esteem. People who can do this are both hardy and resilient under stress.

It is this ability to sit with, ride out, and work through the physical and emotional discomfort associated with anger that allows us to better meet our needs, wants, and expectations and better cope with frustration. When we help children and teens develop this ability, we empower them to experience themselves and others with increased understanding, compassion, and humanity.

3

The Adverse Effects of Anger

What is it you experience when you feel anger? Maybe you think of times when you were upset, annoyed, furious, enraged, or irritated. But anger is more complex than these words imply. Anger is an emotion, but it also affects your physical state, your thoughts, and your behavior, though you may not always be consciously aware of it. Understanding the experience of anger will provide you insight into the role anger may play in your life and that of your child.

Certain of these reactions typically accompany acute (intense, short-lived) anger. Other reactions, such as sleep difficulties, digestive problems, cynicism, and loss of faith may occur with the development of chronic (long-lived) anger. Here are some of the adverse ways anger can impact us.

- *Physical:* nervousness, muscle tension, increased rate of breathing, increased heart rate, shallow breathing, sleep or eating disturbances, indigestion, skin rash, muscle spasms
- *Emotional:* anxiety, guilt, shame, depression, escalating anger, insecurity, fear, feelings of inadequacy, sadness, embarrassment, self-devaluation

- *Social:* withdrawal, developing friendships with others who are similarly angry, scapegoating, racism and bigotry, hate, aggression, hostility, relational aggression, passive-aggressiveness, negativism, irritability, sarcasm, cynicism
- *Intellectual:* decreased capacity for concentration, blocking, forgetfulness, poor judgment, errors in reasoning or speech or action, decreased quality in comprehension and expression
- *Spiritual:* decrease in spiritual or religious convictions and practices, attitude of hate and vengefulness
- *Global outlook:* pessimism, minimization of the positive, increased sense of helplessness and alienation

Let's look at each of these in more detail.

Physical Reactions

The physical reactions to anger are the same as those aroused by stress in general. Our bodies experience a fight-or-flight reaction.[1] We become aroused, energized, and ready to respond to what we perceive as a challenge to our safety. Our breathing becomes more rapid. Depending on the intensity of our reaction, we may experience an overall tingling sensation, as if we can actually feel our blood rushing more rapidly throughout our body. At the same time, our muscles shift into a tense mode, awaiting further orders.

These reactions are based on an activation of our autonomic system, the group of physiological systems in our body that function automatically without our needing to consciously monitor them. Studies using biofeedback instruments (instruments that measure minor physiological changes) indicate that even mild experiences of anger and irritation impact this system. These physiological changes are observed when an individual is connected to these instruments and directed to think about an anger-provoking incident.

The respiratory, cardiovascular, and neuromuscular systems react automatically when we are angry. As anger persists, other, more long-term physical effects may occur. Research suggests that it is the ongoing state of anger that can lead to serious physical problems. The range of symptoms includes headache, stomach upset, muscular tension, pains, and the escalation of certain illnesses such as asthma, arthritis, and other stress-induced diseases. In fact, in recent years, chronic anger has been shown to be strongly associated with certain forms of heart disease. Anger may lead to chronic illness or symptoms when it is not constructively managed and especially when it is repressed, minimized, and ignored.

The range of physical symptoms occurs for adults as well as for children. Similarly, both may experience more immediate reactions or long-lasting effects.

A young adolescent patient poignantly revealed the physical consequences of mismanaged anger. Carol was a twelve-year-old who had been experiencing severe headaches for almost a month; she was referred to me by her pediatrician after he could find no medical basis for the headaches. Following a detailed interview, it became apparent that she experienced her headaches mostly in the evening during the week. As we talked, she revealed that a little over a month prior to our visit, her mother had started working part time from five o'clock in the evening until midnight.

In a few follow-up sessions Carol became more able to express that she was disappointed, anxious, and angered that her mother had to work those hours. But when her mother asked her directly, Carol denied there was a problem. Carol's fear and guilt prevented her from sharing her true feelings. She reasoned, "How could I be angry at Mommy? She's working so the family can have money." Carol's symptoms stopped very soon after she was able to more comfortably express her feelings to her mother.

Emotional Reactions

At times we may experience anxiety, depression, guilt, or shame and not think they are related to anger. However, they may be experienced as an immediate reaction to having angry feelings or as the only acceptable alternatives to feeling anger. Those who are most uncomfortable with anger may not consciously experience it but be very much aware of other negative emotions.

I have worked with men and women whose depression was related to anger that was too scary or confusing to experience or express. Gradually their needs, wants, and expectations were minimized, denied, or ignored along with their anger. This way of responding to anger led them to feel isolated, misunderstood, and helpless. This is often the outcome when these needs, wants and expectations are very important to us and when they involve our most meaningful relationships—those with our partners, family members, friends, and coworkers.

An extreme reaction to anger is suicide. Recent research supports the idea that it is not just depression that leads individuals to make suicide attempts but a "final-straw" incident in which the individual experiences anger—an incident that furthers the person's sense of isolation, hopelessness, and helplessness.

When children and adolescents hide their anger behind depression, anxiety, guilt, and shame, it is difficult for even the most concerned and caring parent to recognize that they are angry. This was clearly evidenced by Clara, an eleven-year-old who arrived in my office appearing somewhat sullen and timid. Her mother reported that in the months following her divorce, Clara seemed withdrawn, at times irritable, and less cooperative around the house. Her teacher had also reported falling grades. Clara was the youngest in the family and had three older sisters, thirteen, seventeen, and twenty-one. Her oldest sister, to whom Clara was especially close, was planning on getting married within two months. While growing up, Clara saw that sister express anger in a variety of ways, which only seemed to make their mother upset.

It was clear to her parents and her teacher that Clara was sad about the anticipated changes in her family. What they did not realize was that she was very annoyed at her mother's divorce and angry toward her sister for abandoning her. Not wanting to further upset her mother, Clara was quick to feel anger and then guilt about feeling angry. She was afraid to express her negative feelings, as she had seen her mother become upset many times with her older sister. Clara had vowed to be a well-behaved daughter who would not upset her mother. But because she did not voice her feelings, she gradually came to feel isolated in the family. This led to the depressed feelings and the behaviors that resulted in her referral for help. Several family sessions helped everyone communicate more openly about the effect each member of the family had on the others.

In contrast, some children and teens express only anger, and the task for parents is to help them better understand and communicate the other feelings that led to the anger. While this is the goal, anger often leads parents to react first and think later. Or, worse yet, they may withdraw in frustration and give up trying to figure out what really is happening in their children's lives.

Social Reactions

Social reactions to anger may be short-lived or long-term in duration. For example, your child may withdraw to his room for an hour after becoming angry with his older sister about a play she made on a board game. She may become hurt and angry and avoid contacting a friend for months after not being invited to the friend's party.

Pervasive anger and underlying hurt may lead to distrust that inhibits an adolescent from making friends during a time of life when involvement with peers is important for development. Similarly, pervasive anger may serve as the fuel for the verbal adult, adolescent, or child who is cynical and sarcastic in his interactions with others. A teen may express such cynicism and sarcasm toward those who make him angry as well as with others.

Chronic anger may underlie a quickness to feel irritated, annoyed, or frustrated. Such anger can predispose a child to more quickly become hostile or aggressive in facing new situations that may provoke anger, and it can lead to resentment that shadows all of her relationships.

Some children and teens who have difficulties with anger seek the companionship of those who are similarly angry. In doing so, they experience camaraderie and an alliance. This way of responding to anger is often the motivation for those who participate in gangs.

Scapegoating, blaming others for our own shortcomings, is another example of how social interactions may be influenced by anger. Racism and bigotry, too, are examples of how anger can lead to attitudes and behaviors in relationships. Anger may lead children or teens to negatively prejudge others because of their religion, race, ethnicity, or other difference.

Anger can lead to a desire for revenge. Those who are angry may focus on seeking revenge or emotionally or physically hurt others because of their anger and hurt.

Similarly, a more intense level of anger is reflected in hate. An individual may be so angry that he develops a completely negative view of those individuals who he feels have wronged him. Hate involves a level of anger so intense that he may see others as adversaries trying to stifle his every action. Hatred at this level may lead to violence in an attempt to eliminate those who are seen as threatening.

Relational aggression is another type of social reaction to anger. Children and teens may try to destroy or undermine the relationships of those with whom they are angry. They may say negative things or spread rumors about them. They may be passive aggressive, expressing anger by not taking a certain action—for example, a teen who is angry with a friend may not tell her about a party she's been invited to, or a child who is angry with his friend about plays he made on a video game may not inform him of certain strategies he could use in another game. Similarly, a child or teen who experiences sibling rivalry with her brother may demonstrate relational aggression through actions or words that lead to her parents' irritation with him.

Intellectual Reactions

As with the other reactions already discussed, intellectual reactions to anger may be short-lived and limited only to the actual moment when we are acutely angry, or they may be more pervasive and chronic. Anger distracts us from effectively performing certain cognitive activities such as thinking, planning, concentrating, organizing, and expressing ourselves. Effective communication and genuine understanding become extremely difficult when two people are intensely angry with each other. For this reason, the worst time to try to discuss a conflict is when we are angry.

All too often we erroneously react to anger during an argument very much how many of us react to a yellow light when driving toward an intersection—accelerating rather than responding to the light as a signal to slow down and prepare to stop. Prompted by our urgency to be somewhere, we ignore the risks we are taking and race forward. Similarly, in a moment of anger, we fail to recognize or attend to warning signs. We may be aware of a wide range of emotional and physical reactions for a moment, but we quickly try to move forward. We may speak louder and faster, with greater emphasis and increased emotion, as we try to force our view on another person. When arguing, we may feel pressure to prove a point, to take control, to get agreement, or to feel understood. At this point, our internal self-talk may sound something like "I just need to say one more thing and then I'll get her to see the point."

Another way in which chronic anger may inhibit us intellectually is in our ability to plan and organize. Anger may contribute to procrastination and underachievement in both children and adults.[2] This can occur when our feelings of anger compete with our motivation to do well or to complete projects. Certainly other factors contribute to procrastination and achievement, but anger is often a core issue for adults and children who may be angry at others' expectations of themselves as well as their own. The adolescent whose grades suddenly drop, who forgets to hand in homework, or who does not complete assignments might be a youngster who is, in essence, going on strike in response to such expectations. Often what we label as "laziness" or "not caring" may really be expressions of resentment that interfere with achievement.

Children and adolescents who have a learning disability, attention disorder, or physical disability may underachieve. They may also develop anger over the frustration with their difficulties. This anger may further contribute to a reduced interest in and commitment to learning.

Spiritual Reactions

In recent years, psychologists have gained more understanding of the spiritual side of our lives and how it can affect our well-being. Chronic anger can have a negative impact even in this area. The impact may be expressed by the reduction of our faith in ourselves, in our family, in religion, in God, or in our general sense of meaning and purpose in life.

When this occurs, we may lose a sense of balance and structure in life, leading to feelings of emptiness and isolation.

Anger can have a profound impact on our spiritual development, especially during adolescence. This is a time when our ideals are developing and being challenged. It is during this stage of development that a child becomes more aware of the inconsistencies of life and the shortcomings of the adults around him, especially his parents. If such awareness leads to hurt and anger, it can profoundly influence his attitudes of trust and his developing sense of values and morality.

In contrast, although not necessarily an adverse reaction, some individuals become more spiritual or religious as a way of dealing with anger. Certainly spirituality and religion can provide us with guidelines and structure for how we deal with life and especially those experiences that cause us anger. In some cases, however, teens may be so hurt and angry that they seek out spiritual connection with others who, while emphasizing spiritual growth, may also embrace anger and encourage it.

Some individuals who are chronically and severely angry may develop a general attitude characterized by hatred and vengefulness. While these feelings may be targeted toward specific individuals as a social reaction to anger, such people may be predisposed to view others and the world in general with these intensely negative and self-defeating attitudes.

Global Outlook

The sum effect of anger can greatly impact our general outlook, which influences how we experience anger as well as our understanding of anger and our ability to handle it. At the same time, how we experience anger and manage it further contributes to our global outlook. The cumulative effect of these experiences determines our overall sense of competence and our perceived capacity to affect our own lives and the world around us. These experiences shape our sense of the environment as being either supportive and manageable or inhibiting and threatening.

A child or teen who lacks the capacity to understand and manage anger will experience diminished trust in herself and others. In contrast, a child who effectively makes sense of and manages anger experiences greater trust in herself and in others. As such, she is able to maintain a more positive general outlook.

A part of the adolescent's task is to develop a worldview. When an adolescent's outlook is negative, his anger may provide the motivation for turning away from constructive behavior and distracting himself by engaging in such behaviors as social isolation, substance abuse, risk taking, and promiscuity. In contrast, when his general outlook is more positive, such anger may serve as the force behind striving for ideals during his teen years and as a young adult.

It is certainly easy to understand why we may want to avoid dealing with anger—it is a complex and uncomfortable emotion. At the same time, we can also understand the lifelong advantages of making sense of and effectively managing anger. In the next chapter I provide a comprehensive view of anger to help you assist your child in achieving this goal.

4

A Comprehensive View
of Anger

Why is it that one five-year-old is quick to have a tantrum while another child responds calmly to the same situation? What makes one teenage boy spring into aggression while a neighbor's son assertively expresses both hurt and anger about the same event? What leads your spouse to respond to anger in one way and your child to manage anger the way she does? Why is it that some people never seem to experience anger?

In this chapter, I present a model of anger, a framework for understanding anger, that will help answer these types of questions. It will assist you in recognizing when and how specific motivations, thoughts, and other emotions contribute to the experience of anger. It will provide a clear understanding of anger so that you will be prepared to help your child or teen better recognize, understand, and manage his anger. By understanding this model, you will be prepared to more thoughtfully choose, and help your child select, from a wide variety of anger management strategies that I present in later chapters.

Rather than simply present the model, I offer a number of experiences that will help you really make sense of it. Several factors influence when we become angry and how intensely we may experience such anger. How these factors interact contributes to what conditions will arouse our anger and the intensity of that anger. These factors include driving forces in the form of wants and needs that are a part of our personality. In addition, they involve expectations we have of others, the world around us, and ourselves. A final component involves emotions that may precede and lead to anger.

The best way to better understand the interaction of these factors is to engage in the exercises below. They are designed to help you develop an increased capacity for self-reflection and awareness, which is critical for making sense of and managing anger. Taking time to practice them is an essential first step in being genuinely prepared to help your child or teen understand and manage her anger.

Exercise

Recall a recent event in your life that led you to become angry. On a scale of 1 to 10, where 1 represents slight annoyance and 10 your most extreme anger, try to recall an incident that falls between 2 and 7 in intensity. I am asking you to recall this event in order to more closely examine the experience and the range of internal reactions that accompanied it. Be aware that since we often have physical and emotional reactions to what we visualize and think about, merely recalling the event may lead you to feel discomfort. Do not continue doing this exercise if it becomes too uncomfortable for you.

Now, try to make the experience as realistic as possible. Try to visualize all the details of that event. Recall the setting, the people involved, their actions, your behavior, your thinking, your self-talk or dialogue with yourself, and any physical sensations you may have experienced. Picture the objects that made up the scene, including their colors and textures. Imagine the air; was it still or moving, dry or humid? In an effort to make this as real as possible, try to recall any sounds or odors that may also have accompanied the setting.

Now picture what led up to the event. What actually happened, and what were your reactions as you became angry? How was this situation resolved? Think about it for a few minutes. Then write a few sentences describing the incident that led to your experiencing anger.

This is an exercise I have participants do in every one of my anger workshops. In general, the response most people report, regardless of the specific details surrounding the event, is "The event happened and then I became angry." If this reaction was diagrammed, it would look like Figure 4.1.

Now imagine the experience as if it were recorded on videotape. Include what led up to it, what happened, and your reaction. Visualizing the experience this way can help you more clearly reflect on it. Imagine that, as with a real videotape, you are able to fast-forward your tape, rewind it, pause, and, most important, review it frame by frame.

Figure 4.1: Anger follows the event

Go back over the event again, but this time focus more on what you experienced internally—specifically, what emotions you were experiencing. Imagine forwarding the tape one frame at a time; review your reactions at each instant. Pay attention to the moment immediately after the provoking event and right before you became angry. Recall any thoughts you might have had, other emotions you might have experienced, and bodily reactions you may recall following that event.

You may at first find it difficult to identify what other emotions you experienced just before you became angry. However, take time to reflect on the experience. If you find yourself going immediately from the event to your anger, reverse your imaginary video from the moment when you first experienced anger. Take a moment to write down your reactions.

This review usually provides us more details about ourselves. When we review the situation in this way, it becomes clear that the experience may best be described as following the sequence diagrammed by Figure 4.2.

You may have identified conclusions or meaning you gave to the event. You may have identified feeling hurt, discounted, shamed, frightened, devalued, or embarrassed before becoming angry. It can be challenging to identify the internal reactions that preceded your anger; it is a skill that requires practice, but it can be learned. The more we practice this type of self-reflection, the more we learn about ourselves. This ability to reflect on and identify our internal reactions is the basis for making sense of and managing anger.

What I hope you experienced by doing this exercise is the awareness that anger does not just suddenly appear. Rather, in the time between a specific event and when we become angry, there are many internal reactions that have an impact on our anger. So I view anger as being influenced by a sequence of factors both before and after an anger-

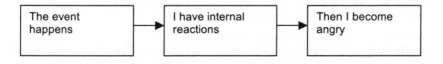

Figure 4.2: Internal reactions follow the event and precede anger

provoking event that determine our reaction to that event. The model described below identifies the major factors that form this sequence.

Motivating Forces

I start with motivating forces because I view anger as a reaction to our experience (or our anticipated experience) of having our needs and desires frustrated or completely unmet. In general, psychologists have most often described human behavior as being based on motivations that are biological or psychological in origin. Motivations derived from our biological makeup include the need for food, clothing, shelter, and the necessary caretaking parents must provide infants and young children for them to thrive.

In addition, we are motivated by needs and desires that are psychological and secondary to those needs that must be met for our survival. These secondary motivations are influenced and determined both by our genetic history and by our environment as we mature from childhood into adulthood. Certainly gender, race, ethnicity, and the values and attitudes of our culture further influence these psychological motivational forces. The pattern of these motivations is derived from and helps form our unique personality. Such motivations become the driving forces that both influence and are further affected by our emotions, thoughts, and behaviors (Figure 4.3). As such, the satisfaction or frustration of these needs and desires influences when we become angry, how we react to anger, and how we handle our anger.

Below is a partial list of psychological motivating forces that are most commonly identified as underlying much of our emotions, thoughts, and behavior. These serve as the background to our experience of any event that may lead to anger. While we have many of these motivations as both children and adults, the order of their importance may vary across our lifespan as well as from moment to moment. Similarly, how much we value one over another varies with our personality. These include but are not limited to the following motivations:

Motivations
Drives
Needs
Wants

Figure 4.3: Motivations

To feel secure	To feel protected
To be nutritionally satisfied	To feel loved (and to lo\
To feel admired	To feel special
To experience interpersonal connection	To be independent
To be creative	To be dependent
To feel centered	To feel accepted
To feel approved of	To feel respected
To feel in control	To feel powerful
To feel optimistic	To experience faith
To feel confident	To feel competent
To be the center of attention	To feel important
To feel challenged	To experience self-acceptance
To experience mastery	To experience structure
To experience self-actualization	To experience novelty

You may be highly motivated by several forces at the same time. At another moment, only one of these forces may be dominant. Upon further observation, you may notice that you feel consistently motivated by a few of these driving forces.

I have found over the years that I tend to seek variety, challenge, and the opportunity to be creative in my work life. I have worked with individuals whose strongest motivation was to be recognized and admired, while others are dominated by their drive for power and the money that may help them achieve it.

Motivating forces similarly drive children and teens. I counseled a ten-year-old boy who appeared very strongly driven by his need to be outstanding. While this can be a positive motivation, when it is extreme it can lead to much frustration and interpersonal conflict. In every area of interaction with peers, he became extremely competitive and felt compelled to be the best. Whether involved in sports or playing video games, his need to be the best often led him to become intensely angry with teammates when they did not perform to his standards, and he became intensely angry with himself when he did not fulfill his self-expectations. His anger toward others was evidenced by name calling, being boisterous, and physical aggression.

Two or more drives may influence us at the same time. Such motivating drives can push us in the same direction to engage in a specific behavior and to have certain expectations. For example, the competitive child described above may also be driven by his need to feel accepted.

In contrast, some motivating forces compete with each other and cause internal conflict. Such inner tension may lead to behaviors that interfere with the satisfaction of either motivating force. One seventeen-year-old girl whom I counseled was strongly motivated by her need for approval. At the same time, she had such a strong underlying dependency that she could hardly make a decision without asking someone for an opinion regarding her actions. She became anxious and then angered if she didn't get the support she felt she needed. This included obsessively asking for feedback from peers and parents when she purchased clothing, and immediately after writing the first sentence of a composition for her English class.

The drives to be creative, to experience stability, to gain admiration, to feel special, and to get approval are just a few examples of how motivations impact our behavior. At certain times it is easy to identify these forces; at other times it is more difficult. This may be true when trying to identify our own motivations as well as when we try to clearly identify the motives of others. However, to the degree you can identify your most significant motivations, you will become more sensitive to your wants and needs. You will become more connected with who you are and what is meaningful to you. To the degree you become sensitive to your wants and needs, you will increasingly make sense of your hurt or disappointments and the resulting anger. You will then be more able to be sensitive to your child or teen as you help him reflect on what is meaningful to him.

At times it may be especially challenging to identify your child's motivating forces. At other times, and with certain children, you may find it very easy. However, to the degree that you become aware of your child's motivating forces, you will have an increased capacity to understand your child, connect with and support him, and help him make better sense of his anger and related frustrations.

Expectations

Of course, our psychological needs and desires are not always satisfied. As a result of the interplay between our genetic history (our biology) and our ongoing experiences (our environmental experiences), we develop a set of expectations regarding the satisfaction of our motivating forces (Figure 4.4). As with motivating forces, our gender, race, ethnicity, and culture strongly impact these expectations and the meaning they have for each of us. When, if, and how these forces are satisfied influence our expectations about whether or not they will be satisfied in the future. Some of these expectations are realistic and some are unrealistic.

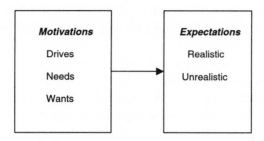

Figure 4.4: Motivations and Expectations

Suppose that a child is born at a time when his mother is not emotionally available to adequately meet his early needs for attention, to feel admired, to experience stability, or to feel protected. Her emotional unavailability may be a result of her needs not being satisfied because of marital conflict, her own depression, family illness, the need to work long hours, or her distraction by feelings surrounding her own parent's death, to name a few. Even a well-intentioned mother may become distracted when faced with any of these challenges. This situation leads to a weakened connection between parent and child. But the parent-child relationship is very important and has the potential to strongly influence a child's beliefs about relationships in general. If in fact the mother consistently cannot reasonably meet her child's needs, he may conclude that the world is not caring and that he is not lovable. This is likely to influence his expectations and, as a result, both how and when he gets angry. This is often the case for young children who appear quick to become angry, demonstrate rebellious behavior, and/or present signs of depression.

In contrast, suppose that a young child experiences a healthy combination of love, support, guidance, and limit setting to promote her healthy autonomy. With this experience as part of her emotional background, she is likely to become an adolescent with a stable sense of inner discipline, a sense of competence, and optimism. When confronting disappointment regarding her needs and wants, she may have a healthy tolerance for frustration, feel confident about her ability to be self-soothing, and be generally optimistic about her ability to cope. This may make her more resilient to frustration of her wants and needs and less likely to respond impulsively or too intensely to situations that might otherwise provoke anger. With this experience, she may be more likely to become an adult who trusts that the world will be a nurturing place. (For a wide variety of reasons, some still unknown, this type of optimism can even develop for many individuals who have been through extremely depriving conditions. Sometimes a relationship with a grandparent, aunt or uncle, teacher, religious leader, or neighbor may provide a very meaningful and positive connection on which to base such optimism.)

The preschooler who has his tower of toy blocks knocked down and immediately begins to rebuild his creation is an example of a child who has developed an overall positive outlook in his expectations. Such optimism is similarly evidenced by the sixteen-year-old who tries out for the school swim team in spite of a rejection the previous year. Similarly, the adult who can experience and discuss the discomfort of anger in a relationship may be an individual who trusts himself, the other, and the relationship. These are all examples of individuals whose expectations may not be immediately satisfied but who have the optimism to move on and not be paralyzed by disappointment or anger.

Clearly, our expectations depend greatly on the cumulative impact of our past experiences as well as our confidence in mastering new challenges. For the most part, no single experience (unless it is highly emotionally charged) can unilaterally influence our expectations and make us optimistic or pessimistic. But certain events can greatly influence the intensity of our expectations.

Children who have experienced frequent relocations may have reduced expectations for developing lasting friendships. A child who is verbally or physically abused may have reduced expectations regarding how others will satisfy her needs.

Children develop many expectations that are unrealistic. They often view the world with "child logic." Such thinking is self-centered and dominated by emotional reactions rather than based on more realistic logical thinking. This type of thinking is active when a five-year-old has trouble telling the difference between the evening news broadcast and a movie. Similarly, child logic dominates the thinking of a six-year-old who may erroneously think that his behavior or thoughts caused the illness of a sibling or his parents' divorce. It may be involved for the adolescent who at eighteen years of age fantasizes about becoming a great ice skater when, in fact, he has never put on a pair of ice skates. An adult is driven by child logic when she maintains the view that she needs to please everyone and must never behave in ways that cause others to become angry with her. Maintaining unrealistic expectations that cannot be satisfied leads to more frequent frustration and dissatisfaction.

Many of us maintain the unrealistic expectations based on child logic long into adulthood. Often we are unaware that these expectations influence our thinking. When, as in recent years, mental health professionals discuss "the child within," our "script," or our "baggage," they are often referring in part to those attitudes, beliefs, and meanings that we developed as a result of child logic. Such logic is a natural part immaturity and self-centeredness of a child. Children rely less on logic and less frequently develop unrealistic expectations when they are gently guided by parents to become more realistic. However, child logic is supported, and even passed on, by a parent whose own expectations are strongly influenced by child logic, communicated both directly (through words) and indirectly (through attitudes and behavior).

Below are a number of unrealistic expectations that are often a derivative of child logic:

- All of my needs must be satisfied.
- If I am good, all of my needs will be satisfied.
- If my needs are not satisfied, then something is wrong with me.
- I need to please everyone all of the time.
- I should be able to please everyone all of the time.
- I should always be able to have my needs immediately satisfied.
- Only my wants and expectations are important.
- My wants and needs should always be satisfied before the wants and needs of others.
- I should always know what my needs are at any given time.
- It should be easy to have my needs satisfied.
- Other people should know what I want or expect without my having to tell them.
- If a person really loves me, he or she will always know what I need or want.
- If a person really loves me, he or she will always help me get what I need or want.
- Satisfying one need or want will always make up for not satisfying another of my needs or desires.
- I need to have all of my needs met or I will be totally rejected, be abandoned, or even die.

Inasmuch as these expectations clearly cannot be satisfied, they predispose not just children but adolescents and adults to quickly respond with anger. In fact, many adults and adolescents experience chronic anger because they have difficulty giving up these unrealistic expectations and expend much time and energy trying to satisfy them.

Aaron Beck, a prominent psychologist, emphasizes that it is a sense of entitlement regarding expectations that yields severe anger.[1] Those who have beliefs of entitlement take for granted that others should behave in ways that will meet their expectations. They fail to realize that such an idea is based on child logic and, as such, are more vulnerable to disappointment and anger. Holding on to these unrealistic expectations of others leads us to be predisposed to become angry toward them, to be angry with ourselves, and to be vulnerable to depression, excessive guilt, and shame.

Take a moment to reflect and try to identify three unrealistic expectations that sometimes influence your thinking and behavior. As you increase your ability to identify unrealistic expectations, you will be practicing a major strategy in understanding and managing anger. As you help your child identify unrealistic expectations, you will assist him in making sense of and handling his anger.

Expectations that are more realistic are based on more mature logic—a cause-effect relationship instead of magical thinking (such as the thought process involved in dreams and fantasy). These more realistic expectations include:

- Everyone has wants and needs.
- Some of these wants and needs can usually be met.
- Some wants and needs will sometimes be met.
- Some wants and needs will never be met.
- Some of my wants and needs will never be satisfied even though they could be.
- Not everyone knows what I want or need.
- Each of us maintains a different priority regarding our needs and wants.
- Others can know my wants and needs when I share them.
- I may not be clear about my own needs and wants.
- I may not be aware of my own needs and wants.
- People who care for me may be aware of some of my wants and needs, but they may not know all of them.
- Even people who love me may not wish to or be able to satisfy my wants and needs.
- I have to wait to have certain wants and needs satisfied.

Being able to distinguish between realistic and unrealistic expectations is a major strategy in making sense of and managing one's anger, and helping a child or teen do so is one of the major ways a parent or caretaker can teach her how to handle angry feelings. The development of this ability is a major step that contributes to the capacity for self-soothing and self-acceptance. By developing more realistic expectations, a child or teen becomes less prone to experience frustration or anger. Guidelines to help children with this essential task are discussed in Chapter 7.

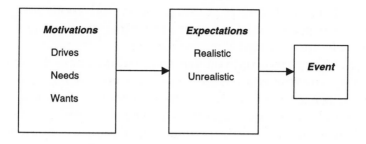

Figure 4.5: The event occurs against a background of motivations and expectations

The Event

Figure 4.5 highlights the next step in the sequence of factors that surround anger: the event.

We live each day with a history that has helped shape our motivations and expectations. We greet events in our lives with this history in combination with the factors that influence our life at the moment the event occurs—a personal pattern of needs, wants, and expectations that affects how we react to that event.

When I discuss events, I am referring to those that have already happened, those that I anticipate will occur in the future, or those that I incorrectly perceive or imagine have happened or will happen. The important point is that the event, whether real or a product of distorted thinking, is experienced as something to contend with.

We must first have an awareness of an event before it can have an impact on us. This leads to a reaction to the event. Our awareness of these reactions may be complete or incomplete, conscious or unconscious. A young child may be very much aware of both an event (e.g., not being able to go on a planned trip to the zoo) and his reaction to that event (feeling disappointed). On the other hand, an adolescent who was rejected by a peer may subsequently react with aggression but have little awareness of the connection between feelings of rejection and her aggression. She may even become hostile in situations that have no relation to the peer who rejected her. If she has not allowed herself to recognize and acknowledge her hurt, she may have little understanding of why she becomes aggressive.

While the list of events that may precipitate anger is endless, each of us can readily identify what will lead us to become angry. On the other hand, we may not be able to identify what makes others angry. Most people have had at least one experience when they said something that unintentionally triggered someone's anger. Unfortunately, many relationships involve a lot of guessing about motivations and feelings. When this happens, we can be very much off the mark in trying to identify what precipitated someone's anger.

As a parent or caretaker, you may be especially puzzled when trying to identify why your child or teen is angry. Certainly most parents can name events likely to cause anger in most children and adolescents. For example, a child will become angry when he is noticeably physically or emotionally hurt, ridiculed, disappointed, devalued, or embarrassed. Similarly, an adolescent may react with anger when his very natural needs for autonomy, peer approval, and feelings of being special are challenged.

In contrast, it may require your best sensitivity to understand what particular event precipitated anger for your child or teen in a specific situation—not least because children's and adolescents' needs are quite variable, change often, and may be experienced more intensely than those of adults.

Appraisal

The appraisal is the part of the experience of anger when we give meaning to the event. In a sense, it is the conclusion we arrive at once we have allowed the event to register in our awareness, and it is based on how well the event satisfies or does not satisfy our motivating needs, wants, and expectations. As with expectations, this appraisal may involve both conscious and unconscious conclusions. Just like expectations, appraisals are influenced by child logic as well as by more mature logic. As such, they may be accurate or distorted (Figure 4.6).

John, a somewhat hyperactive five-year-old whom I engaged in play therapy, would very often throw things at his younger brother, Ralph. John would also humiliate his brother and break his possessions. When directly questioned about his behavior, John was able to admit that he

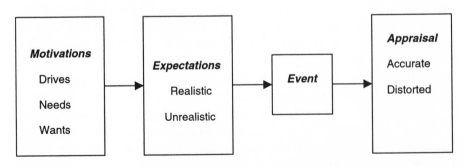

Figure 4.6: The appraisal of the event

was jealous of the toys given to Ralph. He also resented both the quality and amount of attention his parents gave to his brother. Based on his appraisal of these events, John believed that he was not cared for as much as his brother. This is an example of a very self-aware five-year-old who was consciously aware of his reactions, the events that led to his feelings, and the meaning he gave to the events.

An example of a more unconscious appraisal is reflected in my work with Linda, a fourteen-year-old girl. Linda's parents sought treatment because she was increasingly angry and rebellious, isolated herself in her room, and refused to do her share of the household chores. Her behaviors were clear expressions of a variety of emotions, including anger. Unwittingly, Linda had appraised the birth of a new sister and her parents' preoccupation with the infant as signs that they did not care as much for her as much as they did prior to her sister's arrival. Further discussion and exploration with Linda and her parents helped her to realize that her anger was also based on her belief that they now expected her to "completely grow up." In addition, she concluded that her parents no longer sought to be as available for her as they were previously. Likewise, her own struggles and ambivalent feelings about wanting to be independent added to her frustration. She became angry with herself when she felt dependent.

I have worked with many adult couples where one partner was angry toward the other for not sufficiently helping with chores around the house. Often one partner concluded that this lack of cooperation was due to a lack of genuine caring. In some cases, not doing the chores was really an expression of not feeling supported enough. For other couples, not doing the chores was partly related to a partner's underlying depression and dependency. In addition, I have worked with many couples where not tending to a certain chore related to one partner's discomfort or sense of inadequacy in performing a specific task.

Many conflicts between fathers and sons relate to erroneous appraisals of each other's motivations. Rick, a fifteen-year-old I counseled, never seemed to get around to washing the family car even though he was promised ten dollars for doing so. He and his father engaged in frequent arguments about what his father appraised as his son's laziness, lack of cooperation, and lack of motivation. While this was the meaning Rick's dad gave to his son's lack of follow-through, we later identified Rick's dependency and need for perfectionism as factors that played a dominant role in his refusal to complete the chore. In part, he believed that he should not have to work to earn money. In addition, his perfectionism led him to feel inadequate when he could not meet his own standards regarding how the car should appear after washing it.

We may appraise a particular event as being positive or negative in terms of whether it is satisfying or antagonistic to satisfying our wants, needs, and expectations. How negative the appraisal is will certainly influence the degree of our anger. Similarly, the importance of a need that is not satisfied will also greatly influence our quickness to become angered. If you, as an adult, do not get to have your favorite dessert at a restaurant, you may not get terribly upset. In contrast, if someone who promises to meet you at the restaurant stands you up, you would be more than slightly annoyed. Clearly, some needs are more important than others, and the appraisals related to them lead to different reactions.

It is a similar situation for children, although they may be quicker to respond with annoyance. If a six-year-old does not get to have chocolate chip ice cream, her favorite flavor, but instead has to settle for vanilla, she may be somewhat upset or annoyed. If, however, it is her birthday and she receives no ice cream at all, she may become very upset.

Tantrums are another example of how a distorted appraisal influences emotions and behavior. While irritability may be due to hunger, lack of sleep, and other factors, a child who has a tantrum may also have attached a great deal of personal meaning to an event, precipitating his outburst. We may be especially puzzled when young children have tantrums. Parents have reported being astonished over events that have caused their young child to become enraged. This has included being asked to wear a certain kind of coat to school, having a playmate merely touch a favorite toy, and spilling a drop of milk on a sandwich. Each angry reaction was triggered by an unrealistic appraisal of what had occurred.

As stated previously, appraisals may be accurate, or they may be distorted or unrealistic. Like expectations, appraisals are often based on child logic and voiced in the conversations we have with ourselves. Appraisals, like expectations, may be conscious or unconscious. They may be loud and clear enough for us to be aware of them, or they may take place so quickly or quietly that we do not detect them. If they are unrealistic, they will more often than not lead to a predisposition to become angry. Distorted appraisals include but are not limited to conclusions such as:

- The event happened because I was not liked.
- The event occurred because of something I did wrong (when in fact I had no influence over the event).
- The world is not at all safe.
- The world is not caring.
- If this happened, there can be no God.
- If this happened, I should not be religious.
- If my parents did that, they do not love me.
- My whole self-esteem depends on this event.

- My whole future rests on this event (when it does not).
- If this happened, it means nobody loves me.
- If this happened, it means I should not have done what I did (when it does not).
- If this occurred, then none of my needs and wants will be satisfied.
- If this occurred, then all of my needs and wants will be satisfied.
- Since this happened and my needs were not satisfied, I will not be able to satisfy my needs in any other way.
- I might as well give up.
- I have no control over my life.
- I have complete control over my life.

Individuals who are most prone to anger are those who are quick to feel wronged. This is especially the case when they conclude that they were purposely wronged.[2]

Being able to distinguish between appraisals that are accurate and realistic and those that are distorted and unrealistic is a major strategy for learning how to handle anger. Our increased capacity to clearly identify the appraisals we make helps us to better understand the role that our thoughts and feelings play in anger management. We further increase control over our emotional life when we increase our awareness of the appraisals we make about an event, distinguishing between those based on mature logic and those influenced by child logic. Similarly, as we are able to help children and adolescents distinguish between accurate and realistic appraisals and between distorted and unrealistic ones, we help them to be better prepared to recognize, understand, and cope with anger. Chapter 7 focuses on skills to help your child make this distinction.

Expectations Are Satisfied

At this point in the sequence, as depicted in Figure 4.7, we experience either a positive or a negative outcome based on the appraisal of the event.

If we appraise an event as satisfying our expectations, we may feel contentment, a sense of accomplishment, or perhaps a sense of power, mastery, and satisfaction. We may feel satisfaction and control when we experience our motivating needs and wants as being positively satisfied. We may subsequently experience people, and the world in general, as being supportive. This positive response may further affirm and confirm these positive beliefs and feelings and foster for us a sense of self-esteem, confidence, and empowerment.

There are times, though, when positive outcomes may lead to some negative feelings. This can occur when two or more forces are compet-

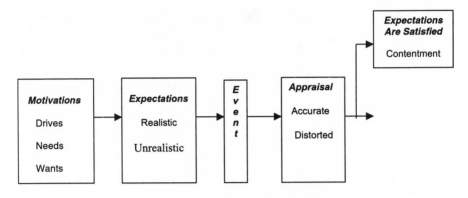

Figure 4.7: Expectations are satisfied

ing for attention and we feel conflicted about our needs or wants. The adolescent who is admitted to the college of his choice may feel extremely pleased but also overwhelmed by the new challenges and expectations he will face when he moves away from home. Though he may be happy to receive the letter of admission, he may become irritable later because of fears and anxieties that accompany the many life changes he will make because of this accomplishment.

For example, a thirteen-year-old girl granted permission to go on her first date may have certain of her wants satisfied, but she may also react with anxiety, confusion, and even anger. She may experience anger if she feels she can no longer be childlike in some of her behavior. She may even be somewhat annoyed at seeing her role in the family changing. Ironically, she may interpret permission to date as an indirect communication that her parents no longer are concerned about her.

Even adults can suffer from this. For example, they may feel conflicted over career success if they see such success as competing with their strong desire to spend more time with friends or family.

While there are some possible negative reactions to having expectations satisfied, I do not want to overplay them. Certainly if important and meaningful expectations are satisfied, the overriding result is positive.

Expectations Are Not Satisfied

As I have previously stated, some of us may experience only anger as our emotional reaction to a negative appraisal of an event. We may fail to be aware of the emotions that actually occur immediately after we appraise the event. These are our immediate or primary reactions based on our appraisal that our wants and expectations are not being satisfied. See Figure 4.8, which diagrams this process.

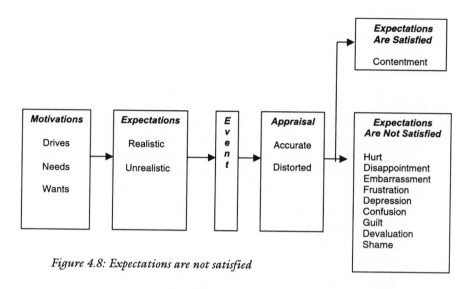

Figure 4.8: Expectations are not satisfied

A three-year-old may become angry when told he must take a bath. However, his anger is usually a reaction to other negative emotions. He may feel fear, a loss of control, or frustration. When an academically driven ten-year-old girl retreats to her room after getting a B+ on a report card instead of an A, she may experience anger toward her teacher, toward the test, or with herself. But her initial reaction, prior to anger, may be disappointment, hurt, shame, guilt, or embarrassment. Any of these emotions may lead to her anger. When a thirteen-year-old raises his voice in angry protest over being grounded, he is really reacting to feeling disappointed, powerless, embarrassed, or devalued. When an irate father yells at the official presiding over his daughter's soccer game, he may be angry at the call. When he yells at his daughter, he may also be reacting to the shame he feels for being the father of a player whose athletic abilities do not meet his expectations.

Any event that causes anger causes emotions such as hurt, sadness, disappointment, shame, embarrassment, frustration, depression, confusion, feelings of rejection, and feelings of devaluation. These are often the initial emotional reactions that most individuals experience for an instant after an event occurs that does not satisfy an expectation. These feelings may be short in duration and not very strong in one's awareness. It is at this point in the model that I find the analogy with videotape so helpful. If we had a videotape of our emotional experience at this point, the immediate emotional reaction may be so fleeting as to occupy only a few frames of the tape. For some of us, this internal experience passes by unrecognized. Instead, we are quick to move on to experience anger or take actions that reflect or express the anger.

Clearly this is a moment to slow down, pause, and reflect in order to more fully make sense of anger—a major goal of many of the strategies that are presented in later chapters.

There is a wide variety of obstacles that create difficulties for children, teens, and even adults in being able to clearly recognize the emotional reactions that precede or accompany anger. Many of us have learned not to tune in to our emotions. As children, we may have been more aware of how we felt. However, over time, many of us have been encouraged to ignore emotions in order to avoid appearing or feeling vulnerable. Some children and adolescents learn to distract themselves from, deny, minimize, or suppress uncomfortable emotions. Some go further and gradually minimize or deny not only emotions but also their wants, expectations, and even needs.

The pattern of tuning out emotions may start very early. For example, as a very young child, I may have negative feelings toward my parents because of some disappointment. At the same time, without full awareness, I may be saying to myself, "Well, I really am hurt and angry, but I am so little, so dependent on them, and so scared of their reaction (or mine). I will make sure I don't show them my feelings, especially my anger." A child may similarly stifle feelings if he is fearful of rejection, retaliation, or abandonment. Some children may conclude, "I am so scared of being abandoned, so vulnerable, that I must not be angry at them." This is just one example of how some of us begin to stifle emotions as well as wants and needs. By so doing, such children and adolescents become adults who are out of touch with their internal life. As they lose connection with themselves, they begin to feel alienated. Not connected to their emotions, they often become less sensitive to the feelings of others. This further fosters their feelings of alienation, a sense of being disconnected from others and self.

These children often become adults who are chronically angry without the awareness of the many hurts they have experienced. Such children and adolescents increasingly feel isolated from others. As they lose awareness of their feelings and needs, they become less able to have them satisfied. This often results in frustration and conflict in relationships and a diminished experience of genuine connection with others.

Children and adolescents may also have difficulty distinguishing among their emotions. Part of this difficulty may be due to factors previously described as well as to a lack of language to clearly differentiate their emotions. These are children and adolescents who may not necessarily need therapy but can be greatly helped by education about emotions.

Some of us may be aware only of a dominant emotion, such as sadness or depression. This is often the situation when we tend to avoid any experience of anger. Such individuals are often described as "anger stuffers," people who lack awareness of anger because they learned that anger is unacceptable, is dangerous, and will chase others away. Many people are stuck at this point because of their inhibited ability to experience anger. Instead of becoming angry with others, they become excessively disappointed and angry with themselves. Subsequently they experience unhealthy guilt, shame, and depression. They may be quick to unrealistically or excessively blame themselves when things go badly in their relationships.

For other people, recognizing and experiencing anger is more comfortable and therefore easier than recognizing and experiencing the emotions that precede anger.

As I have previously described, we often do not want to admit that we feel shame, hurt, disappointment, embarrassment, sadness, frustration, and other uncomfortable emotions. We may feel vulnerable when we admit such feelings—vulnerable in our own eyes and when viewed by others. We may feel more comfortable directing our attention outward, toward the person who we experience as having caused our anger. If I blame or focus my attention on others, I feel less responsible for my feelings. Similarly, this way of handling feelings keeps me from acknowledging that anger is a reaction to my own reactions and that it is determined in part by my own motivations, expectations, and appraisals. Clearly, when I focus my anger toward others, I keep myself from acknowledging and experiencing rejection, shame, hurt, disappointment, and other uncomfortable reactions that result from unsatisfied expectations.

So far, the model reflects a sequence of experiences that lead up to anger. However, from here on, the model becomes a little complicated, as the variety of negative emotions now interacts with bodily experiences and self-talk to affect our experience of anger. Bodily reactions impact thinking, emotions impact bodily reactions (which are themselves impacted by thinking), and so on. The bodily reactions may include any of the physical symptoms described in Chapter 3. They may be subtle and go unnoticed, or they may be so intense that they demand attention. If asked about the experience, some of us may vividly acknowledge and recognize physical reactions. Others recognize the physical reactions only after the expression of anger (see Figure 4.9).

Similarly, self-talk may be subtle or unconscious and go unnoticed, or so intense that we begin talking out loud. The self-talk might also include our reactions, in the form of accurate or distorted appraisals, to the emotions we are currently experiencing. The self-talk might involve self-dialogue that goads us to take some action or helps us to calm down or react differently.[3]

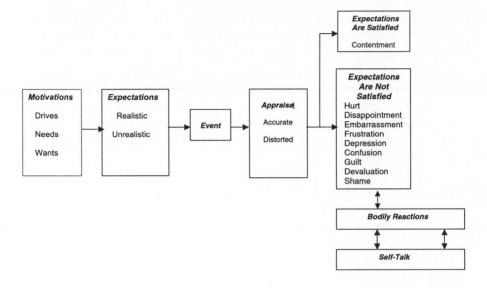

Figure 4.9: The interactions of emotions, bodily reactions, and self-talk

This is a moment when emotions, bodily reactions, and self-talk re-act to and impact each other so as to lead to a fight-or-flight response. This might be considered the deciding moment in anger management. Based on the interplay of these three influences, we engage with anger or pull back. I convey this interaction by arrows that go in both directions, connecting emotions (including anger), bodily reactions, and self-talk (Figure 4.9).

Making sense of anger involves increasing one's awareness of these three factors: emotions, self-talk, and bodily reactions. All strategies in anger management involve addressing one, if not all three, of these activities. Shifting attention to our physical reactions and learning to calm them, becoming aware of and addressing our self-talk, and recognizing the emotions that precede anger are the three basic tasks addressed in all strategies presented in this book.

Anger

Following a negative appraisal, the perception that our needs, wants, or expectations are not satisfied, we react with some form of anger (see Figure 4.10).

The subjective experience of anger, whether experienced on a conscious or unconscious level, provides a driving force and presses us to react. Even if the anger is minimized, denied, or blocked from aware-

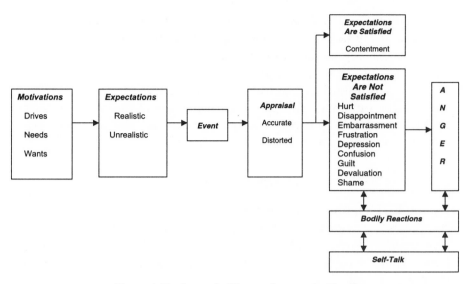

Figure 4.10: Anger, bodily reactions, and self-talk

ness, the experience elicits some kind of a reaction. Our typical pattern of reacting with anger gets played out at this moment. Like the moment that precedes it, this instant is marked by a dramatic interaction of physical reactions, self-talk, and emotions, including anger. However, our unique past pattern of reacting to anger will contribute significantly to our subjective experience at this moment.

At times, factors related to the current situation may very much influence how a child or teen manages anger. An example of this is Casey, a twelve- year-old who very much wanted acceptance from his peers. He really did not experience chronic anger. One evening he was cajoled by several friends into throwing eggs at cars from a highway overpass. The two boys who goaded him on did experience chronic anger in their lives. Such vandalism was just an expression of their anger. In contrast, Casey's strong need for acceptance outweighed his better judgment.

On one level, we may experience uncomfortable emotions, thoughts, or physical reactions that push for and dominate our attention. Even at a low level, this subjective experience competes with other motives, thoughts, and concerns. Our other motivations may force us to quickly suppress or repress anger.

Some people may be very much aware of physical tension accompanied by a volley of thoughts about how to react. Others may experience mild physical tension and self-critical thoughts, blaming themselves for what has occurred. Some might react with a subjective experience of numbness that is replaced several hours or days later by feeling sad, slightly down, or even depressed. And some may experience little self-dialogue or physical tension but aggressively strike out. To the casual observer, this last group of individuals would appear the most impulsive and thoughtless in their anger management.

It is at this instant that our unique past dictates how we experience and manage our anger. And it is only by pausing at this moment to reflect that we begin to experience an increased capacity to choose how we wish to respond and manage our anger.

Handling Anger

Figure 4.11 completes the model of anger and highlights the final component, six categories of strategies that encompass how anger can be managed. While we may handle our anger in a wide variety of ways, I have found that almost all of these strategies can be described by these categories:

1. Physical expression that is direct or indirect
2. Verbal expression that is direct or indirect
3. Acceptance of oneself, others, or the situation
4. Forgiveness of oneself, others, or the situation
5. Reflection
6. Suppression or repression

Physical Expression

When we are angry, we may respond with physical aggression toward the target of our anger. Seven-year-old Bradley handles his anger physically and directly when he hits his four-year-old sister or throws toys at her as a result of his anger with her. However, he may instead manage his anger physically and indirectly by throwing her toys against a wall or hitting his hand against a door in an explosive tantrum. These strategies are indirect in that they are directed away from the person perceived as the source of the anger.

Anger may also be discharged in a physical but indirect way when the physical action is focused on reducing one's physical tension associated with anger rather than expressing the anger. This method of handling anger may be more initially self-soothing and requires greater forethought. Thirteen-year-old Carol may go to her room and listen to music. By doing so, she is able to reduce her physical reactions to anger and become more emotionally calm as well. Rather than directing physical energy toward the object of her anger, Carol has learned to use a strategy that reduces the physical discomfort and tension associated with the anger.

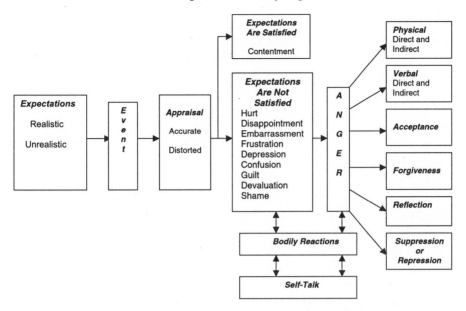

Figure 4.11: The complete model of anger

Common tension-reducing activities include exercise, hobbies, meditation, and even sleeping. Similarly, I include in this category all strategies that demonstrate less constructive ways of handling anger, such as use of drugs, use of alcohol, and eating disorders. Their long-term effect is destructive and does not contribute to positive self-esteem. Nevertheless, they are ways in which people attempt to reduce and contain the physical discomfort associated with anger by distracting from and reducing the tension associated with anger. However, as will be discussed in later chapters, truly healthy anger management involves strategies that are constructive and support self-esteem, not those that simply dull or cover up our discomfort.

Verbal Expression

"You are so stupid! I can't believe you did that! Can't you think clearly? How many times do I have to tell you to leave my things alone?"

Sixteen-year-old Jenny just told her younger brother Mark once again that he should not take her CDs. While it appears that Jenny is being direct in her verbal expression of anger, I categorize this strategy, name-calling and criticism, as an indirect verbal expression of anger. Certainly she is expressing anger toward the person whom she experiences as provoking her anger. But she does not use specific words to describe her feelings. She does not say she is angry, annoyed, upset, or enraged. She does not communicate in words any emotions that may have led her to experience anger. There is no mention of frustration, disappointment, hurt, or confusion. Instead, she shows signs of her anger—she raises her voice, turns red, lifts her hands in the air, and verbally criticizes her brother's thinking and behavior. She is expressing anger indirectly, through her body language and in words that reflect anger.

Even when Jenny calls her friend and discusses her anger toward her brother, she is also managing it indirectly because she is not telling her brother about her feelings. If she enters a note in her journal about the event, she would be expressing her anger both verbally and physically, but still indirectly.

In categorizing verbal expressions of anger, I consider only the actual discussion of anger and related emotions as being direct verbal expressions of anger. The direct verbal expression of anger is the strategy that requires the most maturity and practice. It is especially challenging to use this strategy to relate to people who are important to us. For these reasons, the direct verbal expression of anger may be one of the most difficult approaches for children and adolescents to learn. Strategies to assist children and teens with these skills are presented in Chapter 12.

Acceptance

Acceptance involves being able to sit with, recognize, and experience anger without responding to the pressured urgency to escape the experience, whether by impulsively reacting physically or verbally, by denying or minimizing the anger, or by distracting ourselves. Similarly, acceptance consists of being able to endure the emotional pain associated with anger.

The ability to sit with anger in this way is based, in part, on (1) positive self-esteem, (2) a capacity to be realistic when judging ourselves and others, (3) a capacity to be self-soothing, (4) tolerance for frustration and pain, and (5) practice. Acceptance is a process that many adults engage in as they strive toward increased maturity. Many of us achieve this goal, but to varying degrees.

Acceptance involves truly acknowledging our anger and the emotions associated with it. Acceptance also encompasses being able to accept responsibility for our own motivations, expectations, and appraisals surrounding the event that led to anger. Acceptance involves the ability to acknowledge that another person may have played a part in our reactions. However, real acceptance involves the capacity to recognize that the other person's behavior was based on his or her uniquely personal motivations, expectations, and capacities. It also involves an ability to fully recognize how unrealistic expectations and self-appraisals give rise to anger.

As I have been emphasizing throughout, it is difficult for many of us to accept our anger and all of the emotions that precede it. Strategies to help children and teens with this process will be explained in Chapter 6.

Forgiveness

Forgiveness is perhaps the most difficult yet life-affirming strategy for managing anger. As with acceptance, the ability to react to anger with forgiveness is based on positive self-esteem that includes a tolerance for frustration and a capacity to be realistic in terms of judging ourselves and others. By forgiving, I do not mean that we completely forget, deny, or overlook our anger at a situation or another person. Instead, forgiving means that we are realistic in acknowledging that there are many challenging situations in life that do not nurture or support our needs, wants, or expectations. We can spend a great deal of time being angry and resentful, or we can recognize our hurts and disappointments and gradually move on.

Forgiveness also means that we accept the humanness of people; including ourselves. We accept the reality of life that people occasionally behave in ways that leave us feeling disappointment, hostility, hurt, frustration, shame, rejection, and embarrassment. Acceptance involves recognizing that as much as we may want others to behave a certain way, they may not be obligated to do so. We accept that we too behave in ways that are disappointing, hostile, hurtful, and frustrating for others (and for ourselves). When we are forgiving, we try to acknowledge responsibility for our actions, learn from our mistakes, and improve ourselves. In this way, acceptance of our imperfect nature must occur before genuine forgiveness can be achieved.

Genuine acceptance and forgiveness are also based on an ever-growing ability to see others and oneself as complex, not just a reflection of single or simple behaviors and attitudes. In this sense, being able to accept and forgive involves being able to consider and accept the idea that we may all be doing our best with what we have. It implies that people hurt us and we hurt others. It involves forgiving ourselves when we form unrealistic expectations and appraisals of others and ourselves. It involves forgiving others who form unrealistic expectations or appraisals of us.

Even children and adolescents are able to learn that, as a part of their humanness, others may not be completely available to meet their needs, wants, or expectations. Similarly, a child who can really accept and forgive accepts that he may not be able to meet certain of his own needs, wants, and expectations.

Ultimately, acceptance and forgiveness allow us to direct energy toward the future. Instead of holding on to the past with grievances in the form of chronic anger, resentment, or distrust, we can now move on with our lives. More energy is available to work on the satisfaction of our needs and life goals. We may choose new methods or even seek out other people in an attempt to meet our wants and needs in more-effective ways.

Anger in adolescence is very much related to this increased awareness of the imperfect nature of self and others. Adolescence is an age when we are forced to recognize the realities of our parents' weaknesses as well as some of our own. Very often a teen's anger is related to disappointment surrounding expectations she has of her parents, herself, and what it is like to grow up. These realizations are just a few of the potential sources of anger for adolescents, which will be the topic of later chapters.

Reflection

I want to emphasize that taking time to think about anger does not mean obsessing for months or years. Instead, I am referring to the capacity to interrupt the process of impulsively moving from an internal emotional experience to a behavioral reaction. It is the ability to push the pause button on the playing out of one's anger, allowing for an interruption and subsequent reflection. Just as one can pause the tape to reflect on an image on the videotape, one can learn to pause to reflect on one's reactions during a given moment of anger. The ability to pause at this point is a crucial skill in the management of anger. It is only through developing this skill that we can really take time to more fully think about ourselves and choose how we want to respond to our anger.

This skill takes practice and some maturity for children. Even a young child who appears to have good control of his anger may be limited in the way he can think about his anger. He may understand his anger only as it relates to externally imposed punishment or rewards. He may not really experience a sense of choice based on his needs, wants, and expectations. Nevertheless, encouraging a child to reflect lays the foundation for more flexible self-control and increased tolerance for frustration.

Reflecting on anger leads to new ways to handle anger regarding a specific situation or person. Such reflection increases flexibility and is a necessary ingredient in problem solving. The amount of time for reflection varies. You may decide you need a half hour to reflect on your annoyance with a spouse or a week to decide how to cope with anger on the job. Similarly, a child may be angry with his best friend and decide not to talk to him for several days, while his adolescent sister may choose to withdraw to her room for a few minutes. In both cases, they have paused momentarily to think through their responses to anger.

Suppression or Repression

While reflecting on anger may lead to a conscious choice in how to manage such anger, suppression or repression is a way to avoid the conscious experience of anger. We suppress our anger when we experience it but try to deny, ignore, forget, or minimize the experience. We repress it when, without full awareness, we distract ourselves from more consciously experiencing such emotions.

Certainly there are many situations in our daily lives that lead to annoyance, upset, or more intense anger, and most of us learn to minimize or ignore most of them. Traffic congestion or waiting in line at the supermarket are just two examples of situations that might arouse some level of anger. It can be helpful to be aware of our reactions to these events, reflect on them, and choose to find an alternative way of traveling or shopping. Or, as a result of reflection, we may choose to listen to an audiotape of a book or music while driving or waiting. Both are strategies to avoid annoyance and anger.

Similarly, there are times in a relationship when we may decide not to express or communicate our emotions, including our anger. We may believe that, in the big picture, certain issues are minor. Choosing not to express anger may be an outcome of reflection and a decision that we really do not need to communicate every time we are impacted negatively in our relationships.

However, it is the ongoing suppression of meaningful anger in the context of significant relationships that leads to serious, long-term emotional consequences. A child or teen who experiences anger in response to actions of his siblings, parents, or friends needs to be able to feel comfortable sharing such feelings. If these are smothered or denied, he begins to feel less emotionally connected with others, victimized, and isolated. If he responds by continuing to ignore his anger, he further loses awareness of his emotions, is less likely to make others aware of his needs, decreases his chances for having his needs met, and increasingly feels as though he has little impact on others. He may begin to experience the world in general as being both insensitive and unavailable to satisfy his needs and wants. As a result, he may experience even more intensely and frequently those emotions that lead to anger.

Similarly, as adults, if we never express how we are affected in our meaningful relationships, especially with regard to important concerns, we increasingly feel less heard, less understood, and more isolated; the relationship eventually becomes less meaningful. As emphasized by one of the principles in Chapter 2, the constructive management and expression of anger is just one of the many building blocks for a good relationship.

~ ~ ~

The model of anger presented in this chapter offers increased understanding of the experience of anger. Specifically, I have tried to emphasize how the interaction of motivations, expectations, appraisals, and other emotions impacts anger. It is a comprehensive view of anger that encourages self-reflection. In addition, the model identifies six broad categories of strategies for managing anger, offering a thorough foundation of knowledge for helping your child or teen prepare for anger in everyday life. All of the remaining chapters in this book focus on how you can best help children and teens learn practical skills for the application of this model.

5

How Children and Teens
Express Anger

Children and teens express anger in many different ways. At times it is very easy to recognize their anger, such as when they are hostile or aggressive toward others or are physically destructive of property. We can readily understand why these children and teens attract attention from their parents, their teachers, mental health professionals, and the justice system.

But there are many expressions of anger that are more subtle and may easily escape even your focused attention. The anger underlying these behaviors may not be as apparent as aggression or violence. In fact, while aggression and violence are expressions of anger, most children and teens express anger in other ways. However, these behaviors can lead to lifelong difficulties in relationships, in self-esteem, in careers, and in achieving goals. This chapter will help you to better recognize the wide range of expressions of anger in everyday life.

Little Michael hurls his food off the table to express his irritation at his mother's prompting him to eat. Five-year-old Sally breaks her brother's toy truck in reaction to jealousy about their parents' attention to him. Thirteen-year-old Linda, while typically very easygoing, slams the door behind her as she retreats to her room following a defeat in a tennis match. These are expressions of anger.

In contrast, some adolescents, such as sixteen-year-old Kyle, resort to frequent use of marijuana to calm underlying anger. Similarly, fourteen-year-old Melinda may be getting lower grades as a reflection of her resentment about her father's high expectations for superior academic achievement. Six-year-old Matt withdraws to his room as a way of dealing with the tension and anger aroused by observing parents in conflict. Paul, a nine-year-old with a great sense of humor, may become increasingly sarcastic in his comments. These subtle expressions of anger may go unnoticed when not accompanied by observable hostility or aggression.

Whether expressed overt or subtly, such behaviors are uncomfortable for both parent and child. They lead to tension and conflict in family relationships. They may lead to parents getting angry, or to anger experienced by siblings. And especially when a child demonstrates anger in more subtle ways, parents may feel confused or frustrated by not being able to make sense of such behaviors.

While some young children may be very direct or even aggressive in expressing their anger, others may initially handle their anger in one of several ways. For example, a child may mask feelings of anger. He may experience anger but not admit it or express it, putting up a false front in an effort to please a parent, either out of love or out of fear. His internal thinking or self-talk may run something like this: "I'm just a little kid and I really don't want to upset them. Who knows what will happen if they realize I'm upset or angry? A good kid doesn't get angry. I just won't let them know how I feel!"

Another way of handling anger is for a child to deny it or convince himself that he is not angry. The self-talk might be: "I am angry, but I'm afraid of my anger—I'll chase everyone away with my anger. It's bad to feel angry, so I'm not angry!" While such reactions may not even be a part of one's awareness, they express the variety of reactions one may experience when angry. Some children and teens may even display or express extremely positive emotions in an effort to camouflage their anger and maintain harmony.

A child may also express anger by redirecting it from the original source of his anger. Your child may be angry toward himself but instead express aggression and hostility toward siblings. He may be angry toward others but instead express it toward himself. A child also redirects anger when he slams an object or his hand against a wall. And some children may not show anger at home but instead express it in the classroom or toward peers or other adults.

Developmental Factors That Influence How Children and Teens Express Anger

There are certainly many reasons why each child manages anger the way he or she does. As described previously, the messages we get from parents, teachers, siblings, religious leaders, peers, and others influence our attitudes and behaviors. The particular culture or ethnic group we belong to will further influence how we express anger. The factors that contribute to how a given child expresses anger are as complex as those that help form her personality. However, there are several major developmental factors that contribute to how children express their anger.

The Degree of Dependency or Autonomy the Child Has Achieved

Children or teens who are extremely dependent on their parents may be very fearful of experiencing or expressing anger toward them. Any experience of anger may quickly arouse for them fears of abandonment, rejection, or punishment. These fears may result in managing anger through repression and suppression. They may unconsciously not allow the anger to surface or, when it does, may be quick to deny or minimize it. They may unwittingly distract themselves from experiencing anger. Their discomfort with anger may be based on unrealistic beliefs that lead them to conclude they should never express anger. This way of managing anger may quickly become an ingrained habit, since children, especially younger ones, often lack the capacity to think through and understand the real consequences of expressing their anger. They may automatically take flight from any experience of anger if they associate it with these fears. Similarly, such children may become extremely sensitive about expressing their anger or being the target of others' anger.

A Child Has Fewer Resources than an Adult

Although this statement may appear self-evident, it must be emphasized. Children are immature in their problem-solving skills, in their capacity to understand and to manage their emotions, and in their general intellectual and social abilities. Even the most intellectually bright child lacks emotional maturity. While some may be more emotionally mature than others, compared to most adults they lack the self-awareness and experience needed to identify, differentiate, and understand emotions and the role they play in behavior.

Your child relies on child logic, immature thinking that does not include a sophisticated understanding of cause and effect. In this type of thinking, conclusions are made about events because they occur close in time or they are in close physical proximity to each other. For example, if your child has been wishing for rain and there is a sudden downpour, she may conclude that she caused it to rain. Similarly, a young child who is angry with a sibling may feel quite guilty if the sibling subsequently has an accident. The fact that both young and older children blame themselves following a divorce is often based on this type of logic.

Child logic accounts for many distorted conclusions, unrealistic self-expectations, and self-focused self-perceptions that lead to experiences of anger. At the same time, child logic greatly influences how your child feels, thinks, and behaves in response to his anger. Child logic greatly influences the development of your child's initial habits in managing his anger and may strongly impact his anger as an adult.

Children Differ in Their Threshold for Stimulation

Children react to anger in a variety of ways partly because they vary in how sensitive they are to hurt, pain, disappointment, and other emotions that lead to anger. Certain children are more easily affected than others. Quickness to anger may be influenced by environmental experiences, but genetics also influence one's predisposition to anger. For example, studies suggest that boys are more prone to be aggressive than girls due to genetic or hormonal factors. Even infants differ in the rapidity with which they become angry or distressed. Your daughter may be described as "thin-skinned" if, from day one, she was easily startled by noises or movements around her. On the other hand, your boy may have been very quiet and less responsive since infancy and subsequently; he may not react with anger as quickly. He might then be described as "thick-skinned."

Children Have a Low Tolerance for Frustration

Based in part on their self-centered orientation, children often lack the capacity to postpone the satisfaction of their needs. As such, they may be unable to project themselves into the future and envision their needs being satisfied. They may be quick to feel dominated by the needs of the moment, and any effort to distract them from meeting these needs may seem futile. Recall when you promised your child the thrill of going to an amusement park or getting a favorite toy. You will most likely remember his or her persistent anticipation and inability to focus on anything else. Better yet, recall an event in your own childhood when you anticipated something that was exciting. You may quickly be reminded of the mixture of pleasant anticipation coupled with uneasy frustration that time was not passing fast enough. For most children, anticipating an exciting event makes waiting difficult or unbearable.

It is even more frustrating for children when their expectations are not at all satisfied. Children and teens with a low tolerance for frustration are more likely to become angry when needs or wants are not satisfied.

Children require skills to develop a tolerance for frustration. This tolerance is based on a child's sense that her environment will be consistent and dependable in meeting her needs. When a child has this sort of nurturing environment, she begins to experience herself as lovable and valued. In addition, she develops a sense of optimism that her needs and wants can be satisfied. She can further increase her capacity for frustration by learning skills to reduce the physical tension that accompanies frustration.

Impulse Control Takes Time to Learn

As your child improves his capacity to tolerate frustration, he develops a greater capacity for impulse control, which makes him more able to constructively manage both his experience of anger and the expression of it when his needs and wants are not satisfied. The child who impulsively acts out his anger is a child who has a low tolerance for frustration.

Impulse control takes time to develop and is affected by the intensity of needs and wants. A child can learn frustration tolerance and impulse control by observing you and others who are models for how to manage frustration. He also learns frustration tolerance by hearing messages about how to behave. Through both direct and indirect messages about how to get needs met, a child develops standards for conduct that influence his expectations of others and himself. These standards then impact how he experiences and handles anger.

Children Are Immature in Their Capacity to Be Self-soothing

Children are immature in their problem-solving skills, in their cognitive skills, and in managing their emotions. For this reason, they lack effective self-soothing skills. Self-soothing is the ability to manage uncomfortable emotions in a positive, calming way. In addition, self-soothing involves the capacity to decrease physical tension.

Your child needs to have experiences that help improve her ability to be self-soothing. She develops these skills whenever she successfully manages her uncomfortable emotions and physical tension. It is essential that she have successes in self-soothing, whether by observing how you manage your frustration, through your soothing her, or by learning skills to do so. As your child matures she can continue to master these skills, which are fundamental for constructive anger management.

Children Are Immature in Their Capacity for Introspection

Introspection involves the ability to reflect on our behavior, emotions, and thoughts. In addition, another component of constructive reflection is the ability to observe patterns in our own behavior, emotions, and thoughts. Young children lack this ability and vary in how early they begin to develop it. However, it is this capacity that allows your child to experience both flexibility and choice in deciding how to manage anger.

In general, children become increasingly capable of introspection as they approach adolescence. (I highlight this in various chapters when discussing specific anger management strategies for children and adolescents.) At the same time, all of the strategies presented in this book very much depend on learning skills in introspection.

How Children and Teens Express Anger

I have discussed seven ways children are developmentally different from adults. It is no surprise, then, that children develop a wide variety of anger management strategies that are ineffective, not constructive, and even destructive. The strategies children use are based predominantly on emotionality rather than on more mature logic and reasoning.

Any attempt to help your child better manage and express his anger requires your understanding of how he currently does so. I am sure you are already very much aware of some of the ways your child expresses his anger. However, only by increasing your awareness of both the obvious and subtle expressions of his anger will you be able to help him change his behavior.

One way to increase your understanding of your child's ways of expressing anger is to be attentive to his interpersonal interactions—how your child relates to you, to family members, and to those outside the family. Pay attention to the way your child expresses uncomfortable emotions, and search for subtle evidence of anger that you may have overlooked in the past.

As I've noted, our own discomfort with anger may lead the brightest and most well-intentioned parent to overlook a child's expressions of anger. Such discomfort may lead a parent to communicate directly and indirectly that anger is not acceptable. So when I ask you to become more attentive, be aware that this task may at times be an uncomfortable undertaking. As you can see, helping children to manage anger is not easy. It is a challenge that will take much effort, practice, and patience. Completing the following two exercises is a meaningful first step in this process.

Exercise

Take a moment to think about how your child expresses anger. Describe in a sentence or phrase several ways your child typically expresses anger and several strategies that he uses less frequently.

Review Table 5.1 to help you further assess the ways in which your child expresses anger. This inventory consists of thirty behaviors that reflect different ways children and teens may express anger. Indicate by a rating from 0 to 3 the frequency of such behaviors. Keep in mind two major concepts as you identify your child's responses to anger.

Table 5:1: Child and Adolescent Anger Inventory

Circle the rating that best reflects your observations of how your child expresses anger.

	Not at all	Some times	Often	Very Often
1. Verbal aggression	0	1	2	3
2. Verbal assertion	0	1	2	3
3. Physical aggression	0	1	2	3
4. Displacing anger	0	1	2	3
5. Physical exertion	0	1	2	3
6. Self-destructive behaviors	0	1	2	3
7. Cynicism/sarcasm	0	1	2	3
8. Withdrawal	0	1	2	3
9. Scapegoating	0	1	2	3
10. Passivity	0	1	2	3
11. Forming alliances	0	1	2	3
12. Anxiety	0	1	2	3
13. Physical ailments	0	1	2	3
14. Suicidal behaviors	0	1	2	3
15. Self-denigration	0	1	2	3
16. Self-sabotaging behaviors	0	1	2	3
17. Sabotaging the efforts of other	0	1	2	3
18. Disruptive behaviors	0	1	2	3

19. Underachievement	0	1	2	3
20. Neediness	0	1	2	3
21. Regressive behaviors	0	1	2	3
22. Contrariness	0	1	2	3
23. Negativism	0	1	2	3
24. Pessimism	0	1	2	3
25. Runaway behaviors	0	1	2	3
26. Lateness	0	1	2	3
27. Vandalism	0	1	2	3
28. Shoplifting/stealing	0	1	2	3
29. Substance abuse	0	1	2	3
30. Sexual promiscuity	0	1	2	3

First, as I stated in the introduction, anger is experienced at various intensities. At one time your child may be mildly annoyed, and at another time she may be enraged. The different ways she expresses her anger reflect how angry she is during a specific period of time.

Second, your child may not be completely aware of her anger or that she is in fact expressing anger. Rather, the behaviors may be based on thoughts and feelings that are unconscious.

It is not my purpose to have you become overly preoccupied with looking for evidence of anger in all of your child's activities. You may look at this list and think, "My goodness! What is this psychologist saying? He sees anger everywhere!" Although I list many behaviors as expressions of anger, these same behaviors may also be based on and motivated by other emotions, such as anxiety or sadness. Only by increasing your awareness of your child can you be clear and accurate in understanding the motivations involved in his specific actions. In an attempt to provide further clarification, I have provided a description of each of these categories, including examples of when these behaviors most often reflect anger.

These expressions of anger are not in a specific order. Certain strategies are more constructive than others and may be considered more mature ways of expressing anger. Read the entire list and the descriptions that follow before you rate your child.

Verbal Aggression

Your child displays verbal aggression when he yells at, teases, or belittles others. His verbal aggression may be expressed through name-calling, bullying, or the use of inappropriate language. We are all familiar with children, adolescents, and adults who express anger in this way. Other than physical aggression, verbal aggression may be the most noticeable form of aggression.

Verbal aggression represents an indirect way of expressing anger. I use the word *indirect* to highlight the fact that when a child expresses anger this way, she is showing her anger without directly saying "I am angry." Her raised voice, name-calling, and foul language all reflect underlying anger. It is easier for many people to verbally express anger in this indirect manner. It is more difficult to stand in close proximity, look another person in the eye, and honestly and directly share both the feelings leading to our anger as well as the anger itself. Direct and honest communication leads us to feel more vulnerable. When we are truly direct, we share how we have been affected and not just our anger. Similarly, we talk about it rather than show it.

Your child is not simply trying to communicate anger when he is using the indirect approach; he is striking out in an attempt to hurt someone who he feels has caused him pain, or he is trying to protect himself. This approach also distracts him from experiencing the uncomfortable emotions that so often precede anger: hurt, embarrassment, rejection, disappointment, shame, and fear, among others. It is the use of language to cause pain that makes it verbal aggression rather than verbal assertiveness.

Verbal Assertiveness

We are verbally assertive when we directly and honestly express our anger and discuss what caused it. Words such as *angry, annoyed, irritated,* or *enraged* are commonly used. Verbally assertive statements may even include words that some consider vulgar, but the purpose in this type of expression is to communicate the intensity of our anger rather than to hurt another person.

During an initial family session, Charles, a bright, verbal, and open sixteen-year-old, used assertive language to express how he felt when his mother would not let him attend a specific rock concert. "I was just so angry! I felt treated like a little kid—like what I want or feel doesn't matter. I felt totally discounted, devalued, and belittled. Do you know how frustrating that is?"

While this is not the usual manner of expression for teens, he was verbally assertive in clearly stating his feelings and how he felt impacted. While many adults do not express themselves in this way, it is often even more difficult for children and adolescents to assertively express their anger. This is due to the developmental limitations we previously looked at and the fact that children often lack awareness of their emotions as well as the language to describe them. Also, greater self-control is necessary to state anger in a verbally assertive manner.

Physical Aggression

Some children and adolescents are quick to lose their temper and physically express their anger. Such anger may be directly expressed toward the person who is seen as causing our anger. Physical expressions of anger may include assault or even murder.

In contrast, a child may direct anger toward objects, as when a seven-year-old throws a toy truck across the room after being told he can't watch his favorite television program. In this case, he would be discharging his anger physically, but in an indirect way. He would be using an indirect approach in managing his anger when he hits something with his hand, destroys a possession that belongs to the person whom he sees as making him angry, or hits himself.

Physical aggression very quickly demands our attention. And even more than with verbal aggression, you may feel compelled to rapidly and firmly set limits with a child or teen who is physically aggressive. Physical expressions of anger often have the greatest potential to arouse emotions in others and lead them to be physically aggressive in return.

Displacing Anger

A child displaces anger when she focuses her anger toward someone or something other than the real target of her anger. She may redirect her anger because she feels uncomfortable experiencing or expressing anger toward a person whom she loves or fears. Kathy, Paul, Susan, and Brian provide examples of how anger is displaced.

Kathy, a usually quiet five-year-old, was described by her parents as scolding and hitting the family dog after being admonished by her mother for not sitting still during dinner.

Paul, a tall and rapidly maturing twelve-year-old, initiated a fight during lunch after his teacher told him that he most likely would not be promoted to the next grade.

Susan, age sixteen, was not home in time to get a call from her boyfriend, Jim. She was disappointed and frustrated, and she became angry. In part, she was annoyed with herself for not getting home in time. Instead of experiencing this annoyance and self-criticism, she became annoyed with Jim for not calling her later. Similarly, she became annoyed with her sister, Beth, who was taking a shower and missed getting to the telephone in time to speak to Jim.

Brian, a classic underachiever, often expressed anger toward others for his own inability to follow through with his homework. He would blame and at times express anger at his teacher for giving the assignment, for not reminding him to take the book home, and for his own failure to study. His parents indicated that he often blamed the school in general for his own difficulties in completing his assignments.

When your child displaces anger, he is trying to avoid being responsible for his own feelings and actions. Too, he may avoid acknowledging anger and discomfort toward himself.

A youngster may also displace anger when shame is the basis of her anger. Since shame is extremely uncomfortable, she may instead focus her anger on those who have led her to experience this intensely unsettling emotion.

Physical Exertion

James, a high school junior and a member of the school wrestling team, lifted weights daily as part of his exercise regimen. From time to time he became angry, sometimes regarding school, sometimes about his relationship with his girlfriend, and sometimes over his relationship with his family. He came to realize that one of the ways he could soothe himself and reduce his tension was to engage in a strenuous exercise program. In doing so, he redirected his energy related to his anger and channeled it toward more constructive goals.

Pamela was a rather intense and competitive young runner who participated in both short- and long-distance races. When questioned directly, she indicated that she enjoyed the running for its own sake as well as for the competition when she raced. However, she later added that some of the motivation was driven by a belief that she had to prove something to others. She even reported that, to some degree, she was motivated by anger related to never feeling competent in athletics when compared to her brothers. Her self-talk included "I'll show them!" To some degree, her anger contributed to her competitive drive.

Some teenagers engage in physical exertion to the point of exhaustion as an indirect way of coping with anger. In this situation, the adolescent frequently pushes himself to the point of exhaustion because of self-directed anger for not meeting a self-imposed standard. This can be a form of self-destructive behavior.

Self-Destructive Behaviors

Self-destructive behaviors are behaviors that a child or teen engages in that have a potential to cause self-injury. They are complex in their meaning and origin. They are often seen as expressions of anger that are directed toward ourselves instead of toward others. In this way, self-destructive behaviors are a special form of displaced anger. Your child or teen may direct anger toward herself if she experiences extreme discomfort in directing her anger outward. This may occur when she is fearful of expressing her anger or alienating others. Similarly, she may exhibit self-destructive behaviors when she is angry or disappointed with herself for not living up to expectations that she has established for herself.

Self-destructive actions may be conscious and planned or based on unconscious motivations. A child or teen may hurt himself without being aware that he is attempting to distract himself from uncomfortable emotions such as anger and hurt. This may occur by direct self-injury, through substance abuse, or when teens and children engage in risk-taking behaviors such as riding recklessly, doing dangerous stunts on skateboards, or responding to dares by peers.

Cynicism and Sarcasm

Statements of disbelief, doubt, or suspicion demonstrate cynicism. Sarcasm is reflected in comments that reflect bitterness and mockery. Sarcasm may also have a humorous component, often evident in double meanings. Those who are bright and verbal and yet do not express their anger in a more direct and obvious manner often use these expressions of anger.

Even young children can be sarcastic and cynical. They may come across as skeptical in their general outlook, frequently make wisecracks, and consistently expect that things will go wrong or that they will be disappointed or hurt.

Young children who are cynical may be verbal and appear mature in some ways. However, they are often very much in need of nurturance and reassurance. In fact, their anger is often a derivative of the hurt and disappointment they experience in their lives. They often perceive their environment as somewhat lacking in nurturance and support. They may tend to associate more with adults while they look down on their peers, in part because they may feel inadequate around peers but special when they are with adults. Similarly, such children may feel too inhibited to express their true feelings. As a result, they often feel ineffectual and lack genuine interpersonal connectedness with others. They often feel misunderstood while hoping that adults will magically know what they feel and need.

The adolescent who is constantly cynical may have much difficulty relating with adults because of conflicts with authority. In fact, some of his anger may be related to the disappointment he experiences in seeing adults more realistically than when he was younger. This type of adolescent may also doubt the sincerity of others partly because he himself is not open about his true feelings. As he masks his emotions, he develops doubts about the sincerity of those around him.

Parents may find a sarcastic youngster as somewhat appealing. This appeal may stem from the fact that his comments are humorous, reflect his brightness, and imply a more mature capacity for abstract thinking. In addition, adults often admire sarcasm in children and adults if this is a trait they like in themselves. Finally, some parents may derive vicarious pleasure if their child is expressing some form of anger that they themselves never do.

As you can see, this form of expressing anger reflects a higher level of maturity and is somewhat more socially approved of than certain more destructive approaches.

Withdrawal

Children and adolescents who feel that they have little impact on others may withdraw as a way of responding to their anger. They may not express their anger due to intense fear of anticipated rejection. In some cases they experience others as being angry with them for being angry. Shame and guilt about anger may also motivate a child to withdraw.

One child I counseled became more isolated when his older sister returned home from college during the holiday break. Another young girl, described earlier, had angry feelings related to her mother having to work part time, and she became increasingly silent, withdrew, and experienced headaches.

Withdrawal may be a child's best strategy for coping with anger or with the uncomfortable emotions aroused by anger. The withdrawal may be a constructive way to limit the impact of whatever is provoking the anger. Similarly, it may be an attempt to maintain self-control. Thus, withdrawal can be a constructive coping strategy, intended to control anger by avoiding the situation.

Your child may choose to selectively withdraw. She may tend to withdraw from specific people, at certain times, or under special circumstances. Her withdrawal may in fact be an effective and healthy form of self-protection. In this case her withdrawal may represent good judgment.

Children with poor self-esteem are often quick to give up when facing a new challenge. At times they are unrealistic in their expectations about their performance and are quick to conclude they have failed. Withdrawal may be an attempt to avoid the overwhelming discomfort of the hurt, disappointment, and anger directed at oneself. This type of withdrawal is a factor in underachievement for children who have highly unrealistic expectations of themselves.

Some children who have more severe emotional difficulty may withdraw into fantasy as a way of responding to anger. Very young children fantasize as a natural part of play. They engage in fantasy situations in which they experience power, impact, and control over their surroundings. However, a distressed child may withdraw into fantasy for extended periods of time.

Withdrawal may be due to other factors such as shyness or depression, and so it is important, just as it is in reviewing any of the behaviors described in this list, to focus on the pattern of such behavior. Does your child withdraw after conflicts with a sibling, following a visit to a divorced parent, or immediately after playing with a neighbor? Notice if the withdrawal occurs on specific days of the week or at specific times of day. The key issue is recognizing if withdrawal closely follows incidents that may have aroused anger.

Scapegoating

Scapegoating is a special type of displacing anger. Scapegoating involves blaming another person for a mistake we have made, for our ill fortune, or for our own actual or perceived weaknesses. Scapegoating targets one person or a whole group of people as the object for our anger. Racial prejudice is certainly one form of scapegoating.

Your child may resent a younger child's dependency and vulnerability because he is uncomfortable with these traits in himself. Your teenager may direct her anger toward bright children because she feels intellectually inadequate.

This type of misdirected anger is often an element in teenage gangs. Members of one gang react to members of others not as individuals but as part of a pack that is perceived as either weak or threatening.

Scapegoating reflects stereotyping of individuals based on a common factor. Individuals may be targets for scapegoating because of their skin color, where they reside, their place of origin, the type of clothing they wear, religion, gender, or sexual orientation. In each case the scapegoated group becomes the target for misdirected anger.

Passivity

A child or teen who is passive may exhibit much difficulty in assertively stating his needs or opinions. He may be uncomfortable stating his views even about minor issues such as his identifying his favorite television show, what kind of food he likes most, or the kind of game he prefers to play with his friends. He may at times feel victimized by his peers and family members as a result of not playing an active role in the decision-making process. Passive children often feel they do not deserve to express their feelings or thoughts. Poor self-esteem often contributes to this difficulty. In fact, the passive child may seem more down or depressed than angry. And yet depression may at times be related to unexpressed anger and hurt.

Passivity may also be a response to a fear of rejection. A child may choose to be passive if he feels others will reject or become angry with him for stating his views out loud. In addition, he may be passive because he has confused being assertive with being aggressive. In this situation, your child may experience any assertion as an act of aggression.

A passive child is often trying to protect her family by not getting them upset. She defers her wishes so that others are more likely to have their wishes satisfied. The passive child may be very well behaved and never express her anger. However, as she continues to be passive, she may increasingly feel less understood, less known for who she is, and as though she has little impact on the world around her. This alienation and helplessness further fuel her anger.

Anxiety

Physical and emotional anxieties are often associated with angry feelings. Your child or adolescent may experience physical tension and apprehension associated with anger. His discomfort with anger may lead him to quickly suppress it when he experiences it, or he may unwittingly repress it. At those times he may experience anxiety in place of his anger. He may view anger as a violation of his own standards, or he may fear losing control of his anger. He may experience anxiety associated with both of these situations. In contrast, he may experience only anxiety if the unconscious anger, anger that is blocked from his awareness, begins to surface to awareness.

In order to determine if your child's anxiety is a reaction to anger, observe if she becomes anxious prior to or following an anger-provoking event. Be alert to the physical signs of anxiety as well as to activities that may be attempts to mask her anxiety. For example, many teens try to reduce their physical tension and anxiety through substance abuse, sexual promiscuity, or alcohol abuse. These inappropriate self-soothing activities are intended to reduce anxiety, some of which may be based on anger.

Since anxiety has many causes, determining when, and if, anger plays a role is a challenge that requires careful observation.

Formation of Alliances

One way for a child or teen to channel angry feelings is to ally herself with another person who is similarly angry. An angry child experiences camaraderie with other angry children. Such children sense a common ground as a factor in their friendship. In contrast, some passive children seek an association with an aggressive child in order to experience vicarious pleasure in being around someone who openly demonstrates anger.

Shared anger may also be the underlying motivation for bonding and attachment in the formation of gangs. In addition to experiencing anger, teens may also be attracted to gangs because of a need for affiliation with others who share similar attitudes, experience, or identities. They may identify with each other because of their similar social class, feelings of alienation, or ethnic background. But underlying anger is often a contributing reason for their shared involvement. Group aggression allows gang members to share in their expression of anger with the support, encouragement, and participation of peers. Unfortunately, this is a destructive expression of anger.

Sometimes group participation is motivated by a desire to appropriately channel anger. Some adolescents form groups to achieve shared goals such as raising money for an illness, doing volunteer work in a hospital, or cleaning up a neighborhood.

Physical Ailments

Emotional stress can cause or worsen physical illnesses. Headaches and gastrointestinal upset are just two symptoms that children may experience in reaction to such stress.

In my practice and workshops, parents have provided examples of how their children's physical ailments reflected the influence of emotional factors. A five-year-old boy ran fevers each time his father had to leave home for a business trip. An asthmatic fourteen-year-old girl had a severe flare-up in her symptoms each time her parents had a loud and frightening quarrel. Steven, an eleven-year-old boy, experienced sleep difficulties after each weekend visit to the home of his divorced father and newly blended family.

These are not imaginary ailments. They are ailments that are the result of, or exacerbated by, emotional stress. They may be caused by anxiety, depression, or anger. The way to determine if such symptoms are influenced by emotional factors is to observe the pattern of their occurrence. Certainly these ailments occur in all children and teens for a variety of medical reasons. However, they are more likely to be related to emotional issues if they appear to follow or closely precede especially difficult emotional periods that include conflict, separations, or other changes in the home or family. Physical ailments can often be traced to emotions that are not expressed or acknowledged.

Focusing attention on physical ailments may also be used to get attention. A child may try to obtain attention by eliciting concern regarding his physical well-being. He may be fearful that directly asking for such affection will arouse anger or rejection, or he may have observed this pattern in other family members. I should emphasize that he may not be fully aware of the motivations for such behavior.

Suicidal Behaviors

Increasingly, studies indicate that difficulties in managing anger, in addition to depression, very often underlie suicidal thinking and behavior that leads to suicidal gestures and attempts. Many adolescents and adults who engage in suicidal behaviors report that it is the anger of a "final-straw" incident, coupled with ongoing depression, that pushed them to commit suicidal behavior. Such children do experience depression. However, their suicidal behavior is fostered by anger related to a moment of heightened emotional pain over loss, rejection, abandonment, or feelings of hopelessness and helplessness.

The distinction between a gesture and attempt is important. By gesture, I am referring to behaviors that indicate a child or teen is toying with the idea of suicide but does not really want to commit suicide. A teen may take a dosage of medication that makes him sick rather than takes his life. Another child may cut himself seriously enough to warrant medical attention but not so badly as to end his life. A suicide attempt is an action that is more clearly intended to end a child's life. In either case, these actions should be taken seriously because they often lead to accidental deaths.

Discussions of plans for suicide, threats, giving away belongings, or comments such as "You won't have to worry about me for long" are just a few of the signals that your child may be considering suicide as a way to cope with his emotional discomfort. See Chapter 17 for a description of warning signs of suicide.

Self-denigration

Self-denigration refers to the self-critical thoughts that a child recites to herself. This monologue may be voiced out loud, as when we overhear little children chastising themselves for doing something bad. Most often their self-denigration involves a barrage of self-critical statements following some sensed failure to live up to their own expectations or the expectations of others.

A mother who attended one of my workshops shared an example of self-denigration by Jamie, her six-year-old. She described having entrusted Jamie to watch over Carl, his four-year-old brother, while she attended to a chore in the basement. Though she was out of the room for only several minutes, Carl tripped during her absence and hit his head against the edge of a table, cutting his forehead and requiring several stitches. Needless to say, Jamie was quite distraught. He was later overheard saying to himself, "You're no good! You should have been more careful! It's your fault that Carl got hurt!"

The incident left Jamie feeling overwhelmed and quite guilty about what had happened. But accompanying that guilt was a variety of angry feelings. He was angry with himself for failing to have greater control in the situation. He may have experienced anger toward himself as well as toward his mother for putting him in that position of responsibility. He may also have become angry toward his mother if he believed that she was angry with him for not being more careful. He may have experienced anger, consciously or unconsciously, toward his brother for not being more careful and for doing something that led him to be in a very uncomfortable position in the eyes of his mother and himself. Finally, if he had been experiencing ongoing anger toward his brother, this would further complicate his feelings.

Your teen may silently denigrate or become verbally critical toward others because he is in fact self-critical about qualities within himself. The frequent bantering and the put-downs expressed by children and teens often reflect this type of self-criticism directed outward in the form of verbal aggression. Their verbal barbs may reflect anger related to disappointment with themselves. Such displeasure may be based on the discrepancy between a child's or teen's ideal image of how he should feel, think, or behave and how he actually feels, thinks, or behaves.

This self-denigration may be focused on a variety of attributes, including physical features, intelligence, or personality traits. Children and teens with low self-esteem may especially be highly sensitive to criticism, rebuff, and exclusion. They experience these incidents as confirmation of their lack of self-worth. These children and teens are very often self-denigrating as they approach any new challenge in their lives. Understandably, their self-denigration further reduces their self-esteem. At times this negative self-dialogue leads to self-sabotaging behavior.

Self-sabotaging Behavior

Self-sabotaging behaviors are self-induced actions that negatively affect how a person functions. Thoughts and feelings that are both unconscious and conscious underlie these behaviors. A child is self-sabotaging when she impulsively gives up on new and challenging activities. She may have developed a negative mind-set based on her past performances that leads her to be pessimistic in her expectations. Subsequently, she may quit or fail to engage in tasks, since she is predisposed to anticipate failure. The emotional hurt, disappointment, and frustration lead to further anger and an increased sense of failure. In this way her thoughts and behaviors become self-fulfilling.

I have counseled many youngsters who have been described as having learning disabilities. Many were children whose reading difficulties were additionally influenced by a negative mind-set fostered by their disability. Only after some exploration with these youngsters did they become aware that they were engaging in negative self-talk, an ongoing dialogue that interferes with their concentration on the task. This dialogue consists of phrases such as "You really can't do it, so why bother?" This self-talk is a contributing component for many students who are underachievers as well as learning-disabled. Their disappointment, frustration, and even anger with themselves distract them from paying attention.

I recall ten-year-old Rodney describing his first fishing adventure with his father. While fishing, Rodney became somewhat intimidated by his father's critical comments about his skills in handling the rod and reel. Subsequently, his line became a bundle of knots as he engaged in negative self-talk and labeled himself as incompetent at fishing.

Children who are self-sabotaging quickly give up and often avoid all new challenges. These are the children whose disappointment and related anger lead them to avoid trying out new hobbies. They also resist engaging in unfamiliar social situations, fail to complete academic assignments, and often avoid competitive activities.

One example of self-sabotage is an adolescent who was not accepted for the high school basketball team during the first round of tryouts. In part, because of his anger, he reduced his practice for the next few weeks, only to find that he did not make the team at the next tryout either.

The element of anger that is often present in such avoidant behavior may be directed either toward the self or toward others. Feeling unable to live up to imagined and wished-for accomplishments, the self-sabotaging youngster lacks resilience and is quick to feel defeated and ineffective. When he directs his anger at himself, he remains self-denigrating and self-sabotaging. However, he may also begin to direct his anger outward. Rather than admit that his anger and anxiety are about his own lack of accomplishment or skill, he may project his anger onto others and blame them for setting up obstacles to his success. He may then express his anger by sabotaging their efforts.

Sabotaging the Efforts of Others

Any communication or action by which a child belittles, devalues, or disrupts another person's efforts falls into this category. It is the pattern of such behaviors rather than one single event that suggests these actions are expressions of anger. A child who knocks over his brother's block tower, verbally criticizes or ridicules his sister's efforts to make the volleyball team, or forecasts his brother's failure when competing in a race are some typical examples of this type of behavior.

Such communications, whether expressed at home or in the classroom, are often based on anger that may have its roots in feelings related to competition, jealousy, and hurt. The target of such misdirected anger may be very specific. A child may pick on a younger sibling, a particular schoolmate, or the new kid on the block. Some children are less focused in how they direct their anger and instead engage in bullying or general disruptive behavior.

Sabotaging the efforts of others may also be accomplished through relational anger. Children or teens may spread rumors, form alliances, or criticize peers in an attempt to sabotage their relationships.

Disruptive Behaviors

Behaviors that interfere with the activities of others can be described as disruptive. When your child disrupts the activity of siblings, playmates, or parents, this may be a reaction to resentment, slight annoyance, or intense rage related to needs or expectations that are not being satisfied. These behaviors may be based on very natural needs to be admired or to be the center of attention. At other times they may reflect your child's attempt to get you involved with him to calm anxieties that he may be experiencing. Disruptive behavior may also be a derivative of sibling rivalry and related to feelings of competition for attention, jealousy, insecurity, anxiety, or anger.

The disruptive adolescent may be more overt, brazen, and upsetting in his behavior than when he was a young child. When involved in a group, such teens may try to outdo each other in being troublesome. Behaviors ranging from excessive talking in class to vandalism can be influenced by these needs and related anger.

Some adolescents may be disruptive in a more passive way. For example, your fourteen-year-old may challenge and upset you by his appearance. Many teens who dress in an unusual or eye-catching manner resent the fact that others stare at them. However, they are very often adolescents who need to demonstrate their uniqueness and individuality by their appearance. These adolescents might argue that they do not seek, nor do they need, any special attention.

Underachievement

While some children and teens show their anger through overt or passive behaviors, others show their anger in a very narrowly defined way—through the lack of academic achievement.

Underachievement may best be described as a lack of academic achievement at a level commensurate with one's abilities. The underachiever is a youngster who has sufficient intellectual ability but does not perform the tasks that are essential for achievement. For example, such a youngster reads at or above grade level but refuses to complete assignments. Although a youngster in the elementary grades can be an underachiever, the majority of underachievers are adolescents.

As parents, we are quick to give labels to teens who gradually exhibit falling grades or lose interest in school. We call them lazy, lacking in motivation, rebellious, or "typical adolescents."

However, a refusal to do schoolwork may in reality be a reaction to internal stress, the type of stress that leads to anxiety, depression, or anger. Whether motivated by genuine academic difficulty, the lack of challenge, the crippling effect of unrealistic self-expectations, or distraction from intense emotions about concerns unrelated to academics, underachievement is often the result of anger and resentment. In part, underachievement occurs when children and adolescents are preoccupied with their anger or resentment, which diverts their energies from academic performance. Anger at teachers, parents, siblings, peers, or self is often at the core of this passive-aggressive response to the academic challenge.

Underachievement can also represent a quiet way of rebelling against what is perceived as pressure to please others. This represents an attempt to individuate and to feel less controlled by others' expectations. Although such individuation may appear to be misdirected and self-sabotaging, for some adolescents it is often the first time they ask themselves, "What am I doing for myself and what am I doing for the approval of others?" A child who shuts down in academic performance may be going on strike. She may be communicating resentment about performing for others rather than herself. Such youngsters may express their anger this way without being aware of their underlying motivation.

Neediness

At times, neediness evidenced by children may reflect real or perceived needs based on fears, anxiety, and/or anger. Some children come across as being overly demanding or manipulative. However, it is helpful to remember that when a child is especially manipulative, he is usually trying to change his situation so as to reduce his emotional discomfort, often his underlying anxiety or anger. He is trying to have his needs or expectations met by others when he feels unable to satisfy them on his own.

It is interesting to note that we respond positively to an infant who is crying and frantically waving her arms. With an almost instinctual reflex we want to meet her needs, and we don't hesitate to give her lots of attention in the form of holding her and talking to her. In contrast, usually about the time the child begins to walk and say no we are less inclined to respond with our undivided attention and affection. We may experience her demands for attention as totally unreasonable for a child her age. We may resent her neediness and label her as infantile, too dependent, too demanding, manipulative, or attention-seeking. Our different reactions at these two ages has much to do with our attitudes about dependency and when and how often neediness should be indulged.

Excessive bids for help, statements such as "I can't do it" or "It just won't work," and behaviors that communicate extreme or inappropriate dependency may reflect a child's resentment over having to grow up and assume responsibility. Such behaviors may reflect anger, depression, and an underlying protest: "You are not being a good enough parent! If you were, I would be able to do it" and "Hey! Look at me and give me more attention. Don't take me for granted, even though I don't really need your help for everything anymore!" Such neediness may be expressed in relation to self-management at school and at home.

A young child tearfully complains to her mother that she is not able to button her shirt, when in fact she has been doing so for the last two months when Mom is not around. A fifteen-year-old may ask to be driven to his baseball league games even though he could easily ride his bicycle or take a bus. These are just two more examples of neediness that may be related to a bid for reassurance, a certain level of anxiety, or some feelings of annoyance. When neediness is extreme, it may lead to regressive behavior.

Regressive Behavior

Your child regresses when he displays behavior that he engaged in and which was more appropriate when he was younger. Regression usually occurs in response to the stress of change. Children and teens, as well as adults, often show regressive behavior as a way of coping with depression, anxiety, or anger related to the stress of change. In doing so, they use a strategy that may have been self-soothing and which they found to be partially effective in helping them cope in the past. Each of us may at times resort to past coping strategies when faced with life's especially difficult challenges. For example, your older child may evidence regressive behavior when, following your divorce, he begins to wet the bed again.

A nine-year-old girl whom I counseled exhibited tantrums following a move to another state. Her mother reported that she used to have tantrums when she was five years old.

Julie, a fourteen-year-old, spent a great deal of time in her room playing with her childhood dolls following her breakup with her first boyfriend. Regression is often an attempt to regain a sense of control.

It can be a distraction from the frustration and anger that result from feelings of loss of control.

Contrariness

Children and teens sometimes become contrary in their thoughts and behaviors. In part, this reflects an effort to demonstrate independence and self-assertion. Especially in adolescence, contrariness may demonstrate a teen's initial attempts to develop a unique identity, distinct from that of his parents or siblings. It is a period when teens first develop the capacity to be self-observing and more consciously choose the qualities and behaviors they want as part of their evolving identity.

For many teens, developing a sense of self is a relatively smooth process. But for some, this period is extremely stressful because they lack confidence or a solid foundation on which to build their identity. Instead, they assume a position that is in opposition to those around them. In this way, they try to show themselves and others that they in fact have an identity. The teen who develops an identity focused on being contrary exhibits what is called a "negative identity."

The teen who develops a negative identity demonstrates a high frequency and intensity of contrariness that often reflects anger and negativism in general. It is an attempt by the teen to convince himself and others that he is separate and independent when in fact he is neither.

Your adolescent may be contrary in an attempt to convince you and others that he is not like you. To be similar to you, or even to agree with you, may be experienced by him as a step toward losing his sense of individuality. Therefore, being contrary is his attempt to feel in control. His contrariness may also be an expression of anger related to the inner frustration of lacking an identity. This may be very evident in the youngster who communicates in his behavior the unconscious message "Tell me what to. do or how to behave—I dare you to!"

School Phobia

While any form of school phobia may be based on a variety of factors, including fear, anxiety, or depression, anger often underlies it.

Truant behavior is a statement of opposition to the community and parental expectations. Truancy may be related to feeling misunderstood, either on an emotional level or in the area of learning skills. It may represent a need for affiliation with peers who have similar negative attitudes. Similarly, school phobia may reflect anger about feeling that there is no group within the school with which the teen feels she can identify. She may be a loner who experiences a lack of emotional connection with others. She may be the child or teen who is bullied or scapegoated by others.

Sixteen-year-old Karen became truant when she was rejected by a group of peers, most of whom were cheerleaders. She increasingly sought out other peers who experienced a sense of being ostracized, and she dropped out of competition in both academic and extracurricular arenas.

Stuart, a bright twelve-year-old, became school-phobic following his fifteen-year-old brother's placement in a residential home. He exhibited increased anxiety and depression about going to school. In part this was related to peers teasing him about his brother. The loss of and perceived abandonment by his brother aroused many intense emotions, including resentment toward those who facilitated his brother's transfer from the regular school to the program. Underlying his behavior was resentment toward his mother, school officials, and stepfather, who had married his mother only one year prior to the placement.

Negativism

Negativism may vary in expression from a mood that is experienced for a few hours or a few days to a more enduring and pervasive trait. A child or teenager may exhibit a negative attitude toward a specific teacher or a parent. However, negativism may be more pervasive and reflect an overwhelming negative attitude toward adults and authority in general.

Negativism is often derived from anger due to underlying hurt, an experienced sense of defeat, and even a sense of hopelessness. A child communicates through her negativism her perceptions that people are not reliable, that her environment is not supportive, and that in general the world is not a very good place.

Such negativism is very different from a healthy critical nature, which teens evidence by their increased need to have things proven to them. A critical attitude can remain flexible and open, while negativism implies a rigid mind-set that is closed to being influenced.

In part, becoming more critical in adolescence is a natural reaction to teens' increased awareness of the weaknesses and contradictions of adults and of society as a whole. These disappointments can form a part of their motivation to aspire to certain ideals or develop healthy negativism.

Sally was a thirteen-year-old who lived with her alcoholic father. He was extremely critical and not emotionally available for her. Two years previously, Sally's mother lost her own mother and suffered a prolonged depression. She was not available to nurture or support Sally during this time. Although Sally's mother tried her best to manage the family, Sally experienced her mother as being passive and ineffective. Over time, she developed much negativism about her being lovable and about the capacity of others to help meet any of her needs. This was in part based on identifying with her mother's passivity as well as believing her father's criticisms of her. Her already low self-esteem was further threatened by the anger and resultant guilt she felt toward her parents. Sally felt defeated and hopeless. Friends experienced her as having an angry edge and as being contrary, doubting, and critical.

Children and adolescents like Sally perpetuate decreased self-esteem when they discredit, minimize, or even ignore positive feedback by others. They focus on even the slightest negative interaction as proof that they are unlovable and continue to be negative because the situation is perceived as hopeless.

Pessimism is a partner to negativism. Your child may be pessimistic when he not only feels negative about the present but also believes that the situation will not improve in the future.

Pessimism

A pessimistic child is one who expects the worst to happen. He may doubt that any good can happen, either through his own action or through the actions of others. He may expect that others will not be available to help meet his needs. While hurt and disappointment are the foundation for pessimism, it is often suppressed anger that maintains it.

For example, one high school student I counseled had become increasingly pessimistic about the future following a series of several losses during his second year in high school. These losses included the deaths of a friend and a sibling. Although he previously had participated in extracurricular activities, he greatly decreased his participation during his junior year. His grades dropped and he could not get into the college of his choice, so he decided he would not attend college at all. Clearly he was depressed. Concerned family members, teachers, and friends tried to get him to talk about his depressed feelings. What was not discussed was his anger. Typically a person with multiple losses feels generalized anger at the world, toward God (if he is religious), and even toward those who are still living, including himself.

Pessimism can be paralyzing and may underlie many of the behaviors described in this inventory. In the extreme, pessimism can lead to a sense of helplessness and hopelessness, two basic factors associated with suicidal thoughts and actions of severely distressed teens.

The anger associated with pessimism may be focused on one's family. When this occurs, pessimism may lead to runaway behavior.

Runaway Behavior

Running away from home is clear evidence of anger. It is a strong expression of dissatisfaction in a relationship. And yet certain children and teens believe that they will be happier and healthier if they run away from home. Their anger may be related to real or perceived abuse or neglect, or to a sense of not feeling understood. On the other hand, some children run away from home simply because they have tremendous difficulty following the limitations and expectations set by their parents.

By running away or threatening to run away, a child or teen may be signaling her attempt to avoid interpersonal conflict. Running away may seem to be the only option by which she can manage anger.

Many runaways lack good judgment and end up emotionally or physically victimized. Some are resourceful, have a definite plan, and seek contact with and support from a parent, grandmother, relative, or agency while continuing to attend school. It is a sad fact that some teens are making a wise decision if they carefully plan a way out of an abusive or dangerous situation. In either case, running away is clearly an expression of anger and frustration.

Lateness

Lateness—being late for school or planned family activities as well as coming home after an agreed-upon curfew—may be due to poor judgment, being absorbed in a task at hand, difficulty with assertiveness, or difficulty with independent action (such as leaving a group of friends). Similarly, it may be due to problems with concentration due to attention deficit disorder. Lateness may also reflect a need to test limits, assert independence, and feel a sense of autonomy and separateness.

However, lateness may also reflect strain in a relationship. Being slow to get ready, being late to meet someone, or returning late may be the behavioral equivalent of a verbal communication that says, "So there—I'm not going to let you tell me what to do," "If you treat me that way, I'll show you," "I really do not want to go with you," or "I am in control."

A very vivid recollection comes to mind as an example of how lateness can communicate anger. As a fourth-grade teacher, I had the opportunity to work with children who had behavioral problems. During a hectic morning the class was exceptionally disruptive as they lined up to go to lunch, so as a consequence, I detained the entire class for ten minutes after they became quiet. At first they grumbled. Then they grimaced and, with much resistance, lined up and waited quietly.

At the end of the lunch period (and much to my surprise) the entire class quietly returned to the classroom—ten minutes late. This mass action required cohesive, well-organized planning. They had expressed their anger! I confess that I had to applaud their unity in how they expressed their frustration and anger, but I offered them more constructive ways to express their anger in the future.

Vandalism

Vandalism is clearly an aggressive act. Vandalism may range from slightly defacing property to complete destruction of property in or outside the home.

Children who vandalize are angry. Their aggression is often displaced from the real source of their anger and destructively redirected toward another target. Children and teens often destroy property when, in fact, they are angry with siblings, peers, teachers, or their parents. Their anger may be more pervasive when they feel they are being ripped off by society, and they may resort to vandalism in an attempt to get even for feeling victimized.

Shoplifting and Stealing

A child or teen who shoplifts or steals may be motivated by a variety of factors. Some teens shoplift even though they are not really in need of the items they steal. Shoplifting in this case is often a call for attention based on a sense of neediness that the child may or may not realize or understand.

Some children and teens steal from their parents or from their stepparents. Such behavior usually reflects anger that is not verbally expressed. They may be communicating in a nonverbal way a statement such as "You don't care about me! I'll show you—I'll get something from you anyway!" Often taking things from one's parents is really an attempt to get closer. For example, I worked with one youngster who stole stamps from his stepfather's collection. Similarly, a young adolescent I counseled began taking jewelry from her older sister several months before her sister was scheduled to leave home for college. In both of these cases, the youngsters were really attempting to make contact and preserve their involvement with people who were important to them.

It is also quite common for young children to steal items from a store just to see what it feels like. This may be a way to test limits, an action based on poor impulse control, a rebellion against one's own conscience, or a result of perceived deprivation. It should be mentioned that in most of these cases, the child feels sufficiently guilty and stops the behavior. Certainly this type of stealing is unlike that of the child who repeatedly steals and who victimizes different people—behavior more likely based on underlying anger and a sense of deserving more.

Substance Abuse.

The media devote a good deal of attention to substance abuse by teens, frequently emphasizing the legal aspects of such activities. This focus often leads us to ignore the fact that adolescents use these substances for a variety of reasons. Their use of drugs and alcohol may represent an initial experiment for the adolescent who is exploring himself, wanting to fit in, or simply rebelling. However, ongoing use is a sign of abuse or dependency.

Substance abuse may also be an attempt to reduce or eliminate uncomfortable emotions. The emotional and physical side effects of anger, anxiety, or depression are in fact temporarily reduced with the use of substances. Under the influence of alcohol or drugs, a child or adolescent may easily distract himself from the experience of anger. The muscle tension, irritability, guilt, negativism, and other effects of anger may all be minimized or eliminated by the distracting effects of getting high. Sometimes drug or alcohol use allows some individuals to become less inhibited and to more easily express anger. However, this is not a preferred or recommended way to manage feelings.

Sexual Promiscuity

Sexual promiscuity is another activity that may serve to reduce the overall discomfort of anger, though teenagers may be motivated to engage in sexual activity for a variety of reasons. Their involvement may be based on their natural sexual development, their need to fit in with their peer group, their wish for approval and closeness, or their desire to control, shock, or rebel. Obviously, when sexual activity is a form of rebellion or predominantly driven by a need to control, it can be a derivative of anger.

Frequent and indiscriminant involvement in sexual activity can help distract a teenager from the discomforts of anger. Physical intimacy feels good, and such closeness may be temporarily reassuring to someone who feels insecure, lacks self-esteem, and is very depressed or angry. Physical intimacy may help teens feel more appreciated, especially if parents or other adult significant others are not experienced as caring or available to provide support or nurturance. However, there are risks associated with frequent and indiscriminant sexual activity. These include pregnancy as well as sexually transmitted diseases such as HIV, HPV, herpes, and others.

Teens need and seek alliances. When they experience a sense of emptiness, they often resort to sexual activity to soothe themselves. I have counseled many girls who, by their own report, engaged in sexual activity to feel wanted and appreciated. In many ways, as these girls were later able to understand, they were seeking a male partner who could be a "parent" and provide them with both direction and nurturance. In doing so, they were acting out of an intense need for closeness and much anger regarding their lack of emotional connection with their parents or others.

❧ ❧ ❧

Take time to review the inventory and determine in what ways your child expresses anger. Try to assess if there is a pattern to how your child or teen manages anger. For example, determine if he uses certain strategies in certain situations or with specific individuals. Has he used some of these strategies in the past but is no longer demonstrating them? Are you clearly able to identify major concerns in his life that may provoke anger? Are you able to identify what contributed to your child's having learned one strategy instead of another?

By taking time to answer these questions, you will become more sensitive to your child's specific needs and what areas to focus on when helping him to make sense of and manage anger in his daily life.

II

How to Apply the Model of Anger with Your Child or Teen

6

General Guidelines for Using the Model of Anger

While this model of anger was initially developed with children, adolescents, and adults who demonstrated a wide range of difficulties in understanding and managing anger, this book focuses on preparing your child or teen to develop the knowledge and skills to understand and manage anger long before he or she experiences more serious difficulties related to anger.

The more you apply the techniques in these different ways, the more you will help your child internalize the kind of understanding that leads to increased self-awareness, self-control, tolerance for frustration, and problem-solving skills. Help your child to view these anger management strategies as rehearsals for constructive anger management rather than as strategies to practice only when immersed in the experience of anger.

Teaching Through Modeling

An effective approach to teaching anger management is to model it in your own life. Children learn through observation as well as through discussion. By now you know that this approach toward understanding and managing anger involves your full participation. The more consistent you are in practicing the same strategies that you teach your children, the more likely they are to make them a part of their daily life. While sharing examples of how you apply these understandings to better manage your own anger will be useful, I am not suggesting that you share personal issues that are inappropriate for your child. For example, it may be inappropriate to discuss with your child anger you experience toward your spouse. However, you may want to share with your child your increased understanding of your anger concerning an incident at work, one that occurred while shopping, or a reaction to your child. (Specific communication skills to assertively express anger are discussed in Chapter 12.)

An Informal Approach to Teaching the Model of Anger

Teaching the model of anger is accomplished by discussing its parts and how they fit together, either in the context of an ongoing and spontaneous discussion or as a formal discussion of anger. For example, when your child shares an event that has aroused her anger, you can help her identify the emotions that preceded her anger. Or you may, as part of that conversation or another, help her recognize how unrealistic conclusions and expectations influenced the course of her anger. This approach also allows for a more natural exchange and flow in the conversation. You may share a specific strategy to help her manage her anger related to this event. Focusing on just one part of the model at a time may initially be the most effective approach when working with a child or teen who has only minimally engaged in discussions of her emotions. It may also feel more comfortable to share your ideas as part of the natural flow of conversation with your child.

A Formal Approach to Teaching the Model of Anger

In contrast, depending on your child's ability to understand and your comfort with such discussion, you may want to use a more formal approach in teaching him the model. You may want to discuss and share with him your understanding of the model and how you have used it in your life. The model of anger can be formally taught to one child or to a group. When using this approach, you can clearly state that you will share with them a way of making sense of and managing anger. While this structured format can be used even with young children, it is most suitable for older children and adolescents. First, summarize all of the chapters that have so far been presented. These provide the basis for an understanding of anger that fosters both learning about and applying the model of anger. Ideally, when teaching the model to a group, it should be presented over several sessions so that children have the opportunity to apply what they have learned to their personal experiences.

The Right Dosage

Be alert to how well your child can handle discussions regarding anger. Specifically, remember that your child or teen may only be receptive to a certain dosage of discussion regarding this unsettling emotion. Your teenage son may be very comfortable having a discussion about the anger of a peer or sibling but is not quite ready to address his own anger. Your teenage daughter may be able to directly discuss her anger but not when it concerns you. Finally, your seven-year-old may express his irritation toward you about your not buying him a toy but will not share his deeper anger regarding your impending divorce.

Dosage may also be reflected in the directness of your conversations. For example, as stated previously, boys may engage more easily in discussing feelings when they are involved in shared activities such as driving in a car or taking a walk. Younger children may be more open to discussing anger while engaged with you in parallel play. They may feel much more comfortable in conversations regarding anger when they are playing side by side with toys, clay, crayons, or a simple board game that does not require much concentration.

The Need for Consistency

The need for consistency is an important issue to consider when teaching the material presented in this book. By consistency, I am referring to the need for you to be consistent in your behavior and also for both parents to be equally invested in helping a child learn the model and practice strategies based on it. If you talk about the need to better manage anger and spend time discussing and practicing the model while your spouse ignores, minimizes, or criticizes such activities, your child will be getting mixed messages about anger.

The model of anger and the strategies based on it are strongly founded on encouraging self-reflection regarding emotions and thoughts. Any behavior on your part or that of your spouse that belittles, criticizes, or minimizes these activities will greatly diminish the impact of your teaching. Similarly, be aware that any competing messages from siblings, peers, or other important figures outside the immediate family may also interfere with your attempts to help your child develop constructive ways of managing anger.

A most poignant example of how inconsistency undermines the program was reflected in my work with Adam, a fifteen-year-old whom I counseled regarding academic underachievement. Adam had been angry over his mother's remarriage a year after her divorce. While he experienced deep love for her, he did not feel very attached to his stepfather. It seemed that each time he made progress in being able to more constructively share his feelings with his mother and stepfather, he soon engaged in demonstrations of anger such as ignoring his curfew, not calling home when he was expected to, and periodic outbursts of anger. It took several weeks to find out that his older brother, Aaron, was fueling his anger by frequently expressing his anger toward his mother and stepfather. Adam was torn between wanting to remain close to his brother and reestablishing a more positive connection with his mother.

Applying the Model to Your Child's Anger

As stated previously, the more frequently your child can be encouraged to apply the model to his own anger, the more it will become a natural part of his repertoire. If you find that he is hesitant to address his own anger, suggest he address a situation that left him feeling only somewhat annoyed or irritated. Similarly, in an effort to help him feel comfortable discussing his anger, you may suggest he address an experience that does not directly involve your relationship with him. Instead, have him discuss anger or irritation related to situations or people outside of the immediate family.

Apply the Model to the Anger of Others

As I stated previously, some children and adolescents find it easier to discuss the anger of others than to address or even recognize their own. These situations may involve friends, relatives, or even strangers on the street that you have observed dealing with anger. Again, the goal in such discussions is that with repeated practice, children gradually begin to experience comfort with addressing their own anger.

Similarly, it may even be easier for your child or teen to discuss the anger of others with whom she has no personal relationship. For example, the media, movies, literature, and news reports offer excellent examples of anger you can discuss with your child. Some of you may feel more comfortable initially using these examples because they may be easier to discuss than the anger experienced by you or your child. Chapter 9 is devoted to helping you make use of these resources since it is often more comfortable, and therefore easier, to discuss other people's anger.

Group Anger

The model offers a way of making sense of group anger as well as individual anger. Like individuals, groups are faced with deciding how to manage anger—whether to express it constructively or destructively. When the model is applied to groups, we can better recognize how shared motivations influence expectations of the group. Similarly, we can understand how these expectations influence conclusions that may ultimately lead to anger.

When applying the model to groups, you may wish to consider the wide variety of groups that promote political, religious, or environmental causes. You can also discuss how gangs may unite around a theme of anger. Help your child identify the strategies used by these groups and whether they appear constructive, destructive, or both. Focus also on helping her grasp the concept that individuals often join or form groups as a way of managing individual anger. They seek alliances with those who may share similar anger. They may join forces so that they can combine their resources and energies, gain support, and increase the chances of having their message heard by others.

Another issue to discuss, when applying the model to groups, is the fact that individual members may be more assertive or even aggressive when they are part of a group. One aspect of group dynamics is that some members feel freer to engage in activities that they might not do if alone. They in effect give up some responsibility and, in the grip of strong emotion such as anger, may unfortunately act impulsively rather than proceed more slowly through thoughtful problem resolution. Gang violence is often an outgrowth of this unique aspect of group interaction.

Remain Committed, Persistent, and Patient

Learning to make sense of and manage anger is an ongoing life process. At times you may be anxious to have your child learn all the "right" ways to manage anger, as if there were one final level of achieving anger management that will forever prepare her to manage all situations in an ideal way. You may at times wish that all you had to do is discuss one strategy or have your child read a book. However, it is through repeated practice, application, and shared discussion that your child will become more effective in this lifelong process. This requires commitment, persistence, and patience on the part of both you and your child.

7

Identifying Emotions Associated
with Anger

This chapter provides guidelines and strategies to help you assist
your child in identifying and better understanding emotions that
precede and are associated with anger. In addition, special attention is
given to exploring how anxiety, depression, and shame may be associated with anger. Identifying and understanding emotions that precede
and are associated with anger are essential steps in making sense of anger. A child who recognizes these emotions can more fully understand
the complexity of his anger. Through this process he increases his connection with himself and becomes more aware of his wants and needs.

Emotional Awareness

Helping children and teens make sense of anger involves teaching them
the skills of self-reflection necessary for increased emotional awareness.
Emotions do not occur spontaneously. Rather, they are triggered by
our interaction with others and the world around us and by our
thoughts, other emotions, and neurobiological activities in our body.
Emotional awareness regarding anger includes many different forms of
awareness, described in what follows.

Awareness of the Subjective Experience of Anger

Our subjective awareness of anger involves our overall
this emotion. The awareness may best be described by im
phors.[1] Especially when intensely angry, a child or teen ma
ing "ready to explode" or that she "could go wild." In ...., ...
may use words such as *irritated* or *annoyed* when her anger is less severe. Some children may focus on actions they feel like taking in response to experiencing anger, but do not readily describe their anger.
"I could just punch him," "It makes me want to just run away," and "I
feel like destroying things" are just a few examples of statements made
by children who, while in touch with their anger, focus on actions as a
way of discharging the tension associated with it.

Awareness of Bodily Responses That Accompany and Precede Anger

As emphasized in a previous chapter, anger includes a variety of physical and physiological reactions. A child or teen who has increased
awareness of the physical side of his anger may be aware that his breathing is rapid and shallow, that his muscles are tense, and that when he
gets angry his nostrils flare, he grits his teeth, and his face turns red. Increased awareness of bodily reactions to anger is an important step in
managing anger.

Mixed Emotional Reactions That Include Anger

As we mature, we begin to recognize that we can have mixed or multiple emotions. These may occur simultaneously or in various sequences,
depending on whether we are paying attention to various aspects of the
situation, to another person, or to ourselves. A ten-year-old may experience both pleasant anticipation and anxiety about going to summer
camp for the first time. Similarly, a thirteen-year-old may enjoy a family
camping trip but experience irritation that she is not with her friends.

Hidden Anger

We may lack awareness of certain emotions. As described previously,
our lack of awareness of our emotions or thoughts has to do with how
we focus our attention. For example, anger may be our most noticeable response to an anger-provoking event and dominate our attention, while hurt and sadness remain submerged.

This type of partial awareness may be compared to the partial view
we have of an iceberg (see Figure 7.1). If we attend only to the part of
an iceberg that is above the water, we see just a portion of it. Similarly,
when we attend only to anger, we remain unaware of other related
emotions on which that anger is based and which strongly influence
our motivations and behavior.

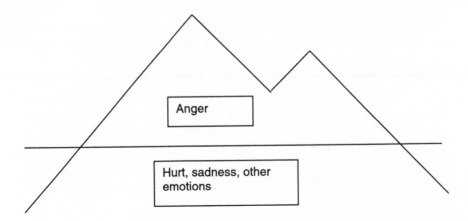

Figure 7.1: Suppressed or repressed hurt, sadness, or other emotions

At other times, sadness and hurt may dominate our attention while anger remains hidden from our awareness. This is reflected in Figure 7.2.

I use the analogy of the iceberg to suggest that we may tend to minimize, deny, or ignore emotions that are uncomfortable to experience. But by avoiding or suppressing our emotions, we become less able to cope with and resolve problems. Our unconscious emotions (and thoughts) influence the emotions and thoughts that we are aware of. It is only when we have access to both conscious and unconscious experi-

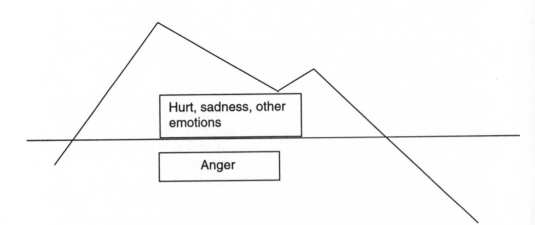

Figure 7.2: Suppressed or repressed anger

ences that we can make the best sense of life situations we encounter and our emotional reactions to them. Similarly, we are most connected with ourselves when we have such awareness. To the degree that we experience only anger and lack awareness of the other related emotions, we lack a more complete self-understanding.

Another way of understanding hidden emotions may be demonstrated by the cube in Figure 7.3. This cube offers an analogy of our ability to shift attention regarding our emotions. At any moment, in regard to an upsetting event, we may focus on anger. Anger can become the foreground to everything else. It can preoccupy our thoughts, emotions, and bodily reactions. In contrast, when we shift attention to the other emotions, anger is no longer the focus of our awareness and we can be more fully aware of the richness of our emotional life. First, view anger as being at the bottom of the front face of the cube, with hurt on the top of the inside rear face of the cube. In contrast, view the cube in such a way that anger appears on the bottom of the inside rear face of the cube, with hurt at the top of the front face.

The notion of suppressed, repressed, or hidden emotions is especially important in regard to anger. At times you may observe your child's anger and conclude that the intensity of his anger is not warranted by the situation. A reaction that seems too intense often suggests that anger about important personal needs has been suppressed; such anger may remain dormant until it is triggered by another anger-provoking event. In response, anger about the recent event combines

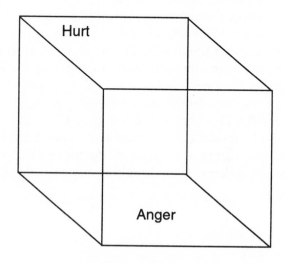

Figure 7.3: The anger cube

with past anger. A child may suddenly have a tantrum about not being allowed to watch a certain television program when in fact much of her anger has to do with jealousy over her older brother being allowed to stay up late.

Another example of hidden anger is a teenager who, while disappointed that his father could not take him to a ball game, later reacts in an irritated manner when his dad asks him to do a minor chore. In fact, some researchers on anger suggest that excessive violence in America is very much influenced by the fact that, as a society, we tend to overly suppress genuine acknowledgment of anger. Our culture frowns on those who display anger and teaches children that they should not experience it. According to this view, violence is then seen as the cumulative impact of such suppressed and repressed anger. (See Chapter 17.)

Strategies to Promote Emotional Self-Awareness Regarding Anger

The strategies discussed in this chapter represent a wide range of approaches for helping your child develop his emotional awareness regarding anger. How effective they are with your child or teen will also depend on her current level of self-awareness regarding anger. I begin with a structured approach that I first described when presenting the model of anger. This time, however, the focus is on helping your child or teen apply the model in order to better recognize and understand the emotions that precede and are associated with her anger.

A Structured Approach

This approach begins by addressing the "moment of anger." We will focus on this point in the anger experience and work backward, just as we did when you were first asked to recall a moment of anger in order to help you learn about the model. The focus starts at the moment of anger because we are usually more aware of anger, or the emotions related to our anger, than we are of our more deeply rooted motivations. The task of recognizing our motivations is often more challenging and requires increased skills in self-reflection. (See Chapter 8.)

While the entire model can be presented to most older children or adolescents in one sitting, the approach described in this chapter will focus only on recognizing other emotions that precede and are associated with anger.

Exercise

Ask your child to recall a recent event that led him to experienc
ger. If the word *anger* seems too threatening, suggest he recall a
when he became annoyed, irritated, bothered, or upset. If he appears
too inhibited to discuss a particular event, you may want to remind
him of an incident when you observed him being annoyed. Identify
an incident that you genuinely believe will be comfortable for both of
you to discuss. Be aware that just thinking about a moment when he
was angry may lead him to reexperience anger and the emotions related to it. As a result, the intensity of aroused emotions can potentially interfere with learning. For this reason, select an incident that
aroused only mild anger. Similarly, at this time you may not want to
discuss anger he experienced toward you. Unless he is already comfortable in expressing such anger toward you, the tension associated
with this type of situation may distract him from learning the process.

Ask your child to rate the intensity of his anger on a scale of 1 to 10,
in which 1 reflects only minimal anger and 10 reflects severe anger. A
rating scale is especially helpful with children and teens because it is often difficult to identify an exact word that best characterizes their subjective experience of anger. Ask him to select an event that led him to
experience anger at a 3 to 5 level of intensity. He should be more comfortable with addressing anger at this level.

Younger children may have some difficulty with ratings. Instead of
using numbers, you may direct them to spread their arms apart to express the level of intensity of their anger—close together for a little anger and wide apart for a greater degree of anger.

Ask your child to recall and then describe to you as many details as
possible about the event and the circumstances surrounding his experience of anger. Coach him to think about and then describe for you the
details of the scene, including the people and situation that led to his
anger, the specific setting, and the time of day. The goal at this moment
is to help him make the recollection as vivid as possible. To do so, suggest he recall the colors, textures, and shapes of objects in the scene. In
an attempt to make the scene even more real for him, direct him to remember what the air was like—whether it was still or moving, dry or
humid. Similarly, ask him if there were any odors associated with this
situation. His recollection will become more vivid as more of his senses
are involved. Suggest he take time to recall the event, which will increase his ability to focus and reflect as well as attend to details that are
external to himself.

The goal at this moment is to help your child recall the details of his
environment, including any actions by other people. He should be encouraged to focus his attention on these external details rather than on

his internal experience—his thoughts, emotions, self-dialogue, or body reactions during his experience. Once he has been helped to revisit the external circumstances associated with the anger-provoking event, he can be encouraged to explore his internal reactions.

At this point, you can introduce your child to the use of the imagined videotape to further help him refine his skills in reflection. Ask him to imagine that this entire incident was recorded on a videotape that he can review in his mind. Suggest he now review the tape again, including all the details he just recalled: the people involved, the setting, the colors, shapes, and texture of the objects in his scene, the air, and any odors associated with the scene. Now, suggest to him that he can move the image backward or forward. He can rewind it, forward it, or push the pause button to freeze it at any moment.

I have found that even young children are familiar enough with videos to be able to create this type of imagery. However, some children and teens need more practice than others, since all of us vary in the degree to which we can create visual imagery.

Now direct your child to forward the tape until the moment when he can recall being impacted by the event, the moment when he was just beginning to experience anger. Suggest he push the pause button and freeze the scene at that moment. Have him scan the scene of that moment, then suggest that, since he is watching this video in his mind, he can even step back and imagine watching himself from the outside, observing his actions and appearance. Next, direct him to shift his attention from looking at himself in the scene to recalling what was occurring inside him while he was in that situation. Specifically, ask him to think about and then describe for you his thoughts (including self-dialogue), his emotions, and any physical reactions that he can recall. Take time to help him focus on each of these reactions in turn. In this way you will help him slow down and shift his attention to self-reflection.

Just as children vary in their ability to visualize, they also vary in their ability to self-reflect. The more you can help your child make this shift in attention, the more self-reflective he will become. Again, suggest that he try to identify his thoughts, self-talk, bodily reactions, and emotions at that moment. Some children find it easier to reflect on their thoughts, while others more easily reflect on their emotions. Similarly, some can readily identify bodily reactions, while others lack such self-awareness. The goal of repeatedly practicing this type of exercise is to help your child become as acutely observant of internal reactions as he is of external circumstances.

When your child has discussed a few details of his internal experiences, you can cooperatively begin to put together a graphic outline of the sequence of elements related to his anger (or other reactions). This can be done with an older child or adolescent by writing down his words; using pictures you draw or cut from magazines along with the words usually works better with a younger child. Creating a graphic representation of his experience will help your child more readily understand the sequence of circumstances involved in anger. Such an outline also helps to emphasize the element of time involved in the entire sequence of factors contributing to the experience of anger, and promotes an understanding of the cause-effect relationship among the factors contributing to anger and anger management.

Suppose your child recalls his best friend refusing to play with him on a particular day. Have him use the imaginary videotape, and ask him to share some of the details of the scene. When he is able to recall those details, have him push the pause button at the very moment when he became upset. Ask him to recall and share his feelings. He may initially report only that he was annoyed. In this case, help him to rewind the tape to the event. You can highlight this sequence by using an outline like that depicted in Figure 7.4.

Figure 7.4: Event and reaction

Alternatively, he may say he became sad. In this case, the outline might look like that presented in Figure 7.5.

As you discuss the event and the details of his experience, you will be adding more details to the outline. Let's assume he is aware of being angry. You can now suggest that he rewind the tape just a little to see if there were other emotions that occurred between the time the event took place and when he experienced feeling annoyed. If he does not readily come up with

Figure 7.5: Event and reaction

other emotions, list some emotions for him to consider. For example: "Well, you were annoyed. I wonder—were you hurt and then annoyed? Or disappointed and then annoyed? Or sad and then annoyed?" As he is helped to attend to those other feelings that occur before the anger, he develops a new "mental set," a new sensitivity or alertness to recognizing these other emotions. Again, remember that each child is different in his capacity to learn these skills, and all children require much practice to effectively self-reflect.

Suppose, that as a part of the discussion, you help your child to clarify that he became sad, hurt, or disappointed. He can now identify the emotions that preceded his annoyance or anger. Your evolving outline may now look like the sequence presented in Figure 7.6

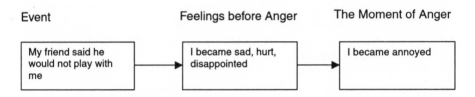

Figure 7.6: Event followed by emotions that lead to anger

By reviewing with your child several incidents of anger using this same approach, he will be developing the most important understanding of his anger: that it is a secondary emotion, a reaction to other emotions. At the same time, by taking time to slowly review the details of his experience, he will improve his skills in self-reflection. His increased capacity to reflect will help him short-circuit his impulse to immediately deny, minimize, ignore, or act out his anger.

While the goal of this chapter is to show you how to help your child recognize his emotions, completing the next stage of this exercise will move him further toward acknowledging his internal dialogue and his physical reactions.

At this point, you can ask your child to forward his tape to the moment when he experienced feeling annoyed, then push the pause button. Initially, you inquired about his emotions at that moment; now inquire further about his self-talk. Encourage him to take time to try to recall what he was thinking, or a dialogue he was having with himself. Share examples from your own self-talk in similar situations as a way to prompt and structure his focused attention. He may discover some self-talk that reflects conclusions and other thoughts that are just observations of what was going on.

Suggest he continue to pause on this one frame of the video and pay attention to any physical reactions he may have had shortly after the event occurred. He may again need prompts or a multiple-choice type of inquiry to help him clarify what he should focus his attention on. For example, inquire whether he felt antsy, nervous, tense, or jittery, depending on which descriptions you believe he can best identify. His observations of self-talk and physical reactions may then be added, so that the outline looks like the one depicted in Figure 7.7. The double arrows reflect the ongoing interplay of emotions, self-talk, and physical reactions that accompany the emotions before anger is experienced as well as the anger.

Now that you have identified and listed the event, your child's experience of anger, and the emotions preceding his anger, try to elicit his

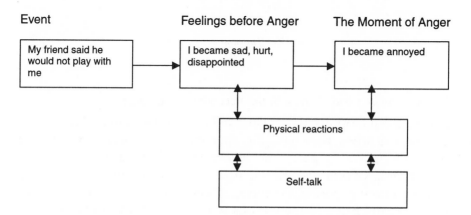

Figure 7.7: Physical reactions interact with self-talk and emotions

appraisal of the event—the meaning or conclusion he arrives at to explain the event. Again, help him by providing some examples of conclusions or appraisals, especially when he is first learning about the model. Specifically, ask him open-ended questions that will provide structure to help him identify his conclusions—for example, "So, what conclusion did you make when your friend said he would not play with you?" or "What did you think about being told ...?" or "How did you explain to yourself that ...?" He may identify one or several conclusions. These can then be added to the outline so that it looks something like Figure 7.8

This exercise emphasizes the general approach in applying the model of anger toward recognizing emotions as well as the physical reactions and self-talk associated with anger. The next chapter focuses on strategies to help children and teens identify their internal dialogue, in the form of specific expectations and conclusions that influence the experience of anger.

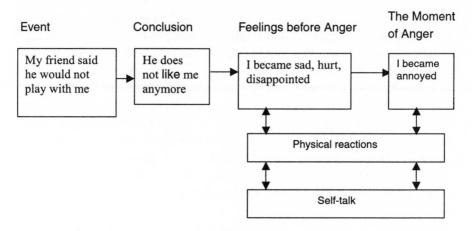

Figure 7.8: The moment of anger

Helping Children and Teens with the Vocabulary of Emotion

Children can more accurately label and discuss their internal emotional experiences when they have the appropriate vocabulary to describe such experiences. In part, they develop this vocabulary through their observations of other people and how they describe and label feelings. Through their exposure to others, children develop the ability to differentiate and name their emotions as well as assess their intensity. The more you provide children with appropriate vocabulary and concepts to discuss anger and help them make distinctions among emotions, the more sensitive they can be to the complexity of their emotional life.

Many young children respond with words such as *good, bad, mad, sad,* or *happy* when asked about their feelings. Young children often lack both the ability to differentiate their emotions and sufficient vocabulary to describe the wide range of their feelings. Even older children may be weak in these skills. When asked how he felt at any given time, thirteen-year-old Warren responded that he felt "good", or "bad" and then added some comments to suggest the intensity of these feelings. At one point in our work together, I suggested he draw pictures to show how he felt during the week. He drew one picture of a house, a tree, and a sun, a second picture of a house with some clouds in the sky with the sun, and a third picture of the house with many clouds. When asked to describe his pictures, Warren responded that the first suggested he was "happy," the second that he felt "good" and "sad," and the third that he was "sad." This was a young man who performed well academically but lacked the ability to identify and differentiate his emotions.

So while a young child may at first only use the word ⟨to de⟩scribe his anger, as he matures he develops a variety of word⟨s that⟩ accurately reflect the range or intensity of his anger. This g⟨rowth is re⟩flected when he is able to use words such as *annoyed, irrit⟨ated, b180⟩ered,* or *furious.*

Below is a list of feeling words that can be used in discussions with your child regarding personal events or the experiences of others. They can be used when focusing on anger management or in any conversation involving emotional awareness. The list offers a broad range of words to describe emotion. Select some words from this list when you are trying to help a child find the right word(s) to accurately describe her emotional experience. In addition, the more you use such words, the more likely they will become a part of your child's vocabulary. They reflect both a variety of single emotions as well as combinations of emotions. Each has a specific meaning. Examples of such words (in no particular order) are:

depressed	cheerful	hopeful	hate-filled
alarmed	powerful	enthusiastic	frustrated
content	impatient	shamed	guilty
warm	good	angry	furious
glad	shocked	pleased	bitter
resentful	regretful	desirous	excitable
grieving	sad	cold	unhappy
agitated	thrilled	awed	loving
concerned	anguished	fulfilled	aloof
amazed	enraged	exhilarated	despairing
fondness	delighted	bored	surprised
sorrowful	calm	happy	sad
terrorized	irritated	annoyed	fearful
anxious	worried	queasy	tense

When children are helped to use words that describe how they feel, they become more sensitive to their internal lives and are better able express these feelings to others. In addition, such awareness helps them become more sensitive to other people.

A part of making sense of and managing anger is finding the word that best matches our subjective emotional experience. This ability is essential for helping children increase the emotional self-awareness that is a basic building block for connecting with oneself.

Working with a Child Who Experiences Only Anger

Your child may report only anger when asked about her emotional reactions to an upsetting situation. Even after you inquire further, she may deny feeling hurt, disappointed, or other negative emotions. Providing empathic responses is especially helpful at this time. For example, you might say to your child, "I know that if I was in that situation, besides feeling angry, I might also feel quite hurt, disappointed, and even discounted, like my feelings don't matter," or "I think many people would feel hurt, disappointed, or even discounted in that situation." The goal is to help her feel less alone, strange, unusual, or weak about feeling hurt, disappointed, or devalued.

As a next step, try to determine if your child experiences other emotions but feels vulnerable or ashamed to admit them to you. He may have difficulty acknowledging that he feels hurt, disappointed, or sad. Keep in mind that his experience of vulnerability, anger, or shame may keep him from sharing other emotions, as may his lack of self-awareness regarding his emotions. You may also choose a very direct inquiry and ask, "Are you aware of other emotions related to your anger?" Another possibility is that he may need permission to acknowledge that he has other emotions. Tell him he does not have to share them, but ask, "Are you aware of what gets in the way of your sharing them with me?" By asking him this question, you are still encouraging his self-reflection. In fact, self-reflection, rather than sharing actual content with you, is the primary goal at this time. Ultimately, his level of comfort should be respected. He may not yet be ready to be open. However, try to figure out which of these factors may be contributing to his not recognizing or sharing other emotions. If you have used one strategy, such as discussion, without much success, try the videotape analogy or diagramming.

Try to determine if your child genuinely does not experience other emotions or if she simply does not want to admit them. She may still be so intensely angry about an event that she is not really available to discuss it. Ask her directly if this is the case. Discontinue the discussion if she still does not come up with other feelings; returning to the subject at a different time or talking about a less intense situation may be more effective.

You may find that children who are extremely uncomfortable with anger may not yet be ready for such sharing. Exploring the anger of others is one way to make such discussions more comfortable. You may also want to think about with whom your child might experience more comfort in discussing the model. For example, he may genuinely be more comfortable sharing his feelings with a grandparent, an uncle or aunt, or even an older sibling.

Young children may just have more difficulty than older children in recognizing their emotions. However, any child who seems to focus on anger and is not available to engage in discussions to increase his emotional awareness may need special help in this process. You may want to seek out the services of a counselor or psychotherapist to assist you in this situation. (See Chapter 17.)

Working with the Child Who Reports Only Emotions Other than Anger

A child may articulate a wide range of uncomfortable emotions but seem unable or unwilling to recognize and acknowledge her anger regarding an upsetting situation. As emphasized throughout this book, there are numerous factors that inhibit the recognition and acknowledgement of anger. The more your child receives messages that it is appropriate to experience and constructively discuss anger, the more open she will be to sharing her anger when it occurs.

Again, being especially empathic can often help such a child become more candid. Really try to put yourself in her situation and identify a variety of emotions she may experience. Rather than indicating just one emotion, suggest several that you might experience or that you believe would be a natural reaction to such an experience. For example, you might state, "You know, besides feeling hurt, I would feel annoyed if that happened to me," "I think anyone would feel annoyed or irritated in that situation," or "You know, I think a lot of people would be somewhat angry or annoyed if that happened."

If he does respond to your empathic comments, try to engage him in discussion of concerns he has about being angry; what he thinks about angry people, what it means to him when he sees others get angry, and what he thinks might happen if he becomes angry. If he directly states that discomfort keeps him from sharing his feelings, you may want to inquire, "Let me know if there is anything I can say or do that would make it easier for you to discuss your feelings with me." This comment communicates your openness and encourages further self-reflection.

These children, like those who express only anger, may best benefit from your modeling how to understand and manager anger, or from applying these techniques to the anger of others before they are comfortable enough to share their own feelings.

Working with the Child Who Responds with Thoughts Instead of Emotions

Some children focus on their thoughts rather than their emotions when asked to share reactions to a situation. For example, when asked how he feels about not being invited to a friend's party, your child might respond, "Well, he should have invited me. I thought I was his best friend! I don't understand!" Here he is responding with his thoughts about the situation and alluding to his expectations. Or he may say, "I would like to call him up and tell him what I really think of him. But no—I think I just won't speak to him again!" These thoughts describe actions he could take to address how he feels, but they do not describe feelings. Even responses such as "Well, he's a real idiot!" are thoughts based on feelings but do not really describe those feelings.

In response to any of these, let her know that she has shared with you what she thinks, and inquire if she could use feeling words to describe how she feels. If she cannot, suggest some in the form of an inquiry, such as "I wonder—were you maybe feeling annoyed, irritated, hurt, or disappointed?" Ask about her experience without providing an answer.

The distinction between thoughts and emotions needs to be made repeatedly when working with a child who is more prone to think rather than to feel. It is a distinction that is frequently overlooked, especially by parents who are more comfortable reflecting on thoughts rather than on emotions. This is an important distinction in anger management. It is reflected in the model of anger, which emphasizes labeling emotions as a part of direct communication about feelings. (See Chapter 12.)

Addressing the Child Who Does Not Recognize or Acknowledge Emotions

Some children and teens seem to be unable to describe feelings at all. They may consistently offer little response to any inquiries regarding their emotions. They may appear puzzled, angry, or bland in their facial expression when you try to initiate a discussion surrounding upsetting or anger-provoking events. They may seem completely unable or unwilling to practice the self-reflection strategies discussed so far.

These children and teens, like those who identify only anger or only the emotions leading to anger, may be more open to discussions of anger when it concerns others. They may be more open with one parent than another. Clearly, in this situation, the parent with whom your child experiences the most comfort should initiate such discussions. As stated previously, if your child feels uncomfortable sharing with either parent, perhaps someone else could be actively involved in discussing anger. An aunt, uncle, grandparent, or teacher, or even an older sibling, may have a relationship that is more likely to include candid sharing and discussion.

When questioned about a specific situation, your child may respond that he is unaware of what his feelings were at the time. Try to determine if he really cannot recall what his feelings were or if he is hesitant to share them with you. Directly inquire which conditions accurately describe the situation. Without asking him directly what his feelings were, guess, and tell him so: "If I were in that situation, I might feel

that way, but I don't know—I'm only taking a guess."
might be getting in the way of his being candid with you.
barrassment, guilt, or shame?

Try other approaches in this chapter and those that f
help may be needed if, after repeated practice, your chilc
has difficulty identifying his emotions.

Another Strategy to Enhance Self-Reflection Regarding Emotions: The "Little Child"

Throughout the day, we form thoughts, make decisions, and take actions based not just on the motivations, emotions, and thoughts we are
aware of but also on others that are not available to our awareness. As
stated earlier, many of our motivations, thoughts, decisions, and actions are influenced by child logic, that less mature way of viewing the
world around us and ourselves.

To the degree that we are aware of these unconscious motivations,
thoughts, and emotions, we are fully informed about ourselves. This
awareness helps us to better understand our needs, to be more aware of
thoughts and emotions that interfere with their being met, and to have
more control over the choices we make in our lives. To the degree that
we lack full awareness of these emotions, thoughts, and motivations,
we move through the day as if we are functioning on automatic pilot,
which takes charge and influences our decisions, actions, and thoughts.
Unfortunately, our automatic pilot is greatly influenced by child logic.

In my work, I refer to the automatic pilot as our "little child." It is
that part of one's thinking and feeling that is overly influenced by child
logic. Our little child represents that part of ourselves that has not fully
developed mature reasoning. The little child represents a part of ourselves that is emotionally immature and often dominated by emotions
instead of reasoning. However, the little child reflects both positive
and negative aspects of a child's nature. For example, the part of us that
is curious, excited, and passionate about life is part of our little child.

At the same time, the child logic of our little child leads to unrealistic
expectations and conclusions in relationship to ourselves and others.
This can lead to overly intense emotional reactions of fear, anxiety, and
anger. One way I have come to view the little child is that it represents
the thinking and emotional development of a four-year-old.

At this point, let me share some examples of Little Bernie, my own
little child, as a way of helping you understand how this concept can be
useful in making sense of and managing anger. I visualize Little Bernie
as being with me wherever I go. He encompasses the part of me that
includes unrealistic fears, thoughts, and anxieties. He also embodies
much of my excitement and passion as well as my curiosity and joy for

..e. For this reason, I do not want to eliminate him. Instead, I see myself helping him become more mature in his reasoning and more able to manage uncomfortable emotions, including anger, without stifling his excitement, curiosity, and joy.

I treat him in a nurturing and supportive way by reaching into the parental part of myself, the part that is most realistic and nurturing. My challenge is to help him to rely less on child logic, to alleviate his fears, reassure him in a protective way, provide him structure, and give him love—all the essential ingredients of quality parenting. This is accomplished through much dialogue with my little child. I engage Little Bernie in dialogue especially at those times when I am puzzled about my feelings, motivations, or thoughts. And, similarly, I engage in this dialogue when I am the most anxious or angry.

For example, several months ago, while driving to my office to present a class on anger management, I came to an intersection with a four-way stop. I braked and waited for a moment as the car to my left stopped. When I started to cross the intersection, the car to my left unexpectedly accelerated. He barely missed me as he sped in front of my car and continued through the intersection. I had intense reactions to the thought that I could have been hit. My heart beat faster, and my breathing became shallower and more rapid. I was no longer thinking about the anger management class. Instead, I was angry—very angry. My internal monologue consisted of statements like "I can't believe that jerk! That miserable @#&%$! Who does he think he is? How could someone be that inconsiderate?"

Almost a block away, I found myself still stuck on these thoughts. I knew that this was a natural reaction to a very irritating and frightening experience. In relating this example, I am not at all implying that my anger was immature or completely attributable to Little Bernie. However, the difficulty in letting it go was, in part, influenced by Little Bernie. When I noticed I was stuck, I began to engage in a dialogue with Little Bernie.

> *Me:* "Okay, calm down. You're okay."
> *Little Bernie:* "But I was scared. He could have killed us! I hate that feeling."
> *Me:* "We're both safe. He was a jerk, his little child is out of control, but we're all right."
> *Little Bernie:* "Maybe this time we should go after him. Can't we do something? Come on, let's get his license plate number."
> *Me:* "No, we don't need to go after him. You may want to get even, but we don't need to do that. What else were you feeling besides scared and angry?"

> *Little Bernie:* "Vulnerable! I hate feeling out of contr[ol] thing can happen to me!"
>
> *Me:* "That is a scary feeling . . . but we're safe now. I'[ll help] us. You know, in spite of how you hope or expect [others to] have, there are some people who are inconsiderate and do fool-ish things. And while it doesn't feel good to feel vulnerable, we're safe now. For all we know, he may really have had an emergency. Maybe he was going to a hospital or going to help somebody."

This exchange took seconds, but it was a way of addressing my anger and calming Little Bernie. In addition, by questioning the part of me that was frightened and angry, I was able to more quickly identify the feeling of vulnerability that underscored my fear and anger.

Dialoguing with one's little child is a way of more clearly identifying the range of thoughts and emotions that influence our conscious thoughts, emotions, and behaviors, especially during emotionally in-tense times. Viewing our feelings as being a part of the little child is a way of stepping back and observing our reactions without being com-pletely caught up in them. This strategy is a way to gain clarity and ob-jectivity in thinking about our thoughts and emotions. It is a strategy for fine-tuning self-reflection.

I have found this concept of a little child to be extremely useful in helping children, teens, and adults to make sense of and manage anger. It is a concept that offers a way of thinking about our thoughts and emotions and how their interaction influences the course of anger. I worked with a twelve-year-old named Russell who reported being irri-table with his father. We practiced dialoguing with Little Russell to help him better understand his feelings toward his father. Russell was one of five children and told me that he felt very much loved by both parents, who took good care of him and often engaged in enjoyable ac-tivities with him. He described going camping, going to amusement parks, and traveling to different countries together. Russell was hesi-tant to discuss his negative feelings in part because he did not under-stand them. After all, he felt so positive about his parents.

I helped Russell become increasingly aware of those times when he felt discomfort. He was encouraged to dialogue with Little Russell in an effort to get to know himself better. Russell was quite reflective and began to write some of his dialogues in a journal, including one about the time he felt discomfort while attending a basketball game with his father, his four siblings, and his mother. While he did not think about it much during the game, he did reflect later that evening and came to the realization that he sometimes wanted to go to a game with just his ather, as it would make him feel special. But such a thought made him feel selfish. He soon realized that feeling selfish was an automatic reaction based on Little Russell's fears and anxieties, which were getting in the way of even asking for what he wanted. He also better understood his increased irritability. He was eventually able to develop more realistic responses to Little Russell and to assure him that he did deserve to at least ask to have his wish satisfied. He also assured Little Russell that he would be all right even if his dad refused his request. He ultimately decided to speak directly to his parents about his concern.

In another situation, I helped a fifteen-year-old high school junior, Lois, to dialogue with Little Lois. She was an athlete who excelled in several sports, including tennis, swimming, and track, and she was also an excellent musician. She was experiencing increased pressure, both from others and from her own self-expectations, to participate in all of these extracurricular activities. However, she increasingly felt overextended in her commitments. She wanted to discontinue her involvement with some of these activities but felt unable to make a decision. She experienced tension and became more irritable in her relationships but could not really identify any other emotions related to what she was experiencing.

Lois practiced engaging with Little Lois. She found herself thinking, "I really enjoy these activities, and I've made good friends doing them. I certainly get a lot of support and admiration from my friends and family. But I am just doing too much. I know that I would feel much less pressure if I dropped one or two of these activities. I am beginning to resent that I have no time to do other things. I know I joined the team because I wanted to, but at times I feel like I'm working so hard for how others will feel about me. I need to balance my time so I can have more leisure time." As she continued these thoughts, she found Little Lois very quickly responding, "You have to do those activities. You should be able to balance all of those activities. A lot of people, including your parents, will be disappointed if you quit any of those teams. You need to continue or people will become angry with you. You have to do it all."

Through increased self-reflection and dialoguing, she became more aware of anger, anxiety, guilt, and fear. She became more aware of perfectionist messages from Little Lois as well as guilt about wanting to give up one of the activities. She felt that she would be disappointing her family, friends, and teammates if she quit any of the activities, but she could not figure out how to take better care of herself. She felt guilty about disappointing others and anxious that they might reject her.

Diagramming the dialogue can help clarify the key elements and emotions involved in a particular situation. The following might best represent the outline for Lois's situation:

Emotions I am aware of	*Little child*
Annoyance	Anxiety, guilt

Lois initially was most aware that she experienced guilt when she even thought about dropping one of her activities. It took her some time to recognize that besides feeling guilty, she was anxious and annoyed as well.

This exercise feels awkward at first and requires very focused attention and self-reflection. The process of dialoguing with his little child helps increase your child's or teen's understanding and helps him gain distance from his thoughts and feelings. It allows him to shift gears and evaluate his reactions from a more reasonable and objective perspective. Subsequently, the process helps him fine-tune his skills in self-reflection. This is the essential task in recognizing emotions that precede or are associated with anger.

The task of stepping outside ourselves and picturing a little child as part of ourselves is somewhat complex and abstract for young children. In general, older children and teens are more capable of learning this process.

Take time to recognize your own little child before using this strategy with your child. Practice dialoguing with your little child until you are reasonably comfortable with the process. The more you have applied it to help you understand your own emotions, the better you will be able to help your child. Think about a recent incident that upset you. Select an incident that led to an anger intensity level of 3 to 5 on a continuum in which 1 represents hardly any anger and 10 reflects intense anger. Use the techniques associated with the videotape analogy in an effort to make the situation as vivid as possible. Review the situation in your mind and recall the details of the scene and the people involved. When you first see yourself experiencing some reaction to the event, push the pause button and focus your attention on recognizing your emotions. (In the next chapter we will apply this same strategy to help you better recognize your thoughts.) Now, take some time and dialogue with your little child. Inquire about what other emotions you may be experiencing. You may find yourself sorting through many thoughts as you identify other emotions. Again, the more practice you have in identifying the emotions that lead to anger, the more you will be available and sensitive to help your own child or teen sort through her own feelings.

When working with older children and adolescents, the videotape analogy can be used in combination with the idea of the little child. However, before applying it in conjunction with the videotape analogy, teach her the concept of the little child and have her practice it until she is able to effectively use it to increase her self-awareness. Begin by asking your child to pause the tape at the moment when she is feeling impacted by the anger-arousing or disturbing event. Direct her to recall what emotions she was experiencing. Suggest that she dialogue with her little child to further identify what emotions she may have been experiencing.

If answers do not come to your child's mind, offer a number of choices, just as you might to a little child who can't quite identify his experience. "Well, you're pretty angry. Maybe you're also hurt or disappointed. Maybe you felt discounted or ignored. Maybe you felt fearful."

Your child may need guidance at this point to help her fine-tune her self-reflection. You can foster such reflection by naming several different emotions and having her indicate which ones seem to best match her subjective experience. The list of emotions presented earlier can also serve as a resource for sorting out and recognizing these emotions.

"Part of You": Another Approach to Recognize Emotions

One approach that is helpful for children of all ages, but especially for younger children, is to discuss different feelings as different "parts" of the child. For example, if you sense your child is angry about something, say something like this: "A part of you is angry *and* another part of you may feel hurt or sad." When we feel uncomfortable acknowledging that we feel a certain way, it is easier to admit that a part of us feels that way or that we feel that way only at specific times. I emphasize the word *and* because all too often we tend to believe we should have one feeling when in fact we have several. Helping children acknowledge that they can have a variety of emotions regarding the same event makes it easier and more comfortable for them to experience and recognize mixed emotions. The videotape analogy and diagramming can also be useful when working with this approach.

Using the phrase "a part of you" is a way to help children address mixed emotions as well as emotions that may not initially be a part of their awareness. Again, rather than providing answers, it is beneficial to help them question themselves to more fully recognize the complexity of their emotions. For example, you might say something like "Well, I know that when I graduated from high school, a part of me was really glad and excited, but at the same time a part of me was somewhat anxious or scared. I wonder if you might have the same feelings" or "I could tell how disappointed you were about not going to the zoo. I wonder if a part of you is also feeling annoyed" or "You've let me know how angry you are. Is another part of you hurt, sad, or disappointed?"

Using "parts" language is a simple but very effective strategy to help children explore beyond their first answer when trying to identify their emotions.

Another Way to View the "Little Child": Riding a Motorcycle with a Sidecar

Another analogy that I have found to be effective in helping children and adolescents recognize their feelings involves the image of a motorcycle with an attached sidecar. First, show your child a picture of a motorcycle with a sidecar, especially if he is not familiar with this kind of image. I use this kind of language: "When you are aware of your emotions, thoughts, and needs or wants, it is like the mature, grown-up, adult, realistic part of you is driving the motorcycle with the little child in the sidecar, always there and along for the ride. You are in control, taking the lead and making decisions. But at times your little child takes over the motorcycle, and then it is as if you are in the sidecar. Sometimes you want to let your little child ride the motorcycle, like when you are playing and having fun. At other times your little child may lead you to have intense emotions that distract you from using good reasoning. When you are unaware of the emotions or thoughts of your little child, you are just going along for the ride. At those times, you need to put your little child back in the sidecar, and you steer the motorcycle."

Anger and Anxiety

Learning to understand the relationship between anger and anxiety is extremely helpful in assisting children and adolescents to make sense of and manage their anger. These two emotions can be related in a variety of ways as reactions to an upsetting event.

As described previously, the flight-or-fight response is a reaction to unusual demands on the body's emotional or physical resources. Our heart rate, breathing rate, and rate of metabolism increase. We become more alert and narrowly focused, while blood flows to our muscles in order to fight or flee from the source of our stress. We experience essentially the same fight-or-flight response when we become angry or when we are anxious. (It is for this reason that the physical relaxation techniques discussed in Chapter 11 can be practiced both as a way of managing anger as well as for managing anxiety.)

Any child who has been the victim of teasing by a school bully is familiar with the fight-or-flight response. In this situation a child may be angry and anxious at the same time. He experiences the fear of being threatened, as well as anger related to being criticized or devalued. These emotions may be experienced simultaneously, and he may feel unable to decide how to respond to them. At some point one emotion may dominate, and he will respond either by moving toward the source of his anger or by moving away from it.

Another example of the interaction of anxiety and anger may be reflected by a child's reactions when she achieves below her self-expectations on a test. She may experience anger toward herself for not measuring up to her expectations and standards. She may redirect her anger at the test or toward the teacher. In part, her anger may be related to underlying anxiety about passing the course, graduating, or meeting her own standards. In this situation, the feelings of anxiety and anger may be simultaneous or alternating. The target of her feelings may also shift as she focuses her anger on herself and then on the teacher.

Anxiety and anger can also be associated in a variety of other ways in addition to causing similar physical reactions. We can experience anger or anxiety and not be aware of the other underlying or unconscious feelings. For example, the boy being taunted by a peer may have grown up hearing messages suggesting that he should not show fear and that he should always stand up to bullies. He may be too uncomfortable to acknowledge fear or to stand up to the bullies. Hence he becomes anxious, but he may minimize, deny, or suppress his anxiety and remain consciously aware only of his anger. Those observing him may also see only his anger and remain unaware of his anxiety.

In an earlier example I gave, a high school student was extremely critical toward his basketball teammates. His intense anxiety about not doing well was unacceptable to him. It was safer to feel anger, which he expressed by severely criticizing his peers.

In these examples, anger may dominate the expression or experience of anxiety. In other situations, a child may appear anxious while not recognizing that his anxiety is generated by the discomfort of anger. This may be especially true for the youngster who has grown up suppressing the recognition and acknowledgment of anger.

A child who repeatedly hears messages that he should not be angry may incorporate these messages as a part of his internal standards. His child logic may dictate that he is bad, sinful, or weak to experience or express anger. His anxiety regarding anger may be so strong that he suppresses or denies anger. When this happens, even the slightest stirring of unconscious anger may lead him to experience anxiety. This is consistent with the experience of anxiety we have when we fail, or anticipate that we will fail, to measure up to our internal standards. When trying to help our child recognize her emotions, she may be quick to focus on facts or feelings that come before anger, rather than recognize her anger. She needs much encouragement, structure, and support to help her reflect on her experiences related to anger.

The experience of a certain level of anxiety can be helpful when we are very angry. Both anger and anxiety serve as signals that something needs attention. Similarly, they offer information about others and ourselves. They motivate us to attend to our emotions and take action. However, the presence of anxiety may lead us to pause and reflect before acting on our anger. Just as when responding to anger, when we take time to pause and reflect on the anxiety, we can form a more carefully thought-out decision about what action to take.

It is particularly problematic when a child does not experience anxiety about his anger; especially when it leads to aggression. This is often the case with children or adolescents who have failed to establish some minimal internal standards to help guide their behavior. Some of these children and teens very impulsively act out aggressively and experience little or no anxiety about their actions. While such children definitely need to make sense of and manage their anger more appropriately, they may also need psychotherapy. Since the lack of such anxiety could lead to serious future difficulties, help for these children should be sought at an early age. (See Chapter 17.)

Anger and Depression

Depression is another emotion that is often linked to anger. In fact, psychoanalytic theory suggests that depression is often an outcome of anger turned inward. Based on this view, we may direct our anger inward in a self-critical way when really we are angry with someone else. We may manage anger in this manner because we believe that anger is dangerous or inappropriate. In this way depression serves to distract us from experiencing the discomfort of recognizing and acknowledging anger. This anger management strategy does not allow for proactive problem solving. When severe, such self-criticism many foster the unrealistic guilt, hopelessness, and helplessness that are associated with depression.

Similarly, depressed children frequently become angry in reaction to feeling down, with the accompanying feelings of hopelessness and helplessness.

While depression may not always be related to anger in this way, understanding the potential interaction between these two emotions is essential to effectively make sense of and manage anger.

For many years, mental health practitioners did not believe that children and adolescents experienced depression. In part, this is because clinically depressed children and teens may not evidence the same symptoms as depressed adults. Not all children are lethargic or express feelings of helplessness and hopelessness. Instead, many children and adolescents show anger and aggression, acting out the discomfort of their depression in a way that camouflages it and distracts them from experiencing helplessness, hopelessness, or despair. Children and teens who exhibit discipline problems and behaviors that lead to problems with the law often may have an underlying depression.

In *The Optimistic Child,* Martin Seligman reports that depression in children and adolescents has risen in the last several decades.[2] He also states that a key identifying factor in a depressed individual relates to that person's explanatory style—how he or she explains why good or bad events happen. According to Seligman, there are three dimensions that need to be considered when understanding how children are either optimistic or pessimistic. These include permanence, pervasiveness, and personalization.

Seligman indicates that children are most vulnerable to depression when they believe that "the causes of the bad events that happen to them are permanent." An example of a pessimistic comment based on permanence is when a child complains, after not being invited to a specific party, "I know Wendy doesn't like me. I'll never get invited to her parties." In contrast, an optimistic response is: "Wendy doesn't know me that well yet. When she gets to know me, I'll be invited." In the first response, he views the cause of the negative event as being permanent. But the second comment reflects a cause that is temporary. The ability to view the causes of negative events as temporary is one measure of optimism.

The second dimension is pervasiveness. This is reflected when we imagine the cause of the negative event as impacting many different situations in our life. The pessimist responds to a defeat with a comment such as "I came in last in the swimming race. That just convinces me I'm not a good athlete. I'm not going to bother trying out for the tennis team." A more optimistic response would be "Well, I'm not really strong at swimming, but I can try tennis."

The final aspect of pessimistic thinking addressed by Seligman is how a person decides who is at fault. Pessimistic children and teens unrealistically blame themselves, while optimistic children blame others. However, Seligman emphasizes that children should not blame others when in fact they caused a bad event to happen. Rather, they should take responsibility for their actions.

Seligman also reported that optimistic children differ from pessimistic children in how they explain the causes of good events. In reaction to a good event, the pessimist is specific and might respond, "I did well

on that test because I'm good in reading" versus "I did well o[]
test because I am smart." The pessimistic child sees the cause of the
good event as being only temporary, while the optimistic child attributes the cause to an enduring trait or quality. A pessimistic child might
respond, "I won the swimming competition because I was in real good
shape today." In contrast, an optimistic child would respond, "I won the
race today because I practice hard and I'm committed to doing well."

How do these findings about optimism and pessimism relate to depression and anger? As will be emphasized in the next chapter, pessimistic thoughts are more likely to lead to expectations and conclusions
that leave us vulnerable to anger. If we see causes of negative events as
permanent, all-pervasive, and completely our fault, we are less likely to
make decisions and take actions to work toward satisfying our needs
and wants. As reflected by the sequence of events depicted in the
model of anger, we would subsequently be more vulnerable to anger
when our needs remain unsatisfied.

If we are pervasive in our pessimistic thinking, we similarly rule out
options to meet our needs and wants. This further increases the likelihood that such needs and wants will not be met and we will subsequently be vulnerable to anger or depression.

Finally, if we overemphasize our role in bad events that happen to us,
we limit our objectivity in determining ways to meet our needs and
wants. This is especially true when we look at one particular anger
management strategy—suppression and repression. As I have emphasized throughout this book, constructively communicating anger is a
way to help other people know us. It is only by sharing our emotions
that we can let people know what is important to us. If we repress or
suppress our anger and the other emotions related to it, we feel less
connected to others. In turn, we feel more isolated and less likely to
have our needs and wants satisfied. Invariably, we feel less special in the
eyes of others, and we become more angry or depressed.

So while depression may not always be viewed as anger turned inward, it can be seen as a distraction to acknowledging and managing
anger—a result of distortions in thinking and beliefs about anger.

Anger and Shame

While shame is listed with other uncomfortable emotions that may
precede anger, shame, like anxiety and depression, may have a very
unique interaction with anger. Shame involves our awareness of not
living up to our own standards, rules, or norms and those standards
perceived as valued by others.[3]

A second component of shame is the negative self-judgment or evaluation of not measuring up to these standards, rules, and norms, which are often felt to be important and internalized as such.

Let us again return to Louis, the high school student who criticizes his teammates during practice. As previously described, his anger may, in part, be due to his anxiety about losing a game. However, Louis did not express interest in any other subject offered in school. He had few close friends, and his self-esteem was very much based on how well he performed as a basketball player. He had few other resources to gain the respect of peers and to bolster his self-esteem. In fact, other than feeling good about his basketball skills, he experienced very low self-esteem. His grades were low as well, and he was in danger of being kicked off of the team because of his academic standing. Underneath his anger and anxiety, Louis's intense feelings about doing well were motivated by not wanting to experience shame. Shame and attempts to avoid shame often underlie the anger of children and teens. It is a very powerful emotion that may be even more uncomfortable to recognize and experience than anger.

Michael Lewis reports in *Shame* that while guilt involves self-reflection that focuses on our specific actions as not measuring up to our own standards or those of others, shame involves an evaluation of our entire sense of self. While guilt is painful, it is not all-encompassing. Guilt often leads to defining an action that can be taken to change the situation, but shame does not. According to Lewis, three key features form the experience of shame: (1) the desire to hide, (2) intense pain, discomfort, and anger, and (3) the feeling that one is no good, inadequate, and unworthy.

Shame is profound and is experienced with the sense of wanting to disappear, hide, or die—to totally escape what we are experiencing at the moment. The desire to hide may take the form of social isolation or withdrawal in an attempt to decrease the vulnerability to potential shame-provoking experiences. Increased inhibition in all forms of self-expression may be another way of hiding.

The pain experienced in shame is extremely intense because while shame may be triggered by hurt, disappointment, rejection, or other negative emotions, it is a global reaction based on an assessment of one's whole self as being flawed. During the moment of shame, we experience this assessment as permanent. This overly critical, global, and permanent self-evaluation leads us to view any action as futile. At such moments, all emotion is stifled and our thoughts are filled with self-doubt. The overriding experience is one of feeling inadequate and unworthy.

Anyone who has experienced shame is familiar with the severe discomfort associated with it. It is for this reason that some children and adolescents (and adults) respond to it by becoming angry. Whether they direct it inward or outward, anger helps distract them from the intense discomfort of shame.

Children and teens (as well as adults) who are easily angered are often individuals who distract themselves from the powerful negative impact of shame by targeting others with their anger. Examples of this are the five-year-old who destroys his friend's sandcastle because he feels inept in building his own, or the ten-year-old girl who constantly criticizes her older sister about a variety of issues because, in reality, she feels academically inferior to her. The adolescent boy who, on the surface, may appear bored and easily annoyed is a subtler example of the influence of shame. His major motivation in not trying new activities may be to avoid the experience of inadequacy that is often a natural part of trying new skills. In this situation, he is motivated to avoid feeling shame that may be aroused when he feels inadequate.

Shame can similarly turn to anger directed toward oneself. Ethan was a five-year-old who had frequent anger outbursts. In one session, he reported being scolded by his mother for making a mess at the kitchen table when he was invited to help her prepare food. He also described being scolded by his father when the family went camping one weekend. In fact, while walking down the corridor to my office, Ethan noticed several children in a room who were playing with clay. He immediately yelled at them, "I'm going to get the police after you. You shouldn't be making a mess—you're dirty." He himself refused to play with clay. Ethan had become angry with himself for not being neat and was redirecting his anger. Ethan's anger was an attempt to distract himself from the shame he experienced when told he could not help his mother because he was too messy. It also appeared that his anger was directed outward in an effort to distract himself from experiencing anger toward himself as well as anger toward his parents.

Shame has been discussed in recent years as a contributing factor for children and adolescents who have committed intensely aggressive acts. Several of these adolescents described feelings of shame that were intense, pervasive, and chronic. Many of those who study such incidents suggest that shame is the driving force for aggression by males.[4] Boys and men are seen as being angry and aggressive in order to distract themselves from experiencing the more internally focused and painful emotion of shame. According to writers such as Michael Lewis, incidents of shame lead some individuals to focus on sadness and anger, while the prolonged experience of shame can lead to depression and rage.

Another aspect of the relationship between anger and shame is that, as with anger, our society communicates strong negative messages about experiencing or expressing shame. These messages, combined with the intense distress shame brings, lead many individuals to deny, minimize, or ignore shame. As with anger, admitting shame is often seen as a weakness and an expression of vulnerability. And, as with anger, the avoidance of this emotion leads to difficulties in relationships with others and oneself.

Clearly, any comprehensive approach toward making sense of and managing anger needs to address the experience of shame. But how can you, as a parent, best help your child deal with shame? Just as with anger, the more you are aware of how shame plays a part in your life and how that emotion may influence your anger, the more you will be available to help your child be sensitive to the powerful influence of shame in causing his anger. The more you create opportunities to discuss shame, the more comfortable and candid he will become in recognizing these feelings.

Shame can be a very powerful motivator, and parents may use it without full awareness of its negative impact. Communications promote shame when they lead to a global sense of inadequacy. In contrast, critical comments that focus on specific behaviors help children and teens to be selective in their self-criticism and self-reflection.

Model your self-awareness of shame. When asking your child to explore his feelings, offer shame as one of the emotions that is a natural reaction to certain circumstances. Help him realize that shame is an emotion that has the potential to be incapacitating when it is not acknowledged. Help him recognize that shame, like anger, offers him information that he can use to make decisions about his life.

Making sense of and managing anger is, in part, based on recognizing the influence of other emotions related to our anger. However, as we continue to apply the model of anger, we begin to further identify how our thoughts influence these emotions that lead us to anger. This is the focus of the next chapter.

8

Identifying and Confronting
Self-talk Based on "Child Logic"

A major strategy for helping children and teens make sense of and
manage anger is to help them better recognize how self-talk influences their experience of anger and how they manage it. Specifically,
when addressing self-talk related to anger, children and adolescents
need to:

1. Identify self-talk.
2. Recognize self-talk that reflects automatic internal dialogue.
3. Clarify self-talk that reflects unrealistic thinking.
4. Challenge and replace unrealistic self-talk by realistic self-talk.
5. Repeatedly practice this process.

Everyone engages in self-talk. Self-talk is the dialogue we have with
ourselves at home, at work, in a car, in a store, when interacting with
loved ones, or while observing people on a bus. We dialogue with ourselves both when we are with others and when we are alone. Some of us
are more aware than others of these ongoing thoughts. And each of us
varies in the amount of self-talk we engage in. However, we may be so
busy, focused on an activity, or engaged with people that we are not
aware of our self-talk. In fact, we live in a time when we are increasingly

bombarded by external stimulation that competes with our ability to listen to our self-talk.

Our society so strongly encourages us to be active and productive that we often lack awareness or even consciousness of such dialogue. In many ways, our culture reinforces the idea that we should be more concerned with the thoughts and attitudes of other people rather than with our own. So while some of the decisions we make every day are based on thoughtful consideration, others are based on an internal automatic pilot. By this I mean that certain decisions and actions are made automatically, seemingly without giving them much thought—but in fact they often are based on the self-talk that goes on without our full awareness. Similarly, they may result from knee-jerk thoughts—rapid and immediate self-talk that is based on child logic and not on more careful evaluation.

The idea that we have thoughts without being aware of them may sound confusing. So let me give some examples of how this works. To begin with, though, it is helpful to understand how we focus our attention, how we can shift our attention, and how when we attend to one area we neglect another.

Imagine you are in a restaurant actively talking with your best friend. At some point in your conversation, you hear two individuals at a nearby table mention the name of your company's CEO. Your interest is piqued. And while you were most likely not tuned into that conversation before, you now continue to talk to your friend while trying to pay attention to that intriguing discussion going on behind your back. You may even find yourself listening only to the dialogue behind you instead of to your friend. This is an example of selective attention.

This same process occurs with our own internal conversations. While we may be very much aware of certain thoughts we are having, other thoughts may be going on at a deeper and quieter level. It is only by attending to such self-talk that we can really become more aware of the wider range of our thoughts and emotions. One example of how you can help children and adolescents better identify self-talk is reflected in my counseling sessions with Matt.

Matt, a seventeen-year-old high school senior, shared with me how excited he was about graduating in two months and how much he was looking forward to going to college. And yet he had been referred for counseling because his grades had dropped in the last few months, he was spending more time with peers, and he was increasingly irritable with family members and friends. For the most part, he was only aware of being tense, and he blamed his irritation on his tension.

I recommended that he try to be aware of when he experienced tension, and, most important, his thoughts that occurred at those moments. Over the course of several sessions he identified becoming most tense when he was thinking about how college meant that he would be away from family, friends, and all that was familiar to him. I asked him what other thoughts he had when he became tense, but he was unable to identify them. I then discussed the videotape analogy and suggested to Matt that he recall his experience of thinking about college and being away from his friends and family as though it had been recorded on videotape. When Matt focused on his feelings of tension as he pictured himself at college during the fall semester, at first he was aware only of his bodily reactions—muscle tension and a tight feeling in his stomach. When I suggested he shift his attention to his thoughts, he indicated that nothing readily came to mind. I then suggested he just slightly rewind his tape and pay attention to any self-talk that may have occurred prior to his experiencing the tension.

Gradually he began to identify his thoughts. "I can picture myself at the college. I'm looking forward to all of the new experiences I will have, including classes, friends, new and challenging activities. This is something I have worked hard to achieve, and I can't wait until I'm there." I then suggested he keep his button on pause and try to listen to any other conversations that might be going on. His face showed a mix of tension and surprise as he shared with me his recognition that a part of his internal dialogue also included comments such as "I'm not sure I can make it. I'll be all alone. I don't think I'm ready to leave my family and friends yet, especially since I was really feeling like I was fitting in. I'm not sure I can handle all of these changes. I'm scared! Actually, a part of me feels like I don't want to go, like maybe I really would rather go to a local college."

By "turning up the volume" on self-talk that he had not really attended to previously, Matt became increasingly aware of how these unacknowledged thoughts influenced his experience of fear, tension, and irritability. He recognized that he had some anger about feeling pressured to make a change in his life while not feeling completely ready and anticipating the loss of close relationships.

Children and teens need to be helped to "turn up the volume" on self-talk so they become more aware of what they are saying to themselves. In order to better make sense of anger, they need to be helped to be more completely aware of the internal dialogue they are engaging in that influences anger. They especially need help in clarifying unrealistic expectations and conclusions that foster negative reactions and related anger. While addressing the physical side of anger helps them to calm bodily reactions to anger, clarifying self-talk is a major strategy to help them make sense of anger and develop more adaptive ways of coping with this emotion.

I have found the use of the videotape analogy to be extremely useful in helping children and teens identify unrealistic expectations and conclusions surrounding anger-arousing events. I suggest you practice it again yourself when you find yourself feeling annoyed, this time focusing on identifying thoughts you had about your expectations going into the situation and conclusions following the event. These are the thoughts and self-talk of your automatic pilot, a part of you that influences your reactions without your awareness.

Automatic thoughts are often unrealistic and based on child logic, which has more to do with wishes and fears than realistic thinking and which leaves you vulnerable to negative emotions and angry feelings. It is when we are unaware of such self-talk that our emotions, thinking, and behavior are most vulnerable to their influence. Without this awareness, our self-understanding and control are diminished. Subsequently, we react more strongly to frustrating events and are more influenced by self-defeating thoughts.

Maintaining unrealistic expectations and conclusions is like driving a car with one foot on the accelerator and the other on the brake. Energy is expended moving forward, but competing energy interferes with that forward movement. Children and teens who maintain such unrealistic thinking unwittingly sabotage their own efforts and those of others. These are children who feel blocked in many endeavors, including developing real connections with others. Their internal brakes keep them from optimally channeling their energy in learning, in play, or in relationships. At the same time, they are vulnerable to hurt, depression, and anger, as they are not aware of the source of their pain.

The more you present these strategies as a type of game, the more children and teens will readily engage in them. The following activity, in addition to using the videotape analogy, is especially useful to help younger children recognize self-talk.

Exercise

First, explain to your child that we all have a variety of thoughts throughout the day and that this is very normal. You may want to share with her some examples of when you have thoughts that you do not regularly share, a part of your internal self-talk. For example, you may want to share some thoughts you have while at work, driving, in the supermarket, or doing chores around the house. In an effort to help her realize this is normal, you can give her permission to spontaneously touch your forehead within a time frame that you decide. This will be the cue for you to shift your attention to your thoughts and share them. At that moment, share your self-dialogue in order to model for her your active attention to such internal talk. While it is appropriate to censor certain thoughts, sharing some of your self-talk will help her better understand how to identify her automatic thinking.

Then touch your finger to her forehead and ask her what thoughts she is having, what she is telling herself at that moment. Reassure her that she may be having thoughts that she does not want to share. Emphasize that the most important goal of this game is for her to be aware of what she is telling herself at that moment. It is also good to emphasize that thoughts are private and others will know her exact thoughts only when she directly shares them.

A major task of this exercise is to help her recognize that many of our thoughts are automatic. These thoughts are the first ones that come to mind. Although they may not be as loud as other thoughts, they influence our behavior throughout the day. It will take practice, but even young children can understand this concept. It is especially helpful if you share some of your thinking that reflects expectations and conclusions. Be sure to share both realistic and unrealistic ones and identify them as examples of such thoughts.

Clarifying Expectations and Conclusions

The most important self-talk to clarify in order to make sense of anger involves unrealistic thoughts. Specifically, it is essential to recognize unrealistic expectations we have for ourselves and others and unrealistic conclusions we make concerning ourselves and others. A child who develops this ability is more capable of making sense of his anger and has achieved a major step in reducing potential anger.

In order to help your child make sense of anger, have her focus on identifying these thoughts when you assist her in "turning up the volume" of her internal dialogue. Without such recognition, these expectations and conclusions become a part of the child logic that influences her relationships with herself and others. At this time, it is helpful to review the lists of realistic and unrealistic expectations and conclusions presented in Chapter 4. The more familiar you are with these examples, the more you can use teaching, modeling, and discussion to help your child recognize them when they occur. It is only after a child recognizes such thoughts that she can then evaluate them as being realistic or unrealistic.

Jean, a seven-year-old, is both hurt and angry because lately her best friend, Hilary, spends a great amount of time playing with a new neighbor, Diane. It is natural for Jean to be disappointed, but her level of frustration or anger depends on how unrealistic Jean is in her expectations and the conclusions she makes regarding Hilary's behavior. If she has the following unrealistic expectations, she will more likely experience hurt and related anger:

Jean's Unrealistic Expectations
1. My best friend should always be available to play with me.
2. My best friend should always choose to play with me rather than with someone else.
3. My best friend should play only with me.
4. If she's really my best friend, she should never disappoint me.

Similarly, the level of her disappointment and resulting anger will very much depend on how realistic her appraisals or conclusions are about the event. If Jean's self-talk involves the following conclusions, she will more likely be angry, perhaps toward herself, perhaps toward her friend:

Jean's Unrealistic Conclusions
1. Since Hilary didn't pick me to play with, she doesn't like me anymore.
2. Hilary probably doesn't want to be my friend anymore.
3. I probably will not have a best friend again.
4. There must be something wrong with me if she chose to play with Diane.
5. Hilary probably doesn't like the games we play anymore.

Jean's expectations and conclusions are unrealistic. Helping children and teens to manage anger involves helping them to put into words their expectations and conclusions and then helping them to recognize which ones are unrealistic.

Children can be helped to identify various components of self-talk by using a diagram like the one below. The first diagram can help Jean see the connection between her thoughts and the event. It can also help her identify those expectations she may experience prior to the event. Greater clarity in her understanding can be gained by helping her to identify and list the unrealistic expectations.

Expectations   *Event*

1. _____   _____

   _____   _____

2. _____   _____

   _____   _____

3. _____   _____

   _____   _____

Using the next diagram, children can identify the internal dialogue that reflects their conclusions following a specific event that may have led to anger.

Event   *Conclusions*

1. _____   _____

   _____   _____

2. _____   _____

   _____   _____

3. _____   _____

   _____   _____

Challenging Expectations and Conclusions

While the first step of identifying self-talk is to help children recognize unrealistic expectations and conclusions, the next step in constructively managing anger is to help them evaluate and challenge these expectations and conclusions.[1] This is not always an easy task. It involves helping children to challenge and change thinking that is based on distorted or child logic, substituting more realistic thoughts for the unrealistic ones.[2] The challenging response is best when:

1. It provides alternative ways of thinking.
2. It is a reminder of reality.
3. It is simple.
4. It is empathic.
5. It results in an improved attitude.

A challenging thought is one that offers an alternative by which we can gauge our expectations and conclusions. Through repetition, the challenging self-talk replaces the unrealistic thought and becomes a part of one's automatic pilot.

A challenging thought draws attention to how the world really is and how people really behave. It uses more mature logic and calls attention to the realistic probability that things will happen in a certain way. Whereas more unrealistic expectations may really be wishes, the challenging thought is bound by reality.

The challenging statement should be simple in wording and in its message. Since it is a message for the child or adolescent to use in challenging himself, it should be a simple phrase. The more concise and simple it is, the more easily it will become a part of her automatic internal dialogue as it influences her expectations and conclusions.

Finally, a challenge is most constructive when it is communicated in a tone that is empathic. It is not meant to be critical. It is empathic in that it recognizes the sense of disappointment you might have in giving up an unrealistic expectation. In addition, it should be empathic when you state it as well as when a child states it to herself. It should be supportive even though its goal is to help a child refocus on the realities of a given situation and alternative ways of thinking more realistically about that situation.

The most important element of this strategy is to help children think about their self-talk, put it in words, write it down, and develop a list of alternative thoughts to challenge the unrealistic ones. We can return to the example of Jean to understand how this works. Below is a list of Jean's unrealistic expectations regarding friendship. On the right side are realistic expectations that she can use in order to help her challenge such unrealistic thoughts.

Unrealistic Expectation	Realistic Expectation
My best friend should always be available to play with me.	That would be nice, but even a best friend has other friends.
My best friend should always choose to play with me rather than with someone else.	A best friend can still be a best friend even if she plays with others. Even a best friend has other friends.
If she is really my friend, she should never disappoint me.	Even my best friend may disappoint me. Sometimes I feel disappointment when things do not go my way. Disappointment is a part of life.

Similarly, below is a list of Jean's unrealistic conclusions and statements of realistic conclusions that can challenge them:

Unrealistic Conclusion	Realistic Conclusion
Since Hilary did not pick me to play with her, she doesn't like me anymore.	Maybe she wants to get to know the new neighbor and still likes me.
	Just because I feel she does not like me, it doesn't mean it's true.
	The fact that I feel hurt does not mean she doesn't like me.

She could play with Diane today, but maybe play with me tomorrow.

Hilary probably doesn't want to be my friend anymore.

Even though I feel that way, it doesn't mean it's true.

I probably will not have a best friend anymore.

I may feel that way now, but I can't really predict the future.

There must be something wrong with me if Hilary chooses to play with Diane.

I have nothing to do with what Hilary says or does.

Hilary probably doesn't like the games we play anymore.

She may like the games we play but want to play different games sometimes.

Below are examples of unrealistic expectations your child may have and statements of realistic expectations that can challenge such thinking.

Unrealistic Expectation

All of my needs or wants must be satisfied.

Realistic Expectation

That would be nice, but it may not be possible.

Some needs and wants can be satisfied, but some may never be satisfied.

I may feel that way, but it doesn't mean it has to happen.

If some of my wants are not satisfied, I will still be okay.

I am still lovable even when some of my needs are not satisfied.

Unrealistic Expectation

If I am good, all of my needs and wants will be met.

Challenging Comments

My being good may help satisfy some of my needs.

Bad things sometimes happen to good people.

Other people should know what I need or want without my having to tell them.

People cannot read my mind. Sometimes they can make good guesses.

If they really know me well, they may be right more often.

If someone really likes or loves me, they should always do what I want.	I may feel that way, but that does not mean it is true.
	Others can like or love me but not behave as I wish they would
	Others can still love me even if they do not do what I want them to do.

Below are examples of unrealistic appraisals and conclusions and challenging thoughts that can help a child become more realistic. Again, the realistic appraisal serves as a challenge to the unrealistic one—it provides alternative guidelines and conclusions based on reality but at the same time is simple and empathic.

Unrealistic Appraisal

The event happened because I was not liked.

Realistic Appraisal

Maybe, maybe not.

I could be liked and likeable, but bad things could still happen to me.

Just because I feel that way, it doesn't mean it's true.

I can't please everybody.

Sometimes events like that happen to people who are liked.

Unrealistic Appraisal

If they did that, they don't like or love me.

Realistic Comment

Maybe they did that and they still like or love me.

Just because I feel that way, it doesn't mean it's true.

They could have done that because they love me.

Maybe they did not intend to do that.

Maybe they had other reasons to do what they did.

I might as well give up.

I could see how I could feel that way even if it may not be true.

That's just one choice among many.

That would be less frustrating or painful.

Disappointment makes me think that way.

As reflected in these examples, the goal of offering a challenging and more realistic conclusion is to help children and teens become more receptive to considering other possible ways of thinking about themselves and their world.

In recent years, repeating positive affirmations has been widely encouraged as a strategy to help people develop positive self-esteem. Examples of such statements are "I am worthy," "I will focus on my positive energy today," "The world has much to offer me," "I will succeed in my goals today," and "I am full of love and I deserve love." Part of the premise of this approach is that if we make these statements to ourselves often enough, they will replace negative self-talk as a part of our core identity. While using affirmations may work to some degree, this strategy is somewhat off target. The process can be compared to covering a cracked wall with wallpaper. The result is a new appearance, but the underlying structure remains flawed.

In contrast, challenging thoughts address the core unrealistic thoughts that are a part of "child logic." Continuing with the analogy described above, this process can be compared to actually mending the wall. These challenges strengthen our core identity by focusing on the structure of *how* we think and not just on *what* we think. This is the strength of the challenging thoughts.

In addition, studies suggest that true positive self-esteem is based on competencies and accomplishment. The ability to respond to unrealistic thinking with more than just positive affirmations reflects skills that help us manage not only anger but also other uncomfortable emotions.

Helping Children Develop Challenging Thoughts

The most important elements of this strategy are to help your child:

1. Think about his self-talk.
2. Recognize his unrealistic thoughts.
3. Put it in words and write it down.
4. Develop a list of alternative challenging thoughts.

Initially, your modeling and discussing challenging statements can help your child arrive at more realistic thinking. In addition, help her brainstorm and identify challenging statements of her own. Another way to help your child identify challenging statements is to ask her to develop challenges she might use in response to a younger child who voices unrealistic expectations and conclusions. Children can often be more realistic in developing challenges for others.

Posting Challenges

Just as we might use motivational posters to encourage movement in a positive direction, posting challenging statements for your child may help serve as reminders of how she can respond to unrealistic thinking. The constant availability of such reminders provides a clear message. Since much of our learning is based on taking in visual information, posting such statements will further foster their commitment to memory. The realistic statements that challenge Jean's unrealistic thinking serve as good examples.

If you know that your child often resorts to a particular unrealistic expectation or conclusion, you may want to post that one along with a challenge. You may suggest your child draw a picture or tell a story to depict the situation in which a character first has an unrealistic thought and then challenges the thought with a more realistic alternative.

I am not suggesting that each time your child is angry you sit down and make a formal lesson of the experience. But the more you introduce these types of realistic challenges into his self-dialogue and the more he is helped to practice this approach, the more he will be prepared to consider alternative responses to his more immediate negative and unrealistic expectations or appraisals.

This approach can be presented formally by parents and teachers by actually having children write down their self-dialogue and responses. At the same time, more realistic responses can be suggested informally, when a child is observed to be angry or irritated. A very gentle but supportive comment might be "I'm wondering if you believe that [state the unrealistic expectation or appraisal]." Then follow up with "But, you know, [state a realistic expectation or appraisal to challenge the unrealistic one]."

The goal is to help children develop a more complete self-dialogue that does not lead them to assume that their first reaction is the only way to explain a specific event.

Modeling the Use of Challenges

Another way to help children and teens challenge unrealistic thoughts is to model this approach. This is helpful for children and teens but is especially powerful with teens. Since teens struggle with issues surrounding feeling controlled, they will be more open to learning this strategy when they hear you discuss it out loud as you apply it to your own situation. You should occasionally share an incident in which you became irritated, annoyed, or angry and realized as you thought about the event that you had certain unrealistic expectations. These should be specifically discussed. Then explain that by reflecting on the event, you recognized a more realistic alternative way of viewing the situation.

Here are two examples of this type of sharing. "You know how I get angry in traffic on the way home. Well, I was thinking more about that. I guess I really assume that people will be considerate, that they won't suddenly come into my lane without signaling and that they'll let me into their lane when I signal. You would think I would know by now, after driving for almost fifteen years, that most people will be okay but there will be others who won't. I think if I remember that more often, I may not get so annoyed."

A real estate agent may share with her son: "Well, I didn't make that sale today, and then, of all things, I got angry at myself. I started thinking it was entirely my fault. Then I stopped and realized that maybe I could have done something differently, but to be honest, that still wouldn't guarantee that I would have made a sale. I was reminded that I can try to influence people, but they will make their own decisions and may not act the way I want them to."

It is the ongoing repetition of these types of communications and reflections on one's thoughts and feelings that can have tremendous impact on children and adolescents. This form of sharing provides examples for our children of how to view their anger and related feelings and thoughts without directly telling them how to think. Such modeling offers children and teens very concrete examples of how they can focus internally on factors relating to anger instead of directing the anger outward or minimizing, denying, suppressing, or repressing it. Such reflection fosters openness to consider alternative ways of self-talk that help children make sense of and express the anger.

Children learn best by example. Consistency in the discussion and modeling of these strategies will have the greatest impact in helping your child make sense of and manage anger.

All strategies in stress management in general, and anger management specifically, involve the ability to think through possible ways of responding to a situation. They emphasize that while we may not be able to control certain situations that cause us stress, we can effectively alter the way we think about such stress. By helping children develop more realistic expectations and alternative explanations of negative events, they develop an increased tolerance for frustration, increased optimism, and an overall resilience to life's challenges.

9

What Does Your Child Really Want or Need?

Your anger tells you more about yourself than it does about the target of your anger. It informs you about what is uniquely important to you. When examined closely, your anger gives you information about your core motivations, including your wishes and needs. It also helps you recognize your values and attitudes. The comprehensive management of anger involves both understanding your core motivations and managing the energy aroused by anger. As a parent, the more you are able to recognize anger as providing information about motivations, the more you can help your child clearly make sense of and manage anger. This chapter provides guidelines and specific skills for achieving this task.

The Importance of Studying Motivations

Why is it so important for anger management that we understand our motivations? For some, anger management focuses only on helping individuals control, monitor, and appropriately channel the energy that is aroused by anger. These strategies are essential as part of a comprehensive approach toward anger management and are presented in later chapters of this book. But when we focus only on addressing the energy aroused by anger, we miss out on the opportunity to explore the richness of information that this emotion provides. As indicated earlier, viewing anger as a sign of a problem is part of managing it in a healthy way. Being able to identify motivations underlying our anger helps us to more fully recognize the problem or concern that we need to address.

Our core motivations have a major influence on what makes us angry. Identifying these core motivations is probably the most complex task associated with making sense of anger. We may be most aware of the anger or other emotions that precede anger but least aware of the motivations that impact anger. The model of anger highlights a sequence of influences beginning with motivations, but it does not communicate the fact that we are aware of some motivations and unconscious of others. Information regarding our emotions, conclusions, and expectations is more available to our awareness than is information about our motivations. It is for this reason that we begin first by identifying anger, then the emotions that precede anger, and next the conclusions and expectations. Finally we need to address the motivations that influence our thoughts, attitudes, values, and associated emotions, all of which play a role in the experience of anger.

The ability to recognize our driving forces facilitates greater self-understanding and results in more flexibility in thinking. More specifically, self-reflection regarding our motivation helps us to:

1. Redirect attention away from the target of our anger.
2. Increase self-awareness regarding our anger and how it relates to what is uniquely important in our life.
3. Decide on the manner by which to express or channel anger.
4. Gain insights into our personality.

When trying to help a child manage anger, I often inquire about the personal meaning of the situation that led to her anger. My goal in asking this question is to encourage self-reflection, in contrast to directing attention outward toward the person or situation that might at first glance appear to be the cause. I support the child in a detailed exploration regarding how the situation or person impacted her. Directing her attention inward also serves to distract her from immediately responding with anger. This ability to short-circuit the impulsive leap from experiencing anger to acting on it is a basic element of many anger management strategies, whether practiced during the moment when we are most intensely angry or after the situation has passed. Counting to ten, focusing on our breathing, and physically relaxing during a moment of anger are just a few ways of disengaging our attention from the source of anger. Self-reflection promotes increased self-awareness regarding anger. Directing attention away from the source of our anger and focusing on ourselves allows for increased self-awareness regarding the meaning of one's anger. Through self-reflection, we can then more clearly identify the needs and wants that are being thwarted.

I am not suggesting that this level of self-reflection should necessarily take place during a moment of anger. As emphasized previously, anger leads to impaired judgment and reasoning. While we may be able to recognize other emotions or thoughts while angry, sorting out motivations is a greater challenge and requires self-reflection when we are more relaxed.

The benefit of directing our attention inward rather than outward is also based on theories of stress management. We can respond to stress by trying to make changes in our environment, by trying to eliminate the external sources of our stress, or by changing how we think about the stress. Similarly, when we try to manage anger, we can focus on changing people and aspects of our external environment, or we can focus on changing how we think about the people and situations that impact us. Much of anger management involves the recognition that we may not be able to change people or situations, but we can have control over how we think about and respond to them. Only after realizing this can we fully identify our needs and wants and more constructively decide how to address them.

Through reflection we gain insights concerning our relationships with others, the world around us, and ourselves. Without self-awareness, we live life on automatic pilot. We think and act throughout the day while driven by needs and wants that we are not fully aware of. We become vulnerable to the influence of others as well as our own impulses. This impacts how we manage not just anger but many other aspects of our relationships. Only by more fully understanding our motivations are we able to make more informed decisions and take actions that lead to more satisfactory relationships with others and ourselves. Following is an example of how you can use the model of anger to help a child increase self-awareness about motivations that may drive his automatic pilot.

A child may become quite upset when his parents refuse to purchase a particular toy for him. Wanting to play, wanting to be like his peers or siblings, or other motivations associated with the particular toy may all contribute to his wanting it. At the same time, when he is disappointed, he may erroneously conclude that his parents do not love him. Clearly, the need for love may not be the primary motivation for wanting a toy, but it may play a part in his reactions when this desire is not satisfied. Applying the insights provided by the model of anger, we may view the sequence of his reactions as depicted by Figure 9.1.

First help your child understand that his anger is related to his feelings of disappointment and hurt. Then help him recognize that he concludes that his parents do not care for him. This belief is based on an unrealistic expectation that if they really loved him, they would buy every toy he wants. A child needs help to evaluate the validity of his belief. Working backward, as we identify factors that contribute to his anger, we may then help him understand that while it is natural for him to be disappointed and annoyed at not getting the toy, a part of his motivation underlying his anger is really his desire to feel cared for by his parents. He may still be somewhat disappointed and angry about not getting the toy. But if his need to be loved and cared for is addressed, he will be better able to understand and manage the intensity of his anger and hurt. He will feel supported and understood.

Recognizing your child's motivations will also help you to more meaningfully address his anger. For example, in the above situation, you may respond with "We want you to know that we love you even if we did not buy the toy for you. You may think or feel that we do not care, but that's not true."

When we first met, Lawrence, age sixteen, described intense rage toward his stepfather for telling him he probably would not be accepted at the college of his choice. While Lawrence had experienced tension with his stepfather ever since his mother married him, three years before, Lawrence had never experienced this intensity of anger. When he finished discussing his anger, I turned to him and inquired, "Help me understand. What does it mean to you that he said that? You say he really did not seem malicious or sarcastic when he shared his opinion. You've told me that he even stated ahead of time that he was being honest and did not intend to hurt your feelings."

In talking about the incident, Lawrence recognized that he felt criticized even if that had not been his stepfather's intention. He soon real-

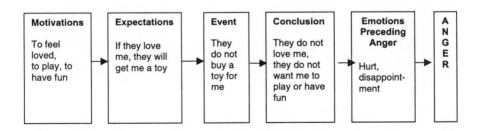

Figure 9.1: Sequence of reactions to not receiving a toy

ized that behind his hurt was his own sense of shame and fear that he himself did not think that his preferred college would accept him. He recognized his self-doubts and how important it was for him to attend that college, as two of his friends and his older brother were attending that same school. The comment made by his stepfather aroused so much anger for Lawrence because he was full of self-doubts. Underlying his anger was his need for support and reassurance regarding his anxiety and self-doubts.

Only after self-reflection could he decide what to do with his anger. Lawrence could have focused only on monitoring his anger and how he expressed it. He could have focused only on managing the energy aroused by his anger. In contrast, after increased self-understanding, he was able to decide not only where to direct his anger but also how to direct it. Since he genuinely experienced his stepfather as being supportive, he decided to be candid with him. He shared how the comment had affected him. He described how his own self-doubts were aroused, and requested that his stepfather continue to be honest with him while being sensitive to his need for support during this time of uncertainty. As a result of this process, he developed a new sense of connection with himself and with his stepfather. His self-confidence increased.

Clearly Lawrence's lack of self-understanding left him vulnerable to feeling criticized and angry. His automatic pilot put him into a defensive mode. Lacking awareness of his underlying sense of shame, lack of confidence, and need for reassurance, he was left vulnerable to any kind of negative feedback and was driven to strike back.

Challenges to Recognizing and Identifying Motivations

While general challenges to recognizing anger have already been discussed, there are very specific challenges that interfere with a child's ability to recognize and identify his motivations. There are three major hurdles to this process:

1. Children vary in their ability to reflect on behavior, emotions, and thoughts.
2. Children are not equally motivated to become more self-aware.
3. Exploring motivations is more complex than exploring emotions or thoughts related to anger.

Another ability that is essential in order to recognize motivations is the capacity to observe patterns in our thoughts, emotions, and behaviors. This requires that we be able to step back and become aware of themes or repetition in our thoughts, emotions, and behaviors. In general, teens, more than younger children, are developmentally capable of recognizing such patterns.

Children and teens vary in their motivation for self-reflection. This motivation depends on a variety of factors that may include modeling by their parents, their own impulsiveness or quickness to act rather than slow down and reflect, their comfort with self-reflection, their sense that self-reflection is somehow associated with being self-indulgent, or an attitude that is not favorable to self-reflection. Children and adolescents, like individuals of all ages, vary in the degree to which they can readily identify their needs and wants. They vary both in their intellectual intelligence and in what has been called their "emotional intelligence," which includes their ability to understand and be sensitive to the emotional life of others and themselves.[1]

Finally, because motivations are often complex, it requires greater self-reflection to identify them than to recognize the expectations, conclusions, or other emotions that are associated with specific anger. For example, children may have several motivations at the same time. A child who has a strong desire for attention and approval may seek to meet these needs by doing well in school. Another child who may have these same needs but experiences anger toward his parents or authority in general may seek to get attention and approval from certain peers by engaging in provocative or disruptive behaviors. He may become the class clown, be truant, or competitively take part in risky behavior.

Children and adolescents may also have ambivalent motivations. For example, a child may want to be treated like an adult and also have the privileges of being a child. A ten-year-old may want to stay up later, like his older brother, but become angry about having additional chores assigned to him because he is more mature. A teenager may want the freedom to drive a car but, at the same time, be fearful of such freedom. He may engage in behaviors that unwittingly lead him to be grounded. As one teen admitted to me, "I'm really not in a rush to have my own car. I know I'll have to earn money to pay for the gas and maintenance, and to be honest, it will be hard to say no when my friends ask me to take them someplace. I am the first one in our group to get a license."

Sometimes we minimize or deny certain fundamental motivations. This creates difficulties for the individual doing this as well as for others. Children and teens who seem to unwittingly engage in a wide variety of activities to make people withdraw from them are one example of this. Past hurt and pain may lead them to minimize or deny their basic need for love and a sense of connection. So they appear to be primarily motivated by a desire to create conflict, tension, and avoidance when in fact they crave emotional connection.

In spite of the challenges involved in helping children and adolescents recognize their motivations, there are a wide variety of strategies that can be practiced to help them achieve this goal.

General Guidelines for Helping Children Identify Motivations

In general, the best way to help children and adolescents identify motivations related to anger is to:

1. Model self-reflection.
2. Allow for discussion of anger.
3. Acknowledge and validate their anger.
4. Help them recognize mixed or competing motivations.

Modeling Self-Reflection

As when teaching your child about any component of the model of anger, the more you self-reflect and become familiar with your motivations and how they influence your life, the more you will be able to assist your child in recognizing her own motivations. Take time to review the list of motivations. Practice recognizing your own motivations throughout the day. Most important, practice applying the techniques I've outlined so that you can more clearly recognize your motivations. Look for patterns in your thinking or behavior in order to identify motivations that are especially important for you. Maintaining a journal or log will further your capacity to recognize them. It takes practice, time, and commitment to become more aware of your motivations, but achieving this is extremely important before working with your child.

Sharing your process of self-reflection is the best way to model self-reflection. Discussing your experiences going through the process is as important as actually sharing some of the motivations that you have identified. It is extremely difficult to ask a child to turn inward and look at his own motivations unless you can model the process for him. This can be done even with young children. Acknowledging motivations such as your desire for admiration, stability, or respect from people important to you can be very effective. By your sharing, you give him permission to address similar issues and encourage him to question himself about his needs and wants.

It is especially important to share your motivations when your needs and wants have not been satisfied. Start with a simple example: "I am really annoyed that television program was canceled. I was looking forward to it, and I'm disappointed. I guess I just wanted to relax and be entertained. Well, let's see—what else can we do for fun?" This highlights a variety of essential factors in making sense of and managing anger. This one conversation identifies anger as a secondary emotion: anger in reaction to disappointment. It also communicates the idea that having an expectation that is not satisfied leads to disappointment. Going further, it identifies the major motivation at this moment: to relax. Finally, the comment concludes with brainstorming about how to achieve your goal even though you were disappointed. Whether your aim is simply to watch a television program or to get more respect from your child, modeling how you process the experience will provide a very specific strategy for helping your child look at his own motivations.

Encourage Discussion About Anger

Encouraging children and adolescents to discuss their anger is a major contribution toward helping them self-reflect about their motivations. I specifically emphasize getting them to discuss rather than express it. By this I mean children should be encouraged and supported to openly voice their anger and other emotions related to it. I am not suggesting they need to be encouraged to express it by acting on it or by being aggressive. Children who are not allowed to discuss anger are not encouraged to move past it. Anger that is not discussed festers, distracts us from the goal of gaining further self-awareness, and very often will be expressed in some other form.

Acknowledge and Validate Anger

Acknowledging and validating a child's anger is also an essential component in helping children and adolescents understand motivations related to their anger. Raymond, thirteen, was referred to me because of his difficulties in school, which included arguments with teachers. He was well behaved at home but acted up in school. As with many adolescents with whom I have worked, Raymond was quite angry about being told he had to see me. As usual, I inquired as to why he came to see me, and he told me his parents had made him come. I then asked him what he thought about seeing me. To this he responded, "I don't want to be here. I was forced to come in!"

"So you don't want to be here, but your parents made you come here," I said. "I can understand your being annoyed about that, but help me understand something else. You say they forced you to come here. How did they do that?" Raymond answered that his parents had threatened to ground him if he did not come for counseling. I responded to Raymond's comment by saying, "Oh—so you chose to come here instead of losing your freedom to be out with your friends. That must be very important to you." I did this because when working with adolescents, I believe it is important to help them realize that although they may be angry about having to go into counseling, they actually choose to come.

Through these interactions I emphasize that it is understandable that they are angry when told by a parent they are going to see me. I then invite them to discuss their anger and related feelings they may have about their choice and feeling coerced to see me.

Help Children and Teens Recognize Mixed or Competing Motivations

Finally, another general strategy for helping children and adolescents better identify motivations is to help them realize that they have mixed or competing motivations. While we may feel strongly about doing one thing, we may have another motivation that moves us in another direction. When meeting with Raymond, I suggested that he was motivated by his desires for freedom and to be connected with his friends.

In general, we feel more comfortable having only a single motivation. But in many situations, as reflected in the above example, several motivations contribute to our behavior. Helping your child identify several possible motivations rather than the one that is "real" or "correct" will assist him in developing more accurate self-awareness.

It can also be confusing when we are pulled in different directions by different motivations. In fact, an important general strategy for working with children and teens in anger management is to help them recognize that it is very common to experience competing motivations. When children are given permission to discuss these mixed motivations, they become more sensitive to, and accepting of, their motivations as well as the realities of life. As a result, they spend less energy trying to convince themselves and others that they have only one motivation.

This was an issue in my discussions with Raymond. I asked him, "So while you chose to come here rather than be grounded, what would you like to be doing instead?" At first he was hesitant and responded that anything would be better than being here. I pushed him to name a particular activity. He surprisingly responded with "I'd like to be home making brownies." I assured him that that sounded like a good idea to me. I asked him whether he liked his brownies with or without nuts and with or without frosting. He smiled and with increased liveliness in his tone described his preference. I then indicated my own preference and suggested, "Well, that makes perfect sense. That is much more enjoyable than coming here to talk about difficulties in school." At that point he became more engaged and able to discuss what was going on.

I was simply recognizing and validating his emotions and attitudes. I was being empathic with him. Such empathy fosters a positive sense of being heard as well as helps a child learn more about himself. He was validated in his experience of anger, frustration, and general discomfort about seeing me. In addition, his mixed motivations were acknowledged and validated.

Though I acknowledged and validated his anger and motivations, I did not say to him, "Well, since you really prefer to make brownies, we're going to let you go home and you can come back when you want to or when you recognize that this is a serious issue." Instead, I listened and acknowledged how his anger and discomfort made sense. I encouraged him to discuss his motivations and emotions without focusing on whether his wants and needs would be satisfied.

Empathy involves acknowledging and validating another's feelings.[2] It also implies listening, recognizing how a child could have the reactions he does, and even being empathic with his negative feelings. This ability to listen to children and adolescents is especially difficult for a parent who strongly wishes to reduce her child's pain or anger. However, being empathic toward a child helps foster his capacity to discuss any component of the experience of anger, including motivations. It helps a child learn that negative or uncomfortable feelings do not have to be "fixed" or removed. But they do need to be acknowledged.

Specific Strategies to Help Children and Teens Recognize Motivations

Direct Questions

So how do you help a child better recognize and understand his motivations and how they may influence his anger? To start with, you may directly ask your child, "Why did you do that?" or "Why do you feel that way?" If you are really fortunate, your child may provide an answer that fully identifies all the elements of anger presented in the model. For example, when questioned about a quarrel with his sister, your son may clearly state, "Mom, the reason I was so angry is that I felt hurt and disappointed. When Sherry took my CDs without asking, I concluded she has no respect for me! And Mom, I expect respect from friends and my sister. I feel I deserve respect, and I want respect. They were my CDs, and she should have asked me before she borrowed them."

If your child answers your question in this manner, skip this chapter and go to the next one, as this type of response indicates a solid self-awareness and comfort regarding anger and the conclusions, expectations, and motivations underlying it. This is certainly a desirable response—but it is one that is rarely given.

Another child may respond by focusing only on his anger or on the action: "What do you mean, why did I yell at her? She took my CDs.

They're mine. She just walked in my room and took them." A third child may share a response that describes other feelings in addition to the anger but does not identify the wish for respect. Some children, when questioned about their expressions of anger, may be vague and offer an answer that they believe will give you just enough information to make you go away. Then there are children who respond, "I don't know."

The "I don't know" response occurs quite often. Think back to how you felt when, as a child, you were asked why you behaved the way you did. Asking why seems to force us to identify a reason and implies that we should provide a mature answer based on cause-effect logic. It also may imply that a child already knows her motivation. Many children shut down for these reasons when asked a why question. I have found that asking a what question is often experienced as being more open-ended. For example, "What led up to your angry reaction?" or "What happened between you and James?" or "What were you thinking that led you to do that?" appear to offer children more direction in reflecting and, subsequently, lead to a more detailed description of what influences lie behind certain actions.

But let's assume you ask why or what questions and you still get a response of "I don't know." Children who are being questioned often say this. It is especially helpful to remember that this response has several possible meanings. For some, the statement "I don't know" is really itself an expression of anger. The child may really be saying, "Of course I know! But I am so angry, I am surely not going to let *you* know!"

"I don't know" can also be a statement of fear, embarrassment, or shame. Your child may actually be saying, "I really do know, but I'm afraid of what will happen if I tell you," "I'm afraid of what will happen to me or what I might do or say," "I'm ashamed to admit what I thought when I did that," or "I'm afraid of what might happen to you; you'll feel hurt, disappointed, or even angry."

Another child or teen may be saying "I don't know" when she really does not have any understanding or awareness of factors leading to her behavior or emotions. This is the more problematic youngster because she is more out of touch with her emotions and motivations. Such children may experience much alienation because they lack awareness of what is meaningful to them, and they require more assistance to help them develop increased self-awareness.

The best way to understand your child when he says "I don't know" is to review your history together, observe his nonverbal expression, and evaluate the tone in his voice. Has he used many feeling words or candidly discussed in some detail his motivations, values, or attitudes? Is he typically timid or fearful? Is he generally unaware? Attending to these areas will help you to more clearly determine whether he is angry, fearful, or genuinely lacking in self-awareness.

Many parents have described behavioral problems that neither they nor the child could explain. These parents were especially puzzled when they were told "I don't know," were met with silence, or received only a vague response. As a result, they often described feeling very estranged from their own child. Whenever I work with a family in treatment, I first meet the parents with the child, then see them separately, and then meet with them together again. I have been thoroughly surprised over the years to find that so many children are quick to describe in detail their concerns and emotions when given the opportunity to privately share their feelings with a stranger. So many of them very candidly articulate their thoughts and feelings about their relationships with their family, peers, and themselves, revealing events that may have led to pain, hurt, shame, or other feelings that in turn lead to anger. It is certainly a positive and healthy sign when children can identify their emotions and motivations. These are children who are aware of themselves but are inhibited about directly expressing feelings of anger. It is more problematic and reflects more serious difficulties when the youngster is not at all able to identify his motivations or the emotions that lead him to anger.

The use of direct questions is often the least effective strategy when trying to help some children and adolescents explore their motivations. Some may feel they have to produce a specific answer. Some, most often adolescents, are very resistant to questions because they experience a sense of intrusion at a time when they desire increased privacy and independence. A simple inquiry may be experienced as an attempt to control them because of the adolescent's concern for privacy and independence. For this reason other types of comments may be more effective in helping these children identify motivations.

Observations and Guesses

Sharing your observations can be especially helpful in encouraging self-reflection regarding motivations. Such observations are best offered as hunches or guesses, not as facts. They should be offered tentatively in such a way that the child does not feel obligated to respond. The goal is to encourage soul-searching. Making observations and guesses can be especially useful when helping a child recognize motivations related to her anger.

Hunches may be based on your observations or on your child's direct communications. Specifically, you may want to offer observations such as "I could tell his friendship is important to you," "It sounds like winning is really meaningful for you," "Wow, you do like being creative," "Well, in spite of what you think right now, we do love you," or "It certainly does feel good to feel special." These comments should be offered without a request for feedback unless your child wants to engage you in discussion. They may be most helpful if offered at a time when your child is able to really hear it—that is, when she is not too distracted by her own thoughts or feelings or the events around her.

Avoid making comments in a tone that is sarcastic or suggests that you can "see through" your child. In essence, your comments should reflect a curious guess, a suggested way for your child to view herself, and a gentle prompt to provide a focus for self-reflection. These comments must be genuine, or they can easily be experienced as devaluing. A parent may respond to a child or adolescent by saying, "It seems like you enjoy being taken care of." This statement may be communicated in a tone that is casual and nonthreatening or in one that reflects anger and is an attempt to ridicule her. Similarly, it may be communicated in a tone that emphasizes your power of perception. Clearly the focus in content and tone should be an empathic response that communicates understanding, validation, and acceptance of a child's motivations.

Present these observations as a concerned parent sharing them for consideration by your child. Present them in a tentative manner, such as "I wonder if ...," "Perhaps ...," or "Maybe ..." Beginning your statement this way will further communicate that it is an observation as opposed to a harshly confrontational statement intended to make your child recognize the "truth."

These same types of statements can also be used when applying the model of anger to other people or characters presented in the movies, on television, in literature, or in news reports. For example, "I wonder if Dumbo was ..." or " Maybe he did that because ..."

"Parts" Language

As described earlier, we feel more comfortable experiencing a single motivation rather than mixed or competing motivations. And yet much of our behavior is influenced by an interaction of several motivations. We may also experience some anxiety and self-doubts when we discover competing motivations within ourselves. Helping children to recognize and understand mixed and competing motivations is another way to help them better make sense of their anger.

One way of doing this is to listen to them describe a particular conflict and then suggest, "Maybe a *part* of you wants to ... and another *part* of you wants to ..." By helping a child recognize mixed and competing motivations, you help him make sense of confusion and tension associated with being pulled in two different directions. This response further recognizes that, in fact, we often make decisions or take actions that address the satisfaction of one need while neglecting another need or want.

An example that comes to mind is reflected in a conversation I had with a thirteen-year-old who was given his own room in the attic. Following this change, he became more irritable with his family as he struggled whether to spend time in his room or in the family room. I suggested, "A part of you wants to be with them *and* a part of you wants to feel more independent. That makes sense."

As I noted before, I purposely use the word *and* to communicate the fact that motivations can compete with each other. All too often, teens make statements such as "I'm confused. At times I want to spend time with my family, and other times I want to spend more time with my friends. Which is it? I feel like I don't know what I want. Is it that I want to spend more time with my family or with my friends?"

Making sense of mixed motivations is best achieved by helping children to drop the *or* when they make such statements and replace it with *and* to best describe the true nature of such motivations. Understanding this idea about motivations helps children and adolescents make sense of anger as well as other emotions related to anger.

Understanding mixed or competing motivations is especially important when a child is aware only of one motivation but feels compelled to act to the contrary. In this situation, she may be motivated to take a certain action, but her automatic pilot may lead her to unwittingly take another action that interferes with the satisfaction of the first motivation. A simple example of this is reflected in the example of Jake, a young man who was extremely motivated to have his peers recognize him as bright. However, he also had much conflict with authority and resented competing for grades to satisfy his need for recognition and to feel special. His inconsistent behavior was an indication that he was responding to competing motivations. For example, Jake did not do many of the assignments in class but evidenced a sharp wit in his answers. He demonstrated extremely solid critical thinking in debates with peers and teachers alike, yet often was the class clown. His jokes reflected a superior level of intellect but were sarcastic and cynical. This was truly an example of motivations related to anger that competed with his strong desire for recognition.

Helping children make sense of and manage anger involves helping them better recognize this inhibiting conflict, when one part competes against another part.

Remain Alert to Minimized or Denied Motivations

Much of anger is related to motivations that are not satisfied. They may not be satisfied for a variety of reasons, but children and adolescents (as well as adults) are often angry when they have minimized or denied important motivations. One example of this is reflected in Rachel's behavior. Thirteen-year-old Rachel had a strong interest in playing basketball and wanted to play on the school team in seventh grade, but she was terribly fearful of what her parents would think of her. They had always maintained strong traditional gender stereotypes and never encouraged any of her athletic interests. She was torn between her desire to compete in a physically active endeavor and her desire to please her parents.

Rachel chose to ignore her strong interest in sports and instead tried to channel some of her competitive drives through her participation in the debate club. By the middle of eighth grade, she had become increasingly testy with her parents. This was most evidenced by her frequent debates with them over their attempts to discipline her. What gradually surfaced in our discussions was her anger related to ignoring her interest in sports.

A fifteen-year-old and the son of a former army officer, Jason was increasingly angry in his early adolescence. During those years, he was involved in conflicts with his father and with other authority figures. He was a bright young man who had excelled academically until the first year of high school, when he began to express resentment toward teachers and became less focused on academic achievement. At the same time Jason became more distant with both of his parents, even though he had previously been close to them. Also, there was a slight shift in the balance of his friendships. Formerly he had been close to peers who excelled academically and talked about going to college. But he had since withdrawn from these friends and developed friendships with peers who were often truant and rarely discussed their future.

Part of Jason's reaction had to do with his feeling that his father wished him to pursue law school or the armed services. In these last few years, Jason had realized that he had a strong passion for art. Jason had become increasingly angry at authority in reaction to his increased irritation with his father. He was extremely intimidated and fearful of expressing his true feelings and interests to his father. His desire not to disappoint his father and his fear of being ridiculed by him combined to create pressure for Jason to deny his real interests. This is an example of how anger may arise when we don't pursue our true motivations. I should emphasize that while Jason was aware of his anger toward his dad, he had little awareness of how this had led him to become angry toward others.

The Little Child in the Sidecar

The analogy of the motorcycle with a sidecar, discussed earlier, helps children and adolescents better understand their motivations. I often use this analogy combined with the image of the "little child" to help them better identify motivations that may not be very apparent to them. I suggest to them that to the degree they are aware of the motivations of the little child and that little child's potential to climb out of the sidecar, they are freer to decide whether or not to act on these motivations. Without such awareness, they may be dominated by them.

A major part of using this analogy is to help children and adolescents "talk" to their little child in an effort to better recognize what it is that motivates him. Children and adolescents can be helped to identify motivations by being encouraged to pretend they are talking to that little child. I once worked with a nine-year-old girl who came to me, in part, due to test anxiety. While the focus was on her anxiety, it also became apparent that a part of her anxiety was related to anger at herself regarding making mistakes. I helped her explore her internal dialogue and motivations by first helping her learn about her little child. I asked her to be aware of self-talk initiated by her little child regarding the test. With several weeks of practice she was able to recognize her little child as saying, "You need to be perfect. You can't make mistakes. You're stupid." Our work together focused on helping her talk back to the little child. She was encouraged to talk back from her most realistic, nurturing, supportive, and reassuring part so that she could calm the little child's expectations but also better understand her motivations. She became more aware of her motivations when she said to her little child, "Mom, Dad, and I will still love you if you make mistakes. Everyone makes some mistakes. You may feel you're stupid, but that doesn't mean that you are!"

My work with the fifteen-year-old high school basketball player who was extremely critical of his teammates, described earlier, also involved using this approach. As he was encouraged to dialogue with this part of himself, he became more aware that his little child was intensely anxious about failure. Thomas was such a perfectionist that he often felt shame when he was given even constructive criticism. With further exploration, he realized that underneath it all, his little child was fearful that "if I make mistakes and don't play well, I will be abandoned." Through this type of dialoguing, he more fully recognized that his needs for security and trust in himself were very intense motivations for him.

With and without our awareness of them, our motivations influence our every action throughout the day. Similarly, with or without our awareness, they play a major role in influencing our anger. To the degree that we can be more aware of them, we become more aware of our true selves. When this happens, we gain connection to and develop greater trust in ourselves. Similarly, we become more authentic. Finally, being more aware of our motivations, we experience more freedom and less emotional confusion about what it is that we want or need.

10

Making Sense of Anger in the World Around Us

So far I have focused on ways you can teach your children about anger by applying the model of anger to their emotions and to those of
others in their life. I also encouraged you to model anger management
for your children. In contrast, this chapter focuses on looking at anger
in literature, movies, television, news reports, music, games, and the
school curriculum. These are rich resources that offer you numerous
opportunities for discussion of anger, whether at home or in school.
Specifically, the goals of this chapter are to help your child do the
following:

1. Realize that the emotion of anger is a natural emotion that
   varies in intensity and duration.
2. Increase his comfort and ease in discussing a very complex and
   highly charged emotion that is experienced in everyday life.
3. Foster problem-solving skills by recognizing the wide variety of
   strategies that are used in managing anger.
4. Recognize and differentiate constructive and destructive anger
   management strategies.

The candid discussion of anger as it is expressed in a wide range of media communicates the message that it is all right to both experience anger and talk about it. In general, we find it easier to discuss and focus on the anger of others than to directly address our own anger. And we can be more open and objective in our learning when we are not distracted by emotional discomfort.

By discussing the examples presented in these media, you will help your child recognize the pros and cons of various anger management strategies and provide greater clarity about how to think when responding to anger. In addition, discussions with your child will strongly communicate your personal values about anger and human interaction in general.

Finally, through discussion of the many ways by which others manage anger, a child gains an increased capacity for coming up with his own ways to manage his anger. It is only by repeatedly drawing attention to the variety of anger management strategies that your child will think of them when responding to his own anger. I am not suggesting that every angry event needs to be discussed. However, the more practice children have with handling this strong emotion, the more likely they are to develop a broad repertoire of anger management strategies. Discussing these examples will also provide you opportunities to better know your child. You will be able to more accurately identify his attitudes, values, problem-solving skills, and understanding of anger, and you will gain a better perspective on how he resolves conflict in relationships.

The examples I provide offer the full range of ways that you can apply the model of anger at home or in the classroom. They offer children the chance to better recognize and understand the sequence of experiences that are a part of anger: motivations, expectations, relevant events, conclusions, moments of anger, emotional reactions, bodily reactions, self-talk, and management and expression of anger. You can work with your child to identify one or more of these components in the material you address.

Choosing Examples of Anger to Discuss

The ideal choices to discuss are those examples of anger that arouse your child's interest but are not so anxiety-producing that she refuses to discuss them. This is an important point because people learn best when interested. The following guidelines should be considered when selecting examples of anger management to discuss with your child:

1. Are the examples appropriate for your child's level of emotional and intellectual development?
2. Are they examples that you are comfortable discussing?
3. Are they examples that your child can comfortably discuss?
4. Do the examples focus on issues that you have never addressed, or do you have some history of discussing such issues with your child?
5. How receptive is your child at the moment you want to discuss the example?
6. How thoroughly do you want to explore the example?

Consider the content of the example and how the anger is expressed when deciding if an example is appropriate for your child's emotional and intellectual development. All too often parents assume that a bright or verbal child can maturely handle a challenging emotional issue, but this is frequently incorrect. Children may exhibit superior intellectual ability as reflected in learning capacity and problem-solving skills when dealing with facts, but they may lack understanding of themselves or others when it comes to recognizing, making sense of, and managing their emotions.

I recommend applying the model of anger to an example that is not too emotionally difficult for *you* to address. While it is not necessary to have complete understanding and make sense of all of your emotions regarding a particular example, selecting an example that is highly emotionally charged may be too challenging and so may distract you from the specific task of effectively teaching the model of anger. For instance, the intensity of your emotional reactions following a conversation with your spouse about your pending divorce may leave you unprepared to objectively discuss an example related to divorce. Similarly, if you are angry with your teen about his returning home two hours beyond his curfew, you may not want to immediately discuss an example of a parent who is angry with her child regarding the same violation of family rules.

Since anger is a highly charged emotion, it is important to consider the level of emotional intensity that your child can comfortably address. As stated previously, while some children are able to comfortably discuss their own anger, others may be too apprehensive to discuss it even in a movie. With a child who easily becomes anxious about anger, initially you may wish to use an example of very low-level anger, and then, as she becomes more comfortable in such discussions, address an example that reflects more intense emotion.

The best way to determine the appropriateness of a particular example is to think about how your child has discussed anger in the past. Specifically, consider how candid he has been, the topics he has been able to address, with whom he has shared such emotions, and what his track record is when sharing with you.

Timing can be extremely important in determining when to discuss examples of anger. Choose a time when your child is not overwhelmed by anger or tension. In an effort to have her better understand your view, for example, you may be tempted to identify an example of anger management that closely parallels the conflict you had with your daughter an hour ago. However, trying to get a particular point across, especially when her emotions are intense, will detract from comfortable sharing now and may lead to apprehension regarding such discussions in the future. Just as it is advisable to ask your boss for a salary raise when he is in a good mood, a child is most receptive to addressing examples of anger when she is relaxed.

Start by sharing your observation of what was most clearly evidenced in the example, be it a person's behavior, emotions, thoughts, or bodily reactions. Initially, avoid asking questions; instead, share some of your own observations in order to foster an experience of comfortable exchange rather than a sense of being interrogated. Avoid leading into the discussion by saying "Now we're going to have a discussion about anger management." The goal is to engage in a way that encourages a natural flow of conversation.

This is not an easy task. It requires that you commit yourself to spending time with your child or adolescent. It requires that you begin to look at your own anger, how you express it, and the expectations, conclusions, and other feelings that lead up to it. The goal is to be able to discuss anger with confidence and sensitivity. This takes practice. As I have made clear from the beginning of this book, much of what I suggest involves learning new skills.

There are many reasons to feel awkward during your first attempts to discuss anger. Most likely you have had very few, if any, adult models on which to rely for these discussions. You may also feel awkward if, in giving an example, you recall similar emotional reactions that you experienced in your own life. You may want to share some of these reactions. Additionally, your child may feel awkward if this way of sharing has not been a natural part of your relationship.

You may be so focused on teaching your child the "right" way of managing anger that you create tension for both of you. Similarly, maintaining a strong focus on achievement can make the exchange feel like a lesson rather than a discussion. Learning these skills is a process that takes time. There is no end point or final stage at which your child will have learned how to respond perfectly in all situations. Instead, by focusing on the process of learning, you help him learn the process of managing anger rather than just specific strategies. Through these exchanges you will do a great deal of sharing, get to know your child better, and foster in him strengths for making sense of and managing the complexity of anger.

Candid expression of thoughts, emotions, and attitudes, especially as they relate to anger—and especially with the older child or adolescent—may lead to disagreement and tension. This is a time to promote open discussion rather than warning how you might punish your child if and when she behaves a certain way. Save that for another conversation when you are focusing on discipline. One approach is to allow for disagreement about your views so that you further preserve mutual sharing in the current conversation.

Be clear in your thinking about how comprehensive you want to be in applying the model of anger to specific examples. You do not need to develop a lesson plan or know in advance exactly where the conversation will go, but you may want to target specific components of the experience of anger when reviewing the example. You may want to focus on helping your child identify the character's motivations, expectations, conclusions, emotions leading to anger, or self-talk, or you may prefer to focus only on how the anger was managed—whether it was minimized or denied, or expressed in a constructive or destructive manner. You may want to identify alternative strategies for managing anger by encouraging brainstorming and then collaboratively developing a list of strategies. Try not to list only the most constructive strategies. Productive problem solving involves openness and the freedom to be creative. It is better to help children identify a variety of strategies without feeling stifled. By sharing a wide array of such strategies you can get to know your child's unique way of thinking and work together to clearly differentiate the constructive and destructive elements of the strategies she tends to use most often.

For example, you could take any one of a number of approaches when you choose to explore a book or a movie in which a classmate is bullying a child. You may want to help your child identify the emotions (anger and others) of the boy being victimized. Or you may want to help your child develop empathy by guessing the motivations, expectations, or self-talk of the bully. Similarly, you may want to focus on identifying strategies the victim can use to cope with his anger. It is best to address only one or a few components when you are beginning these types of conversations. This is especially so with young children and with adolescents who have a history of not being very communicative.

In any of the media described in this chapter you can also find examples to help children understand how anger works in group settings. Literature, movies, and news reports, in particular, offer numerous examples of how individuals join together to address anger. Groups, very much like individuals, experience anger, and the model of anger can similarly describe their reactions. Each group has a dominant motivation and develops expectations about how others should respond to it. Every group, whether motivated by a desire for greater freedom, by a wish to protect the environment, or by another cause, makes conclusions about events. And many groups are united by their experience of being unsatisfied and angry. By applying the model of anger to groups, you can help children and adolescents further identify and understand the difference between constructive and destructive strategies for managing collective anger.

I should emphasize that your child will be most receptive to a discussion of anger in a film, book, or other source when it is just a part of a larger discussion about character and story. Such discussion can flow from a more casual, open, and sharing conversation, rather than a structured lesson in which anger management is the top priority. Reading should be enjoyable and relaxing. While these resources certainly can be used to generate discussions of anger and anger management, this focus should be secondary to their enjoyment.

In the next sections of this chapter I discuss specific media and provide guidelines that identify specific concerns for each.

Television

Children and adolescents spend a great amount of time viewing television. They are presented with characters in cartoons, sitcoms, dramas, and the evening news. They see people who manage anger with a variety of strategies in various situations. All of these provide opportunities for a discussion of anger.

Following a cartoon, you can explore with your child how the characters responded to being annoyed, irritated, or more intensely angered. Share some of your observations and elicit from your child the feelings behind the anger, the expectations that you assume the character had, and any conclusions made. Evaluate the expression of anger by the character in terms of how it matched the offense (did the punishment match the crime?). How could the character have responded differently, or in what ways was the response constructive or destructive? This is an opportunity to help the younger child distinguish between how cartoon characters manage anger in contrast to how real people respond to it.

While your focus is anger management, by helping your children make this differentiation, you will help them develop increased knowledge about what is real and what is fantasy. Rather than discuss every cartoon, choose just a few. In this way you will not overly infringe on your child's enjoyment of cartoons. Similarly, I am not suggesting you spend a great amount of time in such discussion. Just discuss a few of the elements of the cartoon as they may help your child understand what is behind anger and how it might be managed. Sitcoms on television also offer many examples of the ways people manage anger. The wide variety of personalities presented on television offer a range of possibilities. The examples generated on sitcoms and drama may be suitable for some young children but will be most relevant for older children and adolescents.

News events presented on television certainly provide material to discuss, as they address anger related to all aspects of life. (See "News Reports" in this chapter for further discussion of this resource.)

Movies

Movies, more than television programming, offer you freedom to choose specific content for discussion. You can select movies on videotape that are age-appropriate and that address anger related to peer relationships, divorce, loss, illness, or any other of life's challenges.

Determine whether you will watch the movie individually or together. If you have young children, however, view it with them. You may want to first assess how comfortable your older child or adolescent might be watching it together before you make that suggestion; some may feel more comfortable viewing the movie alone.

There may be occasions when you believe it would be helpful to discuss the movie immediately after viewing it. Other videos may be so thought-provoking or deal with such severe anger that you may choose to discuss them several days later.

Even Disney classics provide plots and scenes in which characters experience and express anger. These are especially helpful resources for discussions with young children. While entertaining, good-spirited, and just fun, movie classics targeted for the younger viewer include scenes in which characters are angered and scenes in which characters experience anger as a reaction to other feelings and struggle with how to manage their irritation. For example, *The Little Mermaid* has a scene in which Ariel and her father express anger toward each other when she desires to go against his wishes. These movies similarly offer the opportunity to help children differentiate between anger and aggression and recognize that aggression is an outcome of an animal's drive for food, a reaction to feeling threatened, or a response to anger. These movies are especially recommended with younger children so that very early on you can assess their attitudes toward such subjects as well as begin to help them understand the differences between anger and aggression.

Numerous movies feature teenagers and the anger they experience as they face the unique struggles of adolescence. Whether the motivation is to seek peer acceptance, to seek independence, or to develop an individual identity, characters are often met with challenge and frustration. (See the Appendix for specific suggestions.)

While not every adolescent is an angry young man, many face similar struggles negotiating the changes and demands of his age. The variety of movies reflecting the experiences of adolescence include some that are emotionally light and others that examine core issues in adolescent development in a very emotionally intense way. They also vary in the level of anger experienced by the characters. While these movies present teens dealing with very different circumstances, they often touch upon universal themes that challenge youth and contribute to their anger.

These movies can serve as an excellent resource for generating school-based discussions of anger management as well. The ideas presented in movies can be used as part of a formal lesson on anger management or as a complement to teaching core subjects such as social studies, composition, thinking skills, or drama. This application will be further discussed later in this chapter.

Literature

Whether you are dealing with a young child or an older adolescent, fiction and nonfiction alike offer a wide variety of situations in which characters are faced with emotions leading to anger ranging from slight annoyance to full-blown rage or anything in between. The books you use do not have to portray outright violence in order to be a good resource for discussion. Characters who experience disappointment because they don't get their way, children whose toys are taken, sibling rivalry, peer rejection—these are just a few of the very common scenarios with which children can identify.

Literature, like movies, allows you greater choice in addressing specific and personal issues that may involve anger management. Scenarios presented in books can provide a bridge for discussion of divorce, forming a blended family, responding to loss, coping with peer pressure, or managing a disability.

Teens may be especially interested in books that describe groups of individuals who have united in response to perceived grievances. In addition to discussing the many groups that unite for a constructive cause, it is also helpful to address groups that form gangs focused on violence. Applying the model of anger can provide teens with insights regarding how expectations, conclusions, and child logic contribute to aggression as a way of responding to anger.

If you are helping a young child learn to understand and manage anger, I recommend you read the entire book to him. Share in the reading with a somewhat older child, and let older children and adolescents read the book on their own. When you read with a young child, you may want to share predictions about how characters will behave. However, for the most part, interruptions are distracting and should be kept to a minimum. Even when reading such books with young children, waiting until the story has come to its conclusion can allow for increased engagement and reflection.

When discussing a book with an older child, you may want to share discussion after specified chapters. You may even share predictions about various characters, based on the components in the model of anger. Such predictions may be based on a discussion of identified motivations, expectations, or conclusions or on an assessment of the character's anger management skills.

Literature, like movies, is an especially good medium for use in the classroom. Addressing issues of anger management through books and short stories can be integrated into the core curriculum, whether the main focus is literature, oral expression, written expression, comprehension skills, problem-solving skills, current events (see below), or history. No matter whether you are studying the works of Shakespeare, stories of contemporary youth, or the literature of political movements, you will find a broad array of examples of individuals coping with anger at every level of intensity.

News Reports

Whether presented on television, in magazines, or daily newspapers, news reports offer the most readily available examples to which you can apply the model of anger. Conflicts between individuals, within families, and among politicians, companies, or countries, as well as movements motivated by the anger of people who experience being victimized or devalued, are frequently in the news. These all provide examples of individuals and groups dealing with and responding to anger. Each night the evening news presents different scenarios in which people resolve conflicts and respond to the underlying experiences of feeling threatened, discounted, abused, rejected, embarrassed, shamed, devalued, disappointed, or hurt. Each night we see individuals who respond constructively and others who are destructive in the ways they respond to anger.

Select examples based on the criteria discussed earlier. They should be appropriate for your child's age and intellectual level, but most important is that they take into account your child's emotional readiness to handle such a discussion.

Whether you reflect on news reports that present a mild level of expressed anger or those that describe extreme aggression, such reports offer very relevant topics for discussions of anger management. These reports are especially important when we want to help children and teens understand that violence is just one reaction to anger. News reports of violence, such as the recent school shootings, lead us to ask the following questions:

1. What do you believe kept the people involved from seeking out other coping strategies?
2. What other emotions were involved besides anger?
3. Are weapons too readily available?
4. Was their response to anger influenced by parental attitudes?
5. What part does the media play in influencing what children and adolescents do in response to their anger?
6. How do bullying, ridicule, and peer rejection promote anger?
7. What could they have done to manage their hurt and feelings of rejection?
8. Were the perpetrators of these acts just disturbed?
9. What expectations of others and themselves may have influenced their actions?
10. What conclusions might they have come to that influenced their thinking and behavior?
11. What do you think kept them from talking with others about their feelings?
12. Do you believe that they would have been less likely to act the way they did if they had talked more with others about their feelings, whether peers or adults?
13. Do you believe the anger was mostly related to very recent events, was mostly related to events that occurred in the last few months or years, or had to do with a long-term buildup of anger?

Rather than asking these questions, you may want to share some of your own answers to them in form of an open-ended comment. Comments such as the following may more readily generate open discussion with certain children than asking a more directed question.

- "I'm totally confused about what led up to that, but maybe ..."
- "You know, he must have felt a lot of pain to have had that much anger."
- "I don't know. I think everybody has some experience of not belonging to the in-group. I remember when I was in junior high school—there was a really popular group, and no matter what I did, I couldn't seem to be accepted by them."
- "I wonder what would have happened if they ..."
- "Maybe they felt that no one would really listen to them about how they felt."

Less extreme expressions of both verbal and physical anger are reflected daily in current events. These include politicians expressing anger, incidents of domestic violence, and environmentally-minded groups that take illegal action to demonstrate their outrage over contested laws. All these highly charged situations are presented daily on radio, television, and in the newspapers, and they can be addressed with children and adolescents to help them make sense of and manage anger.

It is important to be selective in choosing news events to discuss with young children. As highlighted in the list of criteria for choosing examples, they need to be appropriate to a child's level of emotional and intellectual development. Young children may not be ready to observe or discuss intense displays of aggression or anger related to more mature topics. Similarly, their lack of mature abilities to self-soothe and to distinguish between real and makebelieve renders them vulnerable to experiencing fear and will contribute to their difficulties in handling and making sense of more serious events. At the same time, if children witness such news events, they can be helped by reminding them that:

1. Such events are rare and not all people are aggressive.
2. They will not be victimized just because it happened to someone else who is like them in terms of age, race, religion, or other status.
3. While the world can be dangerous, it is not always that way.

Children need to be reassured that acts of rage and aggression are infrequent even though they are often described in news reports. It can be reassuring to young children to be told that most individuals manage the anger of everyday life in a wide variety of ways other than aggression. Most individuals are not as impulsive as one might believe by observing the many examples of aggression presented in newscasts. Keep in mind that the fears or anxieties you express will also influence your child's feeling of safety and security.

Children can be helped to avoid developing alarmist thinking by reassuring them of their safety. This also requires helping them articulate specific fears so that you can address these individually in addition to providing general reassurance. Through discussion you can better recognize if their fears are related to being a victim, seeing a parent victimized, or even losing self-control. Such discussions offer insights regarding a child's sense of security as well as concern about aggression.

Emphasizing that the world is not always dangerous communicates a positive general outlook in spite of some of life's harsh realities. This can also be achieved by discussing the pressure news stations are under to provide news.

Games

Many ordinary play activities provide invaluable examples of anger. Even young children sometimes respond with variations of anger in the context of play with parents or in play with peers. Children react with annoyance when they feel they are being teased, when they are confused, and when they feel thwarted in achieving some goal. The challenge of building a tower of blocks, being asked to take turns or share toys, and the experience of competition are all occasions that may lead to some reaction of anger.

The model of anger can be helpful both in gaining insights about a child's reactions and for helping her understand and manage her frustration and related anger. The model can be used to help a child articulate other emotions related to her anger. For example, she may be helped to recognize her experience of disappointment or shame about her own performance. She can also be helped to identify both realistic and unrealistic expectations and conclusions about performance, sharing, and play in general.

Charlie was a very bright eight-year-old who exhibited low self-esteem, was often irritable, had recently been completing only half of his school assignments, and increasingly looked and acted sad and depressed. While Charlie was not very open or talkative during our initial meeting, he expressed an interest in playing checkers. After the start of the game, Charlie made some moves that did not follow the rules of ordinary checkers. At first I wondered whether he just did not know the rules, but then I guessed that he was always allowed to win. After his next unusual move, I said, "Wow! I can tell it's important for you to win!" Over several sessions, he was able to discuss the disappointment and shame he experienced over his performance, not just in playing checkers with me but in many activities involving competition with peers, his older brother, and even his parents. He reported having conflicts with peers over a video game, quarrels over card games with his brother, and tantrums with his parents when playing Monopoly.

Video games offer another source for discussing the expression of anger. Whether one focuses on issues of competition and achievement or the content itself, parents can better know their child and help him manage anger by monitoring these activities. Much has been said about violence in video games, and the debate continues about how these games influence a child's behavior. Overall, research indicates that children and teens are influenced to become more aggressive when observing violence. This is most true for those who are already prone to being aggressive or violent. However, such findings tell you little about how your child or teen reacts to such viewing. The only way for you to know how your child manages his anger is through your observations and by making a commitment to foster open communication in general, especially surrounding issues of anger management. Other guidelines to help you assess a child's potential for aggression are presented in Chapter 17.

In addition to the types of games described here, new types of games have been available in recent decades that focus on helping children better understand and manage emotions. Beginning in the early 1970s, educational publishers began developing these games mostly for use with children who exhibited emotional difficulties. They were most frequently integrated into special-education programs or used in individual and group psychotherapy with children and adolescents. They were gradually incorporated into pilot studies and some mainstream classes. However, most of these activities were intended for small group interaction and were not really suitable for entire classes.

The goal of these programs, often called affective development programs, included the improvement of self-esteem, helping children differentiate and label emotions, and assisting them with social interaction skills. They offered teachers and psychotherapists materials that helped generate discussion about very relevant issues of emotional life.

In recent years there have been significant changes in the focus and availability of such materials. There is now a wide variety of games and structured activities to help children and teens learn about and explore specific areas of emotional development, such as identifying emotions, developing empathy, building social skills, resolving conflict, and handling anger. Such programs are now also designed for all children and not just for those with problems. The format of these activities encompasses board games; stories; decks of cards that offer vignettes, suggested role-playing activities, and questions regarding emotions; the use of puppets; workbooks; and audio- and videotapes with various exercises.

Although originally targeted for use by teachers and therapists, these resources are increasingly available for parents. While you may still find a wider variety of such activities offered in teacher-supply stores, bookstores that cater to therapists, and catalogs aimed at teachers and therapists, many of them are available in general bookstores and those specializing in books for children. (See Appendix.)

While the model of anger discussed earlier provides a comprehensive view of anger, a good number of these activities focus on only one or several of its components. Some may be very helpful in addressing self-talk. Others focus specifically on brainstorming to select and identify appropriate anger management strategies. Still others are more basic and help children and adolescents clarify and differentiate emotions that are involved with anger.

As with those resources previously described, children can most readily and comfortably engage in these games when the quality of the interaction remains playful. And, as I've noted, tension may arise if you focus primarily on being "right" while playing the game. Involvement in such activities may be trivialized or sabotaged or may lead to withdrawal when a child is predisposed to be highly competitive or values intellect and achievement more than exploring his emotional life.

Another concern to keep in mind when selecting a game is the issue you want your child to address. You may want to help him cope with sibling rivalry, and so you select a game that addresses this concern. However, this will not guarantee that a child will automatically open up and share his inner thoughts and feelings. As emphasized throughout this book, children and teens have a certain comfort level when dealing with certain topics. While one child may very candidly discuss her anger about her parents' pending divorce, another may initially feel comfortable only talking about divorce in his friends' families or that of characters presented in a story. A third child may leave the room when the topic of divorce is even hinted at while playing a game.

The games that offer the most creativity and flexibility are often the most effective. These can easily be adapted to the emotional needs and interests of your child. One game that allows for unlimited creativity is a variation of a storytelling game in which children and teens engage in creating the ending or filling in the gaps of a story. This offers an excellent format for children and adolescents that can be used individually or with several children at a time. Children are told a story and asked to create different outcomes that may reflect different ways of dealing with anger. Similarly, they can be offered a story of two children reacting differently to the same event and then asked to describe what they assume are the expectations or conclusions of each child. Vignettes can involve not being invited to a party, feeling picked on by a peer or a teacher, coping with a physical illness or accident, being grounded, or competing with a sibling for computer time.

Emotional Education and Anger Management in the Schools

Though parents' efforts at home are invaluable, only when schools become similarly committed to anger management education will children and adolescents more fully attend to making sense of and managing anger. This can be achieved by directly teaching the model of anger or by applying it to core subjects that are already a part of the curriculum.

For over thirty years I have supported the implementation of programs in schools that help children better understand and manage emotions. My personal interest in this subject extends back to my own childhood. I remember being perplexed in elementary school by the absence of any discussion of emotions. In part it was this interest that led me to pursue graduate work in school psychology before focusing on clinical psychology. Even in that graduate program, the focus was on helping children who were experiencing severe problems rather than on addressing the emotional needs of all children.

While schools are increasingly recognizing the need for emotional education for all children and teens, not very many focus on this extremely important subject area. For far too long, many schools likened the discussion of emotion to the teaching of values. Parents and school boards not only questioned the relevance of such education but were confused about what should be part of such a curriculum. As a result, it was thought that this subject should be taught at home rather than in the classroom. Another obstacle that has contributed to a lack of focus on emotional education has been teacher concern that some material may be both too personal and too difficult to manage.

Emotional education was also neglected because little research could strongly support teaching specific theory and skills related to understanding and managing emotions. In fact, most of the early programs emphasized strategies for improving overall self-esteem rather than identifying specific skills that children and adolescents could learn to better understand and manage their emotions.

In recent years, however, based in part on well-researched programs, schools are increasingly recognizing the importance of encouraging healthy emotional skills and development. *The Optimistic Child,* by Martin Seligman, offers very specific skills that can be used in schools to foster optimism.[1] *How to Raise a Child with a High Emotional Quotient,* by Lawrence Shapiro, identifies a wide variety of skills related to emotional growth.[2] Each of these books is based on years of research regarding the development of various emotional skills. From helping children reduce catastrophizing attitudes to increasing empathy and helping children raise their tolerance for frustration, these books offer very specific guidelines, examples, and exercises to allow children to better recognize, understand, and handle their emotions.

In *The Optimistic Child,* Seligman identifies specific thought processes and how they promote optimism or pessimism. He also emphasizes that children develop genuine self-esteem not from being told how good, smart, nice-looking, or creative they are but by developing specific competencies and the optimism to move beyond initial frustration. It is for this same reason that making sense of and managing anger deserves full recognition in the classroom. Children need to develop a sense of competency with regard to anger.

Anger management education can be integrated into the daily routine of teaching through two major approaches. The first involves formal education in which time and resources are formally allocated to support such teaching. The school can approve such education as a specific core subject. Making it a formal part of the curriculum communicates to students that this area of study deserves attention and resources and is as important as the study of other core subjects.

William White emphasizes another approach to highlight the importance of emotions in the schools. He advocates that teacher certification in Texas require teachers to learn strategies that help them understand what roles anger and empathy play in the lives of their students.[3]

Similarly, by designating emotional education as part of the curriculum, children and teens have a greater opportunity to more directly discuss emotions. Making it a formal subject for study gives children and adolescents permission to examine their emotions in a supportive environment instead of being left on their own to try to figure them out.

One direct approach is to teach the model of anger. While it is best to focus on only one component at a time when working with young children, teens have a capacity to grasp several components of the model in one sitting. Through discussion, they can be led to provide examples of situations in which anger was experienced and assisted in better recognizing expectations and conclusions, emotions leading to anger, bodily reactions, self-talk, and anger management strategies. This is not intended to be therapy. It is education about managing a very complex emotion. All of the chapters in this book may be presented to children in language that they can understand. The actual model can also be presented in the same way it is presented in the book, through discussion of each major contributing factor, one at a time. And, just as it is strongly suggested that you practice the exercises before you use them with your children, teachers will need to practice them to fully understand their application and usefulness.

The second way in which education about emotions can be integrated into teaching is by weaving it into the subject matter of the specific content areas that are already a part of the curriculum. The resources already discussed, including literature, movies, and news reports, can provide numerous examples for the school setting. Also, history is a chronology of people who have taken political action or even made war because of feelings of abuse, discrimination, fear, anxiety, and a range of other reactions that contribute to anger.

Advocating the formal teaching of anger management in schools will complement your efforts at home. In addition, your children will value the necessity for anger management to the degree that you, and the schools, emphasize the importance of this subject.

Whether the subject is geography, history, or literature, teaching by inference has been found to be one method that helps children identify with the circumstances described in the core content. A teacher employs this method when she asks, "If you lived in a dry area that did not have bricks or large trees, how would you live? What kind of food might you eat? What would you wear?" These questions lead to greater involvement in learning as the child places himself in the situation and tries to arrive at the answers rather than having them presented to him in a lecture format. This approach makes learning relevant and can be used at home as well as in school.

You can teach anger management through this approach by asking the following questions regarding the characters in a book or movie:

- "In the situation we just described, would you have been as angry as Corey?"
- "What feelings would have made you angry?"
- "Would you have handled your anger the same way Corey did in the story?"
- "What were the advantages and disadvantages of the way he managed his anger?"
- "What expectations do you sense he had? Were they realistic?"
- "If you were his best friend, what other possible ways of managing anger might you have suggested to him?"

Finally, fully recognizing the importance of anger management education in the school setting requires that teachers be alert to situations that necessitate immediate discussion. While the primary mandate of schools is to help children learn, events that arouse anger in the classroom need to be directly addressed. Whether in school or at home, children and teens are less available to take in information when they are distracted by intense emotions. All too often teachers attempt to ignore such anger in an effort to maintain a focus on education. However, the reality is that when children are angry, the emotion may dominate their attention and subsequently interfere with their ability to learn. When anger is not directly addressed, children expend a significant amount of energy trying to ignore, minimize, or deny it.

I recall an incident that occurred while I was a fourth-grade teacher in the South Bronx during the late 1960s. Ten minutes after the class had settled down to start the day, one child's mother came storming into the room with a leather belt, looking for her son in order to punish him for an incident that had occurred at home prior to his coming to school. I escorted her out of the room after helping her become calm. The class soon settled down, and I led them in a discussion of their reactions to the event. Children shared their emotions about the event as well as their views about discipline, anger, and conflict with parents. This discussion was not mandated by the curriculum and in fact took some time away from a science lesson. However, it would have been extremely unfair if I had pretended that they had not had emotional reactions to what had just occurred, and suggested they immediately take out their science books. Whether in the classroom or at home, ignoring anger often leads to increased anger. By contrast, the more children and teens are allowed to candidly but appropriately express anger (and the range of emotions associated with it), the more they will feel connected and become open to learning and communication.

Another example of integrating a discussion of anger management into the core curriculum involved a fifth-grade class I taught. Along with the rest of the school, we attended a presentation about the neighborhood police. Afterward we returned to our homeroom and I instructed the class to write a composition about what they had just observed. One young man, who had a history of chronic anger, was very adamant as he stated, "I hate policemen. I'm not going to write about them." I responded that he could write his composition about the feelings, thoughts, and experiences that influenced his attitudes. At first he looked surprised and somewhat puzzled, but he began smiling as he sat down to write. I was focusing on the goal of writing, on purposely giving him permission to share his perspective without immediately challenging or stifling it, and on furthering his candid expression of emotion.

As a result, he handed in the longest composition he had written up to that point. His sentences were more expressive and complete than in any previous composition. His writing described incidents that led him to believe that certain officers took advantage of their authority. His classmates and I shared that we could understand how his experiences influenced his feelings. However, we also shared observations about how much more secure we felt because of the services that police provide. I did not try to challenge his perception. Rather, I encouraged him to express his views and tried to help him broaden his perceptions. Once he had expressed himself and had heard feedback that acknowledged an understanding of his feelings and thoughts, he was freer to be open to hear other views. His experience and the feelings aroused by it had been validated. This supported him in trusting his perspective while encouraging him to be open to other perspectives. This was another occasion that reminded me of the need to help children, in school and at home, to express in words whatever they are feeling. Only when children are encouraged to candidly express themselves do they become more receptive to new information.

Anger management education needs to be a part of the regular curriculum and not just a reaction to unusual events such as the one that occurred in Littleton, Colorado. It needs to be presented as an organized program that receives as much support as traditional core subjects. Only through the implementation of such proactive programs in class and at home will we provide children and teens an education that addresses the whole person. And, whether at school or at home, teaching anger management is a process that is greatly fostered when we draw on the rich examples of anger in everyday life.

11

Relaxation: A Primary Task in Managing Anger

The strategies presented in this chapter are aimed at helping children and teens reduce the level of physical tension that is a natural part of anger. While these strategies are useful with children and teens facing the anger of everyday life, they are especially useful for those who are quick to become angry. Such children may be considered "thin-skinned" and overly sensitive to stimulation. They may be more vulnerable to frustration and thus quick to experience the fight-or-flight response that accompanies anger. Compared to others, these children may actually experience a greater arousal of physical tension that pushes them more rapidly to seek physical release.

Research suggests that both genetic factors and learned experiences may contribute to influence how quickly a child reacts with anger in various situations. Some of these children may at times be especially exasperating to parents and difficult to discipline because they are impulsive and often aggressive. Some may become angry and physically agitated but not really behave in a hostile manner. Both types of child present a special challenge to parents and others with whom they interact. And yet there may be a wide variety of reasons why they are quick to become angry.

Some children and teens are quick to feel slighted or threatened because they feel insecure, inadequate, or just very unsure of themselves. John was one of the members of a therapy group in an inpatient setting for adolescents. One day in a session, the group leader emphasized that unless John changed his behavior, he would most likely end up in jail by the time he was sixteen. Hearing this prognosis resulted in a dramatic and immediate increase in John's feelings of inadequacy. This led him to experience intense rage, and he became loud and physically threatening while in the group. It took several staff members to remove him from the room so that he could regain his composure.

If John was sure of himself, he would have been able to listen to the group leader and even think about the implications of that prognosis. If he felt more secure with himself, he would have been able to more comfortably consider what was stated and then agree or disagree with it. However, he was so unsure of himself that just hearing a negative prediction about his future led him to feel rage. When discussing his reactions later, John told me he thought the group leader should not have said what he did, because it might influence what might actually happened to John. This is an extreme example of the power of words for a youngster who is unsure of himself.

Some children may be quick to experience and express anger because they have seen important adults in their lives handle anger this way or they may have actually been victims of abuse or trauma. Their unresolved anger surrounding such experiences makes them feel easily threatened, and they want to "get even" or in some way exert control.

Finally, other children or adolescents may have a short fuse because they lack problem-solving skills, do not have the skills needed to manage intense emotions, or experience severe psychological problems. These children can benefit from the relaxation strategies outlined in this chapter but need additional help from mental health professionals.

While the techniques I discuss here are useful for all children, they can also be helpful for the child who tends to repress anger. By learning how to relax and calm herself physically, a child can gain a greater sense of mastery. As a result, she will become more comfortable with experiencing anger. Her increased capacity to exert self-control over her physical tension fosters increased comfort with her experience of anger.

The Need to Gain Control over Physical Reactions to Anger

High levels of emotional and physical arousal related to anger tend to inhibit information processing. Anger interferes with the clear thinking needed to decide how to manage our anger. Similarly, it distracts us from clearly expressing ourselves or accurately comprehending what is being said. When a child or teen is physically agitated, any communication directed at exploring the precipitating events or his thoughts or feelings about the event, or any attempt to use logic to foster improved reasoning, will not be productive. In fact, these attempts to redirect his energies may lead to further escalation of his physical reactions.

Instead, the enraged child needs help in gaining control over the physical reactions that accompany anger. Only as he increases such control will he be able to think about his situation, explore his emotions, and be more open to consider alternative strategies for dealing with his anger.

Specific Relaxation Strategies

The strategies that I describe here are specific, practical interventions focused on helping your child increase self-control over the physical reactions that accompany his anger. They are based on strategies that have been well researched and proven to help individuals develop increased control over physiological reactions. These strategies are based on the premise that we can use the mind to influence the body. I again recommend that you practice these exercises before teaching them to your child. The more comfortable you are doing these relaxation exercises, the more effective you will be at teaching and modeling them.

Certain of these strategies are preventive—skills that you can teach your child when she is relaxed and not experiencing anger. Through rehearsing effective strategies for self-soothing when she is calm, she will experience increased self-control over her bodily reactions when her anger is aroused. Through rehearsal, they will become an automatic part of your child's behavioral repertoire. They teach her to be sensitive to how her body feels when she is relaxed and what it feels like to be in control. This allows your child to develop a memory of the sensations that accompany the feeling of being calm and in control and to achieve a concrete understanding of how she can control her muscles. The goal for these exercises is for your child to be able to call upon the experience of these calm sensations when she is beginning to experience an escalation in her physical reactions to anger.

I strongly recommend that you engage in these exercises with your child when first teaching them. Performing these exercises together teaches him self-soothing techniques but also fosters an increased level of intimacy. To the degree that your child experiences himself as physically relaxed in your company, he will be freer to be more open and expressive with you. We become more open and close with people when we allow ourselves to physically relax in their presence. This quality of intimacy parallels the bonding that occurs when you share any pleasurable activity with your child.

Reducing Muscular Tension

Much has been written about muscle relaxation exercises as they apply to stress management. The "relaxation response" is one approach developed for adults by Herbert Benson.[1] The exercise described here is a variation of the original strategy, adapted for children. It also includes aspects of relaxation used in a form of child therapy known as Theraplay.[2] This exercise should be an enjoyable experience for both of you. When presenting this exercise to a younger child, try to be enthusiastic and playful, as if you are showing him a new game. Focus your discussion on the goal of relaxing, rather than reducing or getting rid of anger. The purpose of this exercise is to increase your child's self-awareness regarding her body and to help her gain control over the reactions associated with anger. By learning how to relax, she will ultimately be able to calm herself when she experiences physical tension associated with anger, anxiety, or fear. Through continued practice, she will increasingly be able to monitor and control her physical tension when she becomes angry.

Exercise

Have your child lie down on her back on a carpet or on a bed. Direct her to place her arms at her sides with the palms of her hands facing down, with her legs straight out in front of her. Kneel or sit by her side and try to maintain relaxed, reassuring eye contact. Present the following instructions in a very calm voice:

"We're going to play a game that is somewhat like Simon Says." Leaning over your child from her right side, hold her right hand and forearm. "Now, I want you to make this arm as stiff and straight as you can, from the top of your shoulder all the way down your arm to your hand and fingers." Point to the respective locations as you talk about them. "Make your arm straight like an arrow and as stiff as a baseball bat. Now raise your arm." Feel along the length of her arm as she does this. "Wow! That sure is stiff all the way from your shoulders to the tips of your fingers. I can feel all of your muscles tighten at the same time. Now close your eyes for a moment and just picture your arm the way it is—feel how tight and tense it can be." Let your child concentrate for a while with her eyes closed.

"Okay, open your eyes. Now comes a tricky part." Maintain eye contact as you say this. "Lay your arm down by your side and make it as soft as a rubber hose. Just let your arm lie by your side. Make it loose and relaxed all the way from the top of your shoulder to the tips of your fingers." Feel along the length of her arm to see that the arm is in fact relaxed. Raise her arm first by holding her hand and elbow, then by holding her hand. "Boy! Your arm really is relaxed! Every muscle from your shoulder to your fingers is so relaxed, just so loose and soft. It feels like it's made of rubber."

Rephrase and repeat the directions as necessary until your child understands them and is able to do the exercise. Pay attention to words that seem to make the most sense to your child—those to which she responds most readily, with clear understanding. Once she is able to relax her muscles, frequently use the word *relaxed* so that she begins to associate the word with her physical state.

After focusing on one arm, direct her to do the same with the other arm. Then have her tense and relax her legs in a similar way.

Vary your words in order to increase the spontaneity and fun that could be a part of this exercise—for example, direct her to tense one arm while she relaxes the other, or have her relax both legs while she tenses her arms. However, try not to make it too confusing or competitive. Do not rush your child or indicate that she has to do it perfectly. The focus is on helping her learn how to relax her body rather than on being "right" or doing it rapidly.

After you have focused on her arms and legs, direct her to tense and relax muscle groups in her face, including muscles around her eyes and mouth. These may take more practice and will require more specific and detailed guidelines. For example, when asking her to tense the area around her mouth, tell her to raise her tongue to the roof of her mouth and press hard as she clenches her teeth. Then direct her to let her tongue return to its usual position and allow her lower jaw to relax. When directing her attention to relax her forehead and the region around her eyes, you may need to gently touch those areas. By physically touching certain points, you will prompt her to further attend to those areas and thereby increase the precision of her control. In addition, you may sometimes want to ask her to close her eyes throughout this exercise. You may suggest, "While we do this, try closing your eyes, and as you tighten or relax different parts of your body, picture them getting stiffer or more relaxed." Closing her eyes and picturing the area is a way to enhance the precision of her control.

As another component of this exercise, take turns and allow your child to have the opportunity to direct you in the same exercise.

When teaching this exercise, ten to fifteen minutes may be plenty of time for a younger child (through age eight), while a slightly older child can maintain concentration for a half hour. How many body parts you work with and how often you take turns should be determined by your child's attention span and her apparent comfort in doing these exercises.

Breathing Exercises

As we become physically aroused during anger, our breathing becomes increasingly shallow, increasing the level of carbon dioxide in our bloodstream and muscle tissue. This, in turn, leads to increased physical tension. This next exercise may be especially helpful to break the cycle of escalating physical reactions in the early stages of anger. The deep inhaling and exhaling I describe will help to maximize the amount of oxygen and minimize the level of carbon dioxide in the blood and tissues.[3]

Quite often, when first learning this exercise, children and teens (as well as adults) are too physically tense or self-conscious to really breathe deeply. Some individuals report feeling uncomfortable when instructed to exaggerate the movement of inhaling and exhaling. Therefore, as with any of these exercises, practice this one initially on your own so that you know what it feels like to breathe deeply and can be totally comfortable when teaching it. It is essential that you experience the relaxing impact of this exercise before you teach it to your child. Your confidence in the exercise will very much depend on how comfortable you feel when doing it and on the level of relaxation you achieve; how confident you are in using this strategy will be communicated to your child. Therefore, the more assured you are when teaching it, the more your child will trust that it will benefit him.

I present this exercise with a focus on practicing with a young child. Adjust the structure of the instructions when teaching it to an older child or teen.

Exercise

Have your child sit in a comfortable chair while you sit about one to two feet in front of him, directly facing him. Hold his hands in yours while maintaining eye contact and provide the following directions:

"We're going to play a kind of breathing game. We're going to take a big, big, deep, deep breath, hold it for a short time, and then exhale, slowly blowing out as much air as we can. I'm going to do it first so that you can see exactly what to do. Watch me." Slowly take a deep breath, exaggerating as you do so. Breathe in from your diaphragm. Raise your chest, lift your shoulders, and, maintaining eye contact, say, "Now I'm going to hold my breath for three seconds, then I'll let it out very, very slowly."

While still holding one of your child's hands, raise your other hand and count to three out loud, counting with your fingers as well to highlight it. Then, very slowly, exhale. As you reach the end of the exhalation, bend over slightly at your waist to really emphasize and exaggerate how much you exhale. Do not do this rapidly.

> Take both of your child's hands and, maintaining eye contact, say: "Okay. Now let's do this together. Slowly inhale. Breathe in slowly ... deeper ... deeper ... more ... good ... a little more ... hold it." Raise one hand and count out loud while you also count with your fingers. "One ... two ... three. Now slowly let the air out. Exhale ... more ... more ... more ... just a little more ... good."
>
> Repeat this exercise three times. Remind your child to breathe slowly, to hold his breath while counting to three, and to exhale just as deeply as he inhales. This should be done slowly; if done rapidly, it may lead to faintness or dizziness. The full impact of this exercise is achieved only when both inhaling and exhaling are practiced.

After you have engaged in this exercise, direct your child's attention to his level of relaxation. Direct his attention especially to his chest, shoulders, and neck. This exercise may not leave him as relaxed as the one previously described. In fact, he may need to practice this exercise for several sessions before he experiences noticeable relaxation. As with the muscle relaxation exercise, clearly state that this technique can be practiced as a preventive strategy, so that he can help himself relax when he is experiencing the physical reactions to anger. Many people find this exercise to be the one strategy that leads to immediate self-control and a relaxed response during a moment of escalating anger.

Visual Imagery

Visual imagery relies on the imagination to trick the body into becoming more relaxed. It is based on the principle that our bodies react physiologically to our thoughts and images. When we have pleasant thoughts and peaceful images, we foster physiological relaxation. In contrast, when we focus on thoughts or images that are tension-provoking, our body reacts with a level of physical arousal that is associated with the fight-or-flight response. These findings have been thoroughly researched with biofeedback technology equipment that helps to detect and monitor our physiological reactions.

This strategy may be somewhat difficult at first, since each of us varies in our ability to visualize or imagine. I should emphasize that while this strategy can be learned, it may be easier for children who are strong in skills such as attending to visual detail, organizing visual information, and visual memory.

Be aware of your child's tendency to daydream as a strategy for coping with stress. Everyone daydreams at times. But daydreaming may become a child's only form of self-soothing to cope with stress. Therefore, when using this technique, emphasize that it is not intended to help your child totally escape from her surroundings; instead, it is primarily directed at helping her to reduce the intensity of her physical re-actions to anger. Try to communicate to your child that the goal of this exercise is to help her feel physically comfortable enough to more con-structively deal with her current situation.

A wide variety of visualization exercises can be found in books, CDs, and videotapes. CDs and tapes frequently feature calm music or the sounds of peaceful environments such as a beach or forest, as well as narration providing directions in a very tranquil and soothing voice. Some of these are designed for general relaxation, while others focus on increasing the relaxation response essential for specific anxiety-provoking situations. These might include relaxation tapes focused on helping people speak in front of a group, take tests, or cope with anxiety related to air travel.

Videocassettes often provide vivid panoramas of beautiful and sce-nic natural settings accompanied by soothing music. These are at-tempts to provide, in a more concrete fashion, the visual details essential to help achieve relaxation. These are not necessary if your child is able to rely on her imagination. However, you may want to ob-tain one of these tapes if your child has attention difficulties, is weak in visual imagery, or does not achieve relaxation after practicing the exer-cise. When purchasing this type of tape, first identify what you think would be the best match with your child's specific interests. Think about her past experiences and ask for her input to identify a relaxing scene.

In contrast to describing a specific scene, I have found that a very ef-fective technique for visual imagery is to present directions that are open-ended and allow for a child or teen to create an image that has personal meaning for her. This is especially important for adolescents, who have a strong need to feel in control of their thoughts.

As with other exercises, practice this exercise first so that you are fa-miliar with it and become aware for yourself of the powerful effects of visual imagery in helping us to relax. You may want to record the in-structions onto a tape so that your child may practice it alone.

Exercise 1

Select a quiet room in which you will not be distracted by family members or noises. Have your child sit in a comfortable chair and tell him to place his hands in his lap or on the arms of the chair. Select a chair that allows him to either stretch his legs out or rest his feet on the floor. In a calm, reassuring voice, say the following:

"Close your eyes and picture or think about a place where you have been, or a place where you would like to be—a place where you feel safe, happy, carefree, relaxed, and peaceful. Take your time to imagine this place. Choose a place where you feel good about yourself, safe, content, and at ease. As you do so, use your imagination and make the scene as real as you can. Make believe you are really there. At times you may find that you are thinking about something else—your mind might wander. That's all right. Just come back to the place that you are trying to picture in your mind. As you imagine your place, think of the colors in your scene. Think about the different objects in your very peaceful and safe place. This is a place where you feel happy, protected, and very calm."

Monitor your child's expression, and continue. "Think about the air around you. Imagine the air against your face. Is it dry or damp? Is it moving or is it still? Try to make this place real for you. Are there any scents that are a part of this favorite place, this very peaceful and safe place? Inhale deeply for a second to help yourself imagine any scents that are a part of your scene. Think about any sounds that are a part of this safe, comfortable, and peaceful place, or if it is quiet, imagine the stillness.

"Look around the scene and picture the objects. Be aware of their colors, their shapes. Notice their lines—are they straight or curved? Are the objects circular, square, rectangular, or other shapes? Now picture the objects and pay attention to how they might feel. One may be smooth, another rough. Imagine all of the different parts in this very peaceful place.

"Now, reach out and touch one of the objects in this very relaxing place. Notice its color, its texture, its lines or curves. Feel it in your hand. This is just one of the many objects that make up this very relaxing, safe, and peaceful place.

"For a moment, shift your attention from your scene to your body. Pay attention to your body. Now pay attention to your chest, and notice how peaceful and calm your breathing is. Don't change it—just notice how relaxed you are as you breathe. Start by paying attention to your neck and shoulders. Notice how relaxed and comfortable they feel, with the muscles relaxed. Now pay attention to your arms. Don't move them—just pay attention to how loose and relaxed they feel by your sides. Now notice your stomach … your buttocks …your legs … your feet … and even your toes. Your arms, hands, legs, and entire body are just so relaxed. You may even feel a slight tingling like they are about to fall asleep. Just enjoy that relaxed feeling for a moment.

"Now, once again shift your attention to your peaceful scene. Look around your scene and notice all of the parts of your scene. Colors, shapes, the air, scents, sounds—everything that make your scene real. After you do this, take your time and open your eyes."

Determine how successful your child was at imagining his special place. Ask him what he experienced and which parts of the exercise were easy or difficult. Ask him to describe some of the details of the scene and if he did in fact become relaxed. As with other exercises, emphasize the fun in the activity rather than the correctness of his attempts.

The following strategies also involve visual imagery but take on a different focus in an attempt to help your child experience increased self-control over his physical reactions to anger. Again, these are exercises that should be used primarily to help him gain control rather than to completely escape from his temporarily uncomfortable reality.

Exercise 2

While sitting in a chair, face your child and ask him to scan you from head to toe. Then say:

"This may be a little difficult to do at first, but I am sure that you will be able to do it after you practice it a few times. Look at me and try to imagine that I am getting smaller and smaller and smaller. Make believe that I am shrinking in my chair—that as I sit here you can see me getting smaller and smaller. My head, my shoulders, my arms, my body, my legs, and my feet are all getting smaller. Imagine that I am so small that my legs appear to be dangling from the chair, unable to touch the floor. Pretend that I am so small that I look like a puppet or a doll sitting in a big person's chair."

Your child may smile and laugh as you say this. That, in part, is the purpose of this exercise. His visual image of you becoming smaller and smaller will be somewhat comical. His bodily reaction to this image stands in stark contrast with, and competes with, the uncomfortable physical reactions of anger. To the degree that his more relaxed muscle tone dominates his physical state, he will be available to experience control over himself. To the degree that your child can do this exercise, he will develop an increased capacity to calm himself when he is in the presence of others with whom he is experiencing anger.

Exercise 3

A variation of Exercise 2 is to have your child picture the anger-provoking person as being covered by a large glass jar or by a clear plastic shield. Clearly explain the purpose of this exercise and remind her that if her images lead her to laugh out loud, she may actually further escalate the other person's anger. Emphasize that the goal is to reduce the physical impact of her anger and not necessarily to completely ignore, dismiss, or in some other way eliminate the emotion of anger.

~ ~ ~

A teenager whom I counseled shared another variation of a visual imagery exercise. He was discussing his father's latest lecture regarding his grades when, with a sense of power and pride, and with more than a slight grin, he candidly revealed, "I'm getting good at it!" I replied, "I think I know what you mean, but tell me exactly what 'it' is." He responded that as his father spoke to him, he would imagine seeing through him to the wall behind him. This youngster was already practicing visual imagery but was using it to help him completely escape from the situation rather than to just physically relax himself. He used this as a major strategy for handling his frustrations and anger when relating to his father and adults in general. I should emphasize that we had not as yet discussed anger management. However, after he shared that strategy, we identified and explored a variety of strategies so that he could be more flexible in his anger management.

Meditation

Older children and adolescents can be taught meditation techniques to help them achieve self-soothing. When used in this way, meditation is a strategy to manage anger and not a way for your child to withdraw from or deny the reality of the situation. There are a wide variety of such techniques to choose from.[4] Some general guidelines for one form of meditation include the following:

1. Have your child find a quiet place where she will experience minimal distraction.
2. Have her sit in a comfortable chair.
3. Have her close her eyes and concentrate on and repeat a word or short phrase.
4. Direct her to say the word or phrase in a way that is synchronized with her breathing.
5. Have her practice this for ten to fifteen minutes and attend to how physically relaxed she feels at the end of the meditation.

When teaching meditation to a younger child, you may help him choose a word that has special meaning for him, a word that has a calming connotation. For example, if you find that holding his special blanket or teddy bear comforts him, you may suggest that he just repeat the word *blankie* or *teddy*. Such objects may have special meaning to him because they provide security and comfort and facilitate self-soothing. They act as transitional objects—that is, they are objects he has become attached to because he associates them with either parents or settings that have provided protection, reassurance, and security. By selecting these words to focus on, you are helping him to give added meaning to the words themselves in addition to, and instead of, the actual object. Another possibility is to decide on a word from a prayer, a song, or a story with which he is familiar.

Again, the goal is to focus his attention on the self-soothing aspect of the strategy. Emphasize that when this strategy is used to help with anger management, he should not expect himself to suddenly stop what he is doing when he is angry and begin to meditate. Instead, thinking of the word he uses will help him recall being physically calm during meditation, and this will help calm him when he is angry.

Years ago I attended a workshop on stress management. The presenter indicated that he had written two words in large letters on the inside of his attaché case. When he was upset or especially anxious, he opened his case to reveal the words "Who cares!"

Physical Activity

This may be one of the most obvious and frequently used strategies to help children and adolescents manage anger. In contrast to the exercises described so far, this strategy is indirect, in that it attends to physical energy and tension that may have arisen due to anger. But the goal of this strategy is not to rehearse relaxation in order to experience more control during a moment of anger. Rather, engaging in structured exercise or physical activity helps to channel the energy anger arouses. Physical exertion leads to a positive sense of accomplishment and the experience of "good" fatigue.

I want to share a word of caution regarding physical activity as a strategy. In the past some professionals have suggested that hitting pillows or plastic inflated dolls is a good way for children and adolescents to vent their anger. They maintain that children and teens who redirect their anger in this way will experience more self-control. This might be offered to help some children or adolescents in counseling who are completely out of touch with their anger. However, most of the recent research on this strategy strongly suggests that, especially for children prone to anger, the encouragement of this type of activity actually predisposes a person to respond physically when he or she is angry—that is, the child is actually rehearsing physical aggression. For this reason, this method of displacing anger is not recommended for the child who is already quick to act on his anger.

Music

You will gain many points with your child, and especially your adolescent, by being aware of her musical tastes. In terms of anger management, try to help her differentiate for herself which music appears to foster self-soothing. This may not be as obvious as it sounds. I have worked with hundreds of adolescents over the years and have found that some can calm themselves by listening to tranquil classical music. Others insist that when they are feeling keyed up and tense, listening to rock or even heavy metal helps them to relax. Others seem to be attracted by rap, which offers them another way to channel their feelings. One recent study evaluating the calming influence of music suggests that individuals vary in how they select music for self-soothing. Certain individuals listen to mellow music for self-soothing. Others first listen to intensely energetic melodies and then follow this with more tranquil music.

Music can provide an echo to our deepest emotions or help to lead us away from the same emotions. Helping your child to identify her personal preferences will provide her with yet another productive strategy for coping with her physical reactions to anger.

The strategies that I have described in this chapter are the most powerful techniques for directly addressing the physical side of anger. Other strategies that have a similar outcome include involvement in activities. Hobbies, reading, watching television, or spectator sports are other less powerful activities useful in addressing the physical side of anger. These are activities that can facilitate enjoyment on their own, as well as a relaxed physical state. But they do not approach the focused intensity of relaxation that can be achieved by muscle relaxation, breathing exercises, visual imagery, meditation, or music.

12

I Need to Think About It

Critical thinking is essential for effectively making sense of and managing anger, and helping children and teens develop skills in how to think is crucial for effective critical thinking. While a variety of thinking skills are fundamental for learning, only in recent years have schools begun to recognize the importance of teaching these skills, including problem solving, analyzing information, and generating alternative solutions. At the same time, studies emphasize that children who are taught specific skills in thinking are more effective in their learning and develop an increased sense of mastery and competence. Developing a broad range of thinking skills is as important for your child's management of anger as it is for meeting any of life's challenges.

All of the theory and skills presented in this book emphasize the need to help your child think rationally and objectively in order to make sense of and manage anger. Such thinking is vital, beginning with the observation of his reactions to the triggering event, the clarification of his thoughts and emotions related to the event, and his decision how to handle his anger. This chapter focuses on four specific areas of thinking that can positively influence your child or teen's capacity for healthy anger management: problem-solving skills, maintaining a realistic perspective, promoting optimism, and fostering creativity.

Using Problem-Solving Skills

Problem-solving skills help your child or teen assess each anger-provoking situation, identify the most effective response from her repertoire of strategies, and then evaluate her actions.[1] Being able to answer the following questions will help your child or teen further master her understanding and management of anger.

1. What is the problem?
2. What are some alternative ways I can address it?
3. In what ways are the above strategies advantageous or disadvantageous?
4. What strategies will I use?
5. How well did it work?

What Is the Problem?

As emphasized throughout this book, anger is a signal that tells us something is wrong. Self-reflection, guided by the model of anger presented in Chapter 4, will help your child or teen more clearly identify the concerns that need to be addressed. Taking time to think about anger is necessary to understand what it means in relation to your child's emotions, expectations, conclusions, needs, and desires. It is only after she identifies her specific concerns that she can then more clearly consider how to address them.

What Are Some Alternative Ways Your Child Can Address Anger?

The second major goal of problem solving regarding anger is to identify what action to take once your child has more fully understood what he wants, needs, or expects. Children and teens are naturally curious and possess the capacity to think through solutions for a variety of challenges. This is especially true when they are encouraged to trust their thinking and provided skills that foster reflection. When children and teens hear your thoughts about anger and ways of evaluating alternative strategies by which to manage anger, they too will learn to identify alternative responses before taking action. Several ways for generating alternative strategies are described below.

Brainstorming. Children and teens of all ages can be helped to brainstorm in order to identify alternative ways of responding to their anger. One technique involves encouraging your child to list as many responses as possible. Encourage her to feel free in her thinking as she makes her list. She could be silly or even unrealistic. The goal of this exercise is to encourage her thinking and give her permission to express herself. Some children need help in getting started and may benefit from your identifying several possible ways of responding.

Effective brainstorming is based on helping children and teens become uninhibited in their thinking. They should be encouraged to list whatever thoughts come to mind without worrying about being right or perfect in their response. I have often offered outlandish alternatives as well as realistic ones to children and teens in an effort to help them think more freely about various possibilities. These were offered only when I was sure the child or teen was able to see the humor in it, rather than act on it, and I used a joking tone. We very quickly identified reasons why the strategy would not really be effective. For example, I have often suggested to a child who believed he was wronged, "You could just get a whipped cream pie and throw it at him," "Give her the silent treatment for a year," or "You could stage a protest march in front of your friend's house." Such absurd proposals very quickly free children to consider a range of possibilities. Also offer several realistic alternatives. The ability to identify several alternative responses provides children with a sense of control and mastery.

Recording stories. Dictating stories into a tape recorder is one approach that can be used with young children. Modeled after the techniques of child psychotherapist Richard Gardner, this approach can take several forms.[2] In one, you can have your child dictate the details of an anger-provoking incident into a tape recorder. He could describe an actual event in his own life, one that occurred to people he knows, or something from a movie or a book. You might encourage a younger child to describe a story in which animals are the main characters. Encourage him to discuss his thoughts and feelings regarding the incident. Have him complete the story by describing one strategy for managing the anger. Then discuss alternative endings with him. You may need to identify several endings first as a way to help him brainstorm.

Another approach, and one that may be especially effective with younger children, is to make a recording together. Start a story about animals or people who face an anger-provoking incident. You can stop the story at various points to ask your child to provide information such as the names of the characters, details regarding the situation, and ways in which the characters manage their reactions. After he has completed the story, recite the same story but offer a more constructive resolution.

Using word pairs. Helping children use certain word pairs is effective in teaching even three- and four-year-olds to reason before acting impulsively.[3] These include word pairs such as *if/then, fair/unfair,* and *is/is not.* These word pairs can be used in identifying alternative behaviors as well as in deciding which ones are most effective. Examples of these follow.

- "*If* I scream at my friend, *then* he may not want to listen to me."
- "*If* I speak calmly, *then* he will more likely hear me."
- "It is *fair* to say what I want; it is *unfair* to demand it."
- "Talking to someone *is* good; hitting someone *is not* good."

A phrase that is more effective with older children and teens is "If I ___, then ___ will happen." The use of this phrase emphasizes the cause-and-effect relationship between actions, helping children to begin to identify the possible outcome of their actions—the advantages and the disadvantages of certain behaviors.[4]

Seeking more information and guidance. Sometimes seeking additional information is a necessary step in identifying alternative strategies for managing anger. Encourage your child to share her thoughts and get opinions from those she trusts. Similarly, support your child's attempts to gather information from others in an effort to get a reality check regarding her experience of a situation.

Foster your child's comfort in seeking guidance, whether he wants to obtain feedback about how he perceived an event or he is considering several alternative strategies for coping with his anger.

In What Ways Are the Identified Strategies Advantageous or Disadvantageous?

Children and teens can be helped to recognize the strengths and weaknesses of the alternative strategies that they have identified. Your thirteen-year-old may decide to jog for half an hour following an anger-provoking event. In contrast, following a rejection from a friend, your seven-year-old may immediately call another friend to plan a sleepover. Answering the following questions will provide guidelines for deciding how effective one strategy is compared to another.

- How effective will this action be in addressing my concern?
- Will my action ignore it, address it just for now, or address it forever?
- How constructive is the action I plan to take?
- How likely is it that my action will achieve my goal?

As with many of the exercises described in this book, children and teens can be helped to ask these questions about their own anger, in discussion about others they know, or about personalities in the media and in books or movies.

What Strategy Will Your Child Use?

At this stage in his thinking, your child may choose a best strategy or several that he feels will work best in combination with each other. Encourage his exploration in more detail about how he will actually handle the situation. An extremely important part of this stage of problem solving is to help your child identify several outcomes that might be described as "worst-case scenarios." Then help your child determine several ways of responding to each one. This step in problem solving is extremely effective because it allows a child to explore his worst fears and identify ways of managing them. Through shared exploration, you will help him to feel more confident and be better prepared to manage even a worst-case scenario.

How Effective Was the Strategy?

This question is one of the most important to answer when trying out new behaviors. By carefully reviewing with your child what went well and what was problematic, he will develop improved guidelines for future behavior. This type of self-monitoring and evaluation is a key component in developing any new skill, since it will help him learn from his mistakes and highlight what was most effective. By doing so, he will be better prepared to meet new challenges instead of treating each one as entirely different from others he has mastered in the past. In addition, this type of self-evaluation will further promote confidence and trust in his ability to manage new challenges.

Using Realistic Thinking

As parents and caretakers, we always want to protect our children from experiencing pain. Our strong determination to do so may at times actually contribute to emotional difficulties and anger in particular. I counseled the parents of Robin, a seventh grader who expressed some doubts about being accepted for the school band. Her parents observed her become increasingly tense and irritable in the days leading up to when she would find out whether she had been accepted. They were so concerned about her discomfort that for several days they tried to avoid discussing it. When they finally asked if she was worried about being accepted, Robin responded that she generally felt positive about it but had some doubts at times.

In their effort to calm Robin, her parents immediately reassured her, saying that they were absolutely sure she would be accepted and that she did not have anything to worry about. Hoping to help her avoid pain, they actually made the situation worse in several ways. Robin was doubtful about her acceptance because she knew she had not practiced as much as she needed to in order to improve her skills. Her parents' suggestion that she had no reason to have doubts actually led her to feel more isolated from them in her experience and that it was not right to have self-doubts. When she did not make the orchestra, she was disappointed as well as annoyed with herself and her parents for convincing her not to worry.

In contrast to simply reassuring her, they could have listened to her anxiety and specifically inquired about what contributed to it. Had they done so, Robin would have perceived them as genuinely empathic. They could have said, "We can understand why you are worried if you believe you did not practice enough. It sounds like you've figured out what might keep you from being accepted. We hope you make it, but we'll just have to wait together." The emphasis in this response is on being realistic, remaining connected, being empathic, focusing on the optimistic possibility, and promoting sharing.

Certainly children or teens do not need to know more about certain issues than they can reasonably handle. But not being honest can have serious impact on a child's trust in himself and others. And it is often loss of trust that most fosters hurt and related anger.

When parents give each other the silent treatment for several days and deny conflict, discuss plans to move to another city at the last minute, or try to deny the real bullying of a younger sibling by an older one, they encourage distrust and increase a child's predisposition to become angry.

Being realistic and candid is extremely important for helping children cope with major family changes. This is especially true when responding to the extremely challenging experience of parental divorce. As indicated previously, empathy involves the ability to see another person's perspective and understand that person's thinking and emotions. Your discussing the reality of an impending divorce gives permission to your child to share her reactions, her thoughts and emotions. Through open communication, she can be helped to sort out her concerns, clarify her feelings, and feel a connection, which is so very important to maintain during this stressful time.

I have counseled many parents who have reported to me that their children did not get upset when they divorced. Often a parent in this situation is overwhelmed and cannot acknowledge his or her own anger because it adds to the tremendous amount of stress already present. As a parent in this situation, you may be tempted to tell your child that he should not be angry. You may indicate to him that much of his life will be the same, that you are not angry, that he should focus on the positive aspects of the change, or that his anger will quickly pass. Any of these responses falls short of being realistic or empathic. Each communicates directly or indirectly that something is wrong with your child for feeling or thinking the way he does, that he should not feel those emotions or think those thoughts, and that he should ignore them. At the same time, you may be directly communicating to him that in order to feel better, he should agree with your view and distrust or stifle his own experience.

In contrast, you would be genuinely empathic when you communicate that it is realistic and natural to experience anger in such a situation, that you recognize he will be going through many changes, and that he may experience a variety of thoughts and emotions. Your connection with your child would be further strengthened by your recognizing and allowing him to discuss hurt and pain associated with his loss and resulting anger. Finally, empathy is reflected in your candidly sharing your understanding that such a transition involves mourning and that he can depend on you to help him through the process.

Similarly, it is difficult for many parents to manage their child's anger toward a new spouse. You may appeal to logic and your own need for harmony when you tell your child she should not be angry with a new stepparent. However, this may not be realistic from your child's point of view. This person may be a stranger to her and may arouse in her conflicts about loyalty to her natural parent. The stepparent may be perceived as an intruder who expects an immediate bond with your child and threatens her relationship with her natural parent. She may still be mourning the loss of her natural parent. These are all very realistic reasons for the arousal of anger and apprehensive thoughts. Trying to ignore this reality or appealing to logic about why such emotions or thoughts should not exist will only lead to further anger.

Being realistic does require being sensitive to your child's ability to handle facts about a particular situation. Certainly you should consider your child's capacity for handling such realism. However, all too often parents underestimate what a child can manage because they themselves may experience discomfort acknowledging uncomfortable thoughts and emotions and internal conflict. But it is through being realistic that your child is given permission to be and express himself. And, as he does so, especially during the most difficult times, he will be helped to maintain connection with you and with himself.

Encouraging Optimistic Thinking

As I noted earlier, how pessimistic a child is may very much influence his tendency to become angry.[5] Children and teens who are pessimistic expect the worst. They anticipate failure in their efforts, rejection by others, and a general lack of support and nurturance by those around them. Again, pessimists and optimists differ in how they explain the causes of both good and bad events. These beliefs form the basis of the inner voice that offers meaning, makes appraisals, and explains events. Specifically, the optimist and pessimist differ with regard to three main patterns in their explanatory style—the way they explain events in their lives. These patterns are permanence, pervasiveness, and personalization.

Permanence. When the optimistic child does well on a science test, she concludes she did well because of her abilities. In contrast, the pessimistic child who does well may conclude that his mood or special effort the night before the test contributed to his success.

The optimistic child explains good events as based on permanent causes, such as her abilities and traits. The pessimistic child explains good events as being caused by more transient or temporary causes.

Similarly, the optimistic child who does not do well on the science test may conclude she did not study enough this time, while the pessimistic child concludes he will never do well in math. The optimistic child explains bad events in terms of the influence of temporary factors, while the pessimistic child thinks in terms of "always" or the influence of permanently fixed traits.

Pervasiveness. Children who explain a cause for an event as being pervasive understand that cause as influencing many aspects of their lives. The optimistic child who does well on the science test may say to herself, "I'm smart," while the pessimistic child may be more likely to say, "I'm smart in science."

When it comes to explaining good events, the optimistic child generalizes her self-assessment; it is global. She is more open to experiencing herself as smart in many areas. The pessimistic child focuses on specific factors as the major cause of good events.

Optimistic and pessimistic children reverse the explanations in terms of pervasiveness when they make sense of bad events in their lives. After doing poorly on a science test, the optimistic child concludes, "I didn't study enough for this test." She identifies a very specific cause for her difficulty. The pessimistic child might respond, "I'm not good in school," reflecting a more global assessment that generalizes to all subjects.

Personalization. The third quality of an explanatory style is personalization, deciding who is responsible when bad things happen. Children *internalize* when they blame themselves and *externalize* when they blame others or the situation for causing an event to occur. Those who habitually blame themselves are more likely to feel excessive guilt, shame, and (associated with this attitude) low self-esteem. Children who routinely blame others experience less guilt or shame and have a tendency to be angrier. Through excessively blaming others, they experience less control over their lives and a diminished sense that they can have a direct impact in their lives.

In general, those who are pessimistic routinely blame themselves in a global way. In response to not doing well on a science test, the pessimist may say, "I am stupid or I am a failure." When she makes this assessment, she is negatively and globally evaluated in a way that is both permanent and pervasive. In contrast, the optimist is more likely to think, "I failed the science test because I did not study enough." The optimist is blaming himself for a specific behavior: not studying enough. His view of the cause is internal, but it is temporary and specific.

These findings regarding optimism and pessimism offer us much-needed direction in helping children and teens develop ways of thinking that foster healthy anger. Specifically, the more you can help your child challenge his pessimistic thoughts and replace them with optimistic patterns of thinking, the more optimistic he will become. Optimistic thinking fosters a more realistic sense of personal strengths and weaknesses and increases your child's experience of having an impact on the world around him. In contrast, maintaining a pessimistic explanatory style leads a child to be more prone to depression. The pessimistic child or teen experiences a lack of impact in creating change and subsequently is more likely to become angry.

Chapter 8, on self-talk, provides specific guidelines for helping your child identify, challenge, and replace unrealistic self-dialogue. Examples of pessimistic thoughts and challenges to these thoughts are described here.

Pessimistic Thoughts	Optimistic Thoughts
I missed four shots in a row; I might as well give up! (*Global, permanent*)	Getting good at basketball does take practice, and I have to miss some shots before I get better. (*Specific*)
I'm a nerd! I have difficulty talking to people I don't know. (*Global, permanent*)	It sometimes is difficult to talk to people I don't know, and I become anxious. I just have to learn some ways to start a conversation. (*Specific, temporary*).
I am sure he won't want to play with me. (*Global, permanent*)	He doesn't know me very well, and so he may not want to play with me. But I could try to figure out what he might like to do together. (*Specific, temporary*)

It's all my fault that you were divorced. (*Global, internalized*)	There were things I did that disappointed both of you, but your divorce had to do with how you felt about each other. (*Specific, external*)
I shouldn't have said that to Mark. I'm just not a good friend. (*Global, internal, permanent*)	I guess I was angry he didn't ask me to be on his team. What I said was mean. Maybe if I apologize, he'll talk to me again. (*Specific, internal*)

As these examples show, optimistic thoughts are not simply thoughts based on a false view that all things will turn out well and that the world is just wonderful. Instead, they offer your child and teen a more realistic assessment of himself and the world around him. As with all skills presented in this book, the more you model optimistic attitudes in your conversations and behavior, the more likely it is that your child will develop healthy optimism. In doing so, you will play a major role in helping your child or teen develop a way of thinking that increases his development of healthy anger.

Criticize in Ways That Promote Optimistic Thinking

How you criticize your child can very much influence her tendency to be optimistic or pessimistic in her thinking.[6] If in your criticism you use language that explains good or bad events in pessimistic language, you promote pessimism. In contrast, when you criticize in language that is associated with optimism, you promote the internalization by your child of that language in her thoughts. Let's return to the example of Robin, described earlier. Below are a variety of comments that her parents could offer if Robin does not make the orchestra. Following each example is an indication of how they may reflect optimism or pessimism.

- "You aren't good at music. I don't think you could ever make the orchestra if you didn't make it this time." (*Pessimistic; global and permanent*)
- "You didn't practice enough these last few months. I believe that if you practice more, you could make that orchestra." (*Optimistic; specific activity and skill*)
- "I think that even if you practice, you will not improve enough to make it." (*Pessimistic; global, permanent*)
- "I think that if you practice, maybe get some extra help, you'll have a much better chance of being accepted." (*Optimistic; specific behaviors*)
- "You're pretty lazy." (*Pessimistic; global, internal*)
- "You will get better when you practice." (*Optimistic; specific*)

Keep a log of your criticism on a daily basis for one week. Review your comments and determine in what ways you may be emphasizing pessimistic thinking or optimistic thinking. In this way you will be better able to review your communications and decide on ways of expressing yourself that foster optimistic thinking by focusing on specific behaviors and the potential for positive change.

Developing Creativity in Thinking

Healthy anger involves having a wide repertoire of strategies for resolving anger. The more you can teach your child or teen to think creatively in general, coupled with all of the strategies discussed so far, the more you will help her develop skills in managing anger. Being creative encompasses a variety of attitudes and skills that foster healthy anger.[7]

While creativity can foster healthy anger, it certainly is not a guarantee of constructively making sense of and managing anger. There are many creative people who experience difficulties in anger management, and creative individuals can demonstrate anger, hostility, and aggression, like everyone else. They may lack empathy, make unrealistic conclusions, be impulsive, or have a variety of difficulties associated with destructive anger. However, you will further strengthen your child's ability to understand and manage anger when you nourish your child's creativity while teaching the strategies contained in this book.

For example, helping foster creativity in children involves helping them trust themselves. It entails looking inward to value their thoughts and emotions. Dealing with anger, as with being creative, involves trusting ourselves but remaining open for feedback and self-evaluation.

An individual who nurtures creativity has allowed his childhood curiosity to flourish. The child or teen who is encouraged to be curious is more apt to have passion for life and to see the uniqueness in different situations. As such, he may rely less on automatic thoughts in reacting to new situations. Similarly, because creativity involves the capacity to take on different perspectives or step back and see things in a different light, the creative child may be more empathic as well as more open to considering the perspective of others who may have contributed to his anger.

Focused creativity requires the ability to postpone judgment or criticism. This ability allows for the generation of new ideas and so is essential in every aspect of anger management. The child or teen who can do this is able to take time to "sleep on it" before taking action.

Creativity often involves the ability to sit with the tension of disorder. Whether we are creating a story, a painting, or a musical composition, we may be pulled in different directions during the creative process. Children who can ride out such tension can manage the frustration of not fully knowing in the beginning where their process may end up. Certainly the ability to tolerate tension is a major component of making sense of and managing anger.

The excessive need to be "right" interferes in the creative process just as much as it hampers effective anger management. Children and teens who are helped to be compassionate and forgiving while still maintaining aspirations to better themselves are more able to cope with such demands by others and themselves.

A key element of creativity is the ability to trust one's imagination while maintaining control over it. Role playing, visualization, and imagining alternative scenarios are just a few ways in which this skill can play a part in constructive anger management.

Being creative means taking risks. The painter, writer, and musician direct their energies in directions that challenge tradition, go against trends, or meet rejection from peers. Many techniques of anger management described in this book involve helping a child or teen take a risk. Your fifteen-year-old son may take a risk by sharing his emotions when to do so would be viewed as not being a real man. Your seven-year-old may take a risk by telling her brother what she really thinks and feels about his invading her room without her permission. Your ten-year-old may take a risk when he admits that something you said to him led him to feel shame. Being authentic and communicating our internal experiences can be just as risky as any creative endeavor, if not more so.

∾ ∾ ∾

Our thoughts and emotions are clearly interwoven and influence every action we take, including how we respond to anger. It is only when your child takes time to think through how to respond to anger that she will constructively manage it. Teaching her skills in critical thinking, instilling optimism, being realistic, and furthering her creativity combine to strengthen her capability for healthy anger.

13

Okay, I'm Ready to Talk About It

This chapter describes specific communication skills that will encourage your child to self-reflect and lead her to value using words
to express her feelings. In addition, it provides specific guidelines to
help your child constructively communicate anger. These skills focus
initially on helping your child look inward to better determine what she
wants to communicate.

Positive Communication

Every relationship we have is very much influenced by the quality
of our communication with the other person. We nurture a healthy
connection when we communicate with others in ways that foster
freedom to express thoughts and feelings, support open self-reflection
and growth, promote healthy self-acceptance, and encourage candid
dialogue.

In contrast, when we communicate with others in ways that inhibit
candid and appropriate expression of thoughts and feelings, discourage
self-reflection and growth, and devalue and hinder open dialogue, we
create a relationship that is marked by tension, frustration, conflict, and

anger. This is a simple principle but one that requires a great amount of attention and practice if we are to be sensitive in our communication with others.

As parents, we nurture open and candid sharing when we communicate with our children in ways that foster their comfort in expressing thoughts and feelings, support their open self-reflection and growth, and promote healthy self-acceptance. Most important, when we encourage and model sharing of thoughts and feelings, we also help children and teens experience the power of the spoken word.

Words and communication take on great meaning for children and teens who are encouraged to express themselves. In fact, it is often said that we genuinely know ourselves most fully by really listening to what we say out loud. When we are encouraged to share our experiences, we are supported in selecting words that most accurately reflect our views, attitudes, and feelings. Through such open discussion children and teens develop increased self-awareness, which also includes the recognition and acknowledgment of inconsistencies in their beliefs and feelings. As such, candid dialogue encourages self-reflection and increased self-understanding.

When children and teens are genuinely listened to and feel understood, they experience a personal and meaningful connection. This does not mean you have to agree with everything your child or teen says or that you have to satisfy his or her every whim. But by listening to and genuinely understanding her perspective and by communicating your understanding, you will foster a bond with your child that promotes self-expression. By doing so, you will also help your child experience the power of words over impulsive action.

The model of anger introduced in Chapter 4 is very much based on this premise. By developing and practicing skills associated with this principle, your child will be intrinsically rewarded for his self-reflection and begin to more meaningfully value discussing and sharing his thoughts and feelings rather than acting on them. A child or teen who values words experiences empowerment and a genuine sense of internal control that cannot be matched by aggressive behaviors.

Effective communication skills are essential for the constructive management of anger. As with all of the strategies presented in this book, the more often you model these skills, the more likely it is that your child will incorporate them as a part of his behavior. We will start by identifying key elements of positive communication.

Listening Skills

Genuine active listening is one of the most essential skills for effectively communicating with others.[1] However, we live in a time dominated by demands that distract us from truly listening in our relationships. This is no less true for parents. Even the most caring of parents may be so preoccupied with teaching their child specific ideas, attitudes, and behaviors that they fail to actively listen to the child. This may also be especially true in our relationships with adolescents, who may not be very open or even available for communication. But only by active listening can we really help children and adolescents develop ways to better understand and manage anger.

Active listening involves listening in a comprehensive way. It involves listening for content but also for what is not stated out loud. It consists of listening to determine your child's mood but also to detect emotions that are not expressed. It involves trying to identify core motivations, expectations, and conclusions when these are not clearly stated. For example, suppose Robert, a fourteen-year-old, complains about an assignment he was given in his English class. He may say, "I can't believe Mr. Lowe gave us such a stupid assignment! I mean really, who cares about the characters in that story? It's boring. How am I supposed to know what made the main character behave the way he did?"

If you listen in one way, you may attend only to Robert's annoyance regarding the task. If you are task-focused, are pressed for time, or direct your attention mostly toward behavior rather than emotions, you may feel compelled to quickly tell him how to behave. Similarly, if you are made anxious by his annoyance, you may try to solve his problem in a hurry. Prompted by your concern that he do well in school, you may immediately remind him that he needs to complete his assignment to get good grades. If you are overly sensitive to his being annoyed, you may try to minimize his annoyance and cajole him into doing the assignment by saying, "It will only take a half hour," "It can't be that bad," or "Sometimes we all have to do things we don't like to do." If you use a behavioral reward program to motivate him for getting good grades, you may remind him that he will be allowed to play with his favorite video game upon completing his assignment. If you too quickly overidentify with your child's pain, you may even call Mr. Lowe for further explanation regarding the teacher's choice of assignments.

Your reaction will depend on what you listen to and how you are impacted by what you hear. In contrast, more in-depth or active listening involves scanning all of the available information your child provides you and being sensitive to the key issues underlying his complaint. For example, through active listening, you might recognize that his feelings of inadequacy or frustration in doing the assignment underlie his complaint. If you listen to his most recent complaint in the context of other issues he has recently discussed, you may understand his complaint as really being a communication about other issues—that he is angry at Mr. Lowe for other reasons, that he is annoyed with the assignment because he was really hurt for not being selected for the school basketball team, or that he is responding to competition with his older brother, an English major in college, by not even trying to complete the task.

Clearly, active listening requires being open to the many possible meanings of what is communicated and the many motivations, emotions, and attitudes that may influence the communication.

Active Listening and the Model of Anger

Active listening, when applied to anger management, involves listening for motivations, emotions, and attitudes that underlie anger rather than attending only to the anger. By listening to your child more actively, you will be more aware of his experience and subsequently more available to help him make sense of and manage his anger. At the same time, through active listening, you will be less reactive to and distracted by his anger. Active listening will help you become a better observer of his experience when he is expressing anger about other events or people in his life, including when he is expressing anger toward you. Focusing on active listening, rather than paying attention to your immediate emotional reaction or thoughts that prompt you to take action, is a major strategy to help you deal with your anger and that of your child.

Active listening is one component of positive communication that helps foster your child's freedom to express his thoughts and feelings, supports open self-reflection and growth, promotes healthy self-acceptance, and encourages open dialogue. Let us return to the example of Robert and his annoyance with the English assignment. If you immediately focus on his need to get good grades, you focus on your expectations for how he should behave instead of on his thoughts and feelings—his internal experience. Similarly, if you only remind him that sometimes we all have to do things that are not enjoyable, or if you remind him of the behavioral reward program and that he will be allowed to play video games when he completes his assignment, you focus on his behavior. Again, you would be giving a response that does not support his self-reflection regarding his emotional experience and thoughts about the situation.

Finally, if you have a knee-jerk reaction to come to his rescue by immediately contacting Mr. Lowe to question the merits of the assignment, you will be encouraging Robert to externalize—to look outside himself for the cause of his discomfort. At the same time, you may be communicating the message that the only way to cope with stress is to try to change others around us rather than reflect on, and perhaps alter our reactions to, feeling stressed.

So if these typical automatic reactions to your child's anger discourage self-reflection, how could you make use of your active listening in formulating alternative responses?

Communication That Reflects Active Listening

While active listening is a major component of effective communication, sharing what you have heard and requesting feedback is the next major task in constructive communication. To do this, you share hypotheses or guesses you may have developed as a result of your active listening. Such communication conveys the message that you are listening beyond the anger and frustration.

Below are examples of comments that demonstrate active listening.

- "I can see you're annoyed. Tell me more about it."
- "Wow! You are really upset. What's going on?"
- "You don't have to tell me the details, but you seem more upset about this than usual."

Returning again to the example of Robert, you might identify the following responses and hypotheses based on active listening.

- "You're sounding fairly angry with Mr. Lowe."
- "Help me understand. What do you feel is stupid about the assignment?"
- "I wonder . . . you talked the other day about feeling Mr. Lowe was picking on you. Are you still resentful about that?"
- "It can sometimes be very difficult to figure out what makes a person do what he or she does."
- "I'm here if you want to talk about it."

Each of these responses communicates a message of support and empathy that fosters sharing, openness, and exploration. Each statement communicates your concern and your willingness to see the experience through your child's eyes. This is the essence of empathy.

Empathy. We are empathic when we can identify with the feelings of others and can recognize their emotions without trying to avoid them or without being overwhelmed by them. Empathy involves the capacity to experience the emotions of another, but with a certain distance.

Our ability to experience empathy for another person allows us to be sensitive to that person's feelings. But effective communication is based not just on being able to experience empathy but also on the ability to communicate our empathy to another person. For example, you may feel empathy for Robert in this situation but choose not to focus your attention on his discomfort. Responses that focus on his need to get good grades or the potential for a reward if he completes his assignment are examples of comments that do not convey empathy. Certainly, there are times you may choose not to communicate empathy. Your annoyance regarding your child's frequent complaints, your lack of time for discussion, or your view that acknowledging negative emotions is a sign of weakness may contribute to lack of empathy in your communications.

However, empathic communication is essential to foster the type of self-reflection emphasized in the approach to anger explained in this book. By being empathic, especially with a child's internal subjective experience (her thoughts, attitudes, and emotions), you are directing attention to those experiences. Rather than directing attention to external issues—her behavior, the behavior of others, or events that involved her—empathy very powerfully communicates to your child that you recognize and can understand her feelings. It tells her that it is all right for her to feel the way she does, and that what she feels deserves attention and should not be ignored. In this way, empathy provides a validation of a child's or teen's inner experience, regardless of whether it is based on realistic or unrealistic thinking. Only after the experience is acknowledged will your child be more available to discuss it and to be helped to decide whether it is based on realistic and objective thinking. This is especially true with regard to making sense of anger.

Such communication is a key element that helps children explore emotions related to their anger as well as the conclusions, expectations, and motivations that play a part in their anger. Empathic interactions foster a bond between you and your child that will enable him to more comfortably engage with you regarding a whole range of issues in addition to anger.[2]

While this discussion has focused on how your communication can promote self-reflection, positive communication will also help your child defuse his anger. Rather than respond to his anger with attempts to distract him from it or help him deny or minimize it, such interaction will help him to acknowledge anger and more constructively accept and manage it. Through such discussion you give him permission to experience anger, and you help him to remember that anger is the reflexive response to a number of internal experiences.

The more empathic you can be with your child, the more she can accept and recognize her thoughts and emotions. However, our ability to be empathic is greatly influenced by our acceptance of and comfort with our own emotions. As I have stated repeatedly, your own discomfort with certain feelings, thoughts, or attitudes may interfere with your capacity to be empathic about those feelings, thoughts, or attitudes in others.

All too often, when we hear a child or teen share emotions or thoughts that do not immediately make sense, or with which we disagree, we want to quickly convince her of what we believe she "should" or "should not" feel or think. We may feel challenged and become concerned about her being childish, unladylike (or, for a boy, unmanly), silly, dangerous, confused, or ignorant. We may become anxious about our own image if others were to hear our child discussing these emotions or thoughts. Similarly, we may become fearful of her emotions or thoughts. As a result, we may tell her to be quiet and not think about a problem, or we may try to distract her from such thoughts or feelings.

These attitudes, whether expressed directly or indirectly, have a tremendous negative impact on a child's development. Such attitudes lead children to distrust or doubt their emotions, not express them, and develop underlying anger as a result of feeling stifled and criticized.

The need to idealize our childhood is another factor that may interfere with our capacity to empathize with your child. Many of us prefer to perceive childhood as easygoing, lacking in tension, and simple rather than as complex. We often wish to maintain this view in spite of numerous reports in recent years about the increasing pressures and challenges children are experiencing. Similarly, we try to keep this perception even as we increase the pressure on youngsters to grow up more quickly and to achieve more.

A commitment to be empathic challenges us to self-reflect and gain self-awareness. In doing so, we become more sensitive to our children and help them develop increased comfort in sharing their thoughts, emotions, and attitudes.

Nonverbal communication. While the content of what you communicate to your child is extremely important, how you say it can either strengthen or weaken your underlying message. Your tone of voice, facial expression, eye contact, and physical proximity are some key elements of nonverbal communication that can foster helping your child manage anger.

Tone of voice. What you share will be heard best when your tone communicates acceptance, support, concern, and presence—a message that you are fully attending to her at that moment. If you are trying to be empathic but speak in an angry, impatient, anxious, or critical tone, your child will hear anger, impatience, anxiety, or criticism. These nonverbal aspects of your communication will distract her from your message and from genuinely experiencing empathy. Even a comment such as "You're sounding fairly angry with Mr. Lowe" can be said in a critical and devaluing tone. Similarly, "I'm here if you want to talk about it" can be said in a tone that conveys frustration, annoyance, or impatience.

Facial expression. Your facial expression, like your tone of voice, can convey either genuine concern for your child's experience or a negative message that undermines the full impact of your verbal message. An example of this is my work with a couple who were trying their best to be empathic with their angry thirteen-year-old son. Both husband and wife grew up in challenging circumstances that left them with many emotional scars and made them uncomfortable with acknowledging the hurt and disappointments of their respective childhoods. For this reason, they were often unavailable to be sensitive to the emotional pain their son experienced. They had learned the message that in the face of emotional hurt, they should just try to ignore it and move on. This message tremendously influenced their views regarding vulnerability and being independent. Their own discomfort with emotions encouraged them to maintain the view that they were helping their son to "become a real man" by encouraging him not to admit to or complain of pain.

When it was suggested that they work at being empathic with his pain and help him talk about it, they very quickly tried out responses such as "I could understand how you could feel that way" and "Maybe a part of you still just wants to be taken care of, like when you were younger." When stated with genuine concern and empathy, these responses are very powerful in creating openness, engagement, and self-reflection. However, both parents' own discomfort with helping their son explore such feelings led them to make these statements in a devaluing and critical tone and with a tense facial expression that reflected disgust and promoted shame. When they said the words "I can understand how you could feel that way," their nonverbal message also communicated the additional message "But it sure is childish or foolish to feel that way." Similarly, when they said "Maybe a part of you still just wants to be taken care of like when you were younger," the teasing and belittling tone in their voices conveyed the additional message "You're just acting like a baby—grow up!" Only after they individually worked at acknowledging their own pain and related anger could they be more genuinely empathic with their son.

Physical proximity. How close you are physically with your child is an important issue in communication in general, but even more so when it comes to empathic communication intended to foster self-reflection and increase the bond with your child. Calling out "I'm here if you want to discuss it" from the kitchen to your child in the living room will dilute the impact of the offer of support. Talking from across the room while reading a newspaper may similarly diminish the empathic quality of a message such as "I can see how you could feel that way." Ideally, being in close physical proximity emphasizes your genuine availability, presence, and concern to discuss such issues. Close physical proximity conveys messages such as "What you are feeling and what you have to say is important to me," "I really am here for you," and "You have my full attention."

Eye contact. Good eye contact really communicates genuine presence and concern. Good eye contact involves not a fixed stare but looking frequently and warmly into your child's eyes. This may not be easy if you are not used to maintaining eye contact when talking with people. Similarly, eye contact may be more difficult when you are talking about personal issues such as your child's emotions and thoughts, especially as they relate to anger.

Some people feel more comfortable talking about more personal issues when they do not experience direct eye contact. Parents often indicate that some of their best communications have taken place in the car. Some children and many adolescents feel uncomfortable with direct eye contact. Be sensitive to this in yourself and in your child. The goal is to be empathic. If eye contact promotes too much discomfort, it is not empathic. Teens who struggle with their need for independence or experience shame or guilt about their feelings may be more likely to feel discomfort with eye contact. For this same reason, while I encourage direct communication, the most effective communication with your child or adolescent may actually take place while the two of you are involved in some activity that is relaxing but does not require so much concentration that you are both distracted from being candid with each other.

Modeling these communication skills is the best way to help your child develop positive communication. Specifically, help him to engage in active listening and attend to his nonverbal communication, including his tone of voice, eye contact, and physical proximity. These can be taught through your modeling them as well as by discussing them with him. Role-play with him so that he experiences what it feels like when you demonstrate different degrees of eye contact or physical proximity while talking to him. Then role-play so that he has opportunities to practice these skills in conversations with you. Remind him that how he states his thoughts and feelings regarding anger is as important as the words he chooses to express them.

While positive communication skills improve communication in general, they are especially relevant when helping your child or teen communicate anger. Candidly expressing anger and the thoughts and emotions surrounding it is a major challenge for most people. It is particularly difficult for children. The guidelines below offer specific direction for helping children and teens address this challenging task.

Help Prepare Children and Teens to Communicate Their Anger

You can best help your child prepare to express her anger when, through discussion and modeling, you help her to:

1. Become calm when deciding how to express her anger.
2. Clearly identify her feelings, thoughts, motivations, and expectations.
3. Identify the goal of her communication.
4. Decide how candid she wants to be in her communication.
5. Select a good time for communication.
6. Practice assertive communication.

Help Your Child Become Calm When Deciding How to Express Anger

As I have emphasized throughout this book, the first goal in responding to anger is to be physically relaxed. Only when we are physically relaxed can our thinking exert control over our emotional and physical reactions to anger. Becoming calm is essential for the clear reflection needed to flexibly think through and formulate our response to anger. Reducing physical tension associated with anger is an essential first step, whether your child achieves this by counting to ten, distracting himself from his anger, running five blocks, performing visualization or breathing exercises, or assertively expressing himself. He may take a few minutes, a few hours, or even a few days to achieve this calmness.

Achieving calmness is also indicated when he finally does intend to communicate what is on his mind. Breathing exercises may be especially helpful at this moment.

Help Your Child Identify Emotions, Thoughts, Motivations, and Expectations

A major step in deciding how to handle anger is for your child or teen to more clearly identify the motivations underlying her anger, the emotions related to it, and her expectations about the situation that provoked the anger. What was the experience that preceded her anger—hurt, disappointment, rejection, unrealistic or realistic expectations or conclusions? Without identifying these important components in the sequence of anger, her communication may remain motivated by her desire to vent, "win," prove she is right, or inflict pain on those who led her to become angry.

James, a thirteen-year-old, frequently became angered when his younger brother, Sean, entered his room and played with his Nintendo without permission. His typical reaction to Sean was to raise his voice and humiliate his brother by being critical and devaluing. Only by sorting out his reactions was James able to be clearer about what he wanted to share with his younger brother. As a result of his self-reflection,

James clearly indicated that while he would like to trust Sean, that trust diminished each time Sean violated it. James indicated that he felt a lack of respect from Sean and that he really wanted to have a good relationship with him. Following James's candor, Sean was also able to more readily admit his feelings of frustration that James never seemed to want to play Nintendo with him.

Chapters 7, 8, and 9 offer a variety of strategies to help your child better identify the many different reactions she may have that relate to her anger. Your empathic communication will further foster her openness to self-reflection. In addition, as described previously, the use of hypotheses is another way of helping children and adolescents look inward and question themselves. Specifically, share with your child your observation about what may be influencing her experience. But be sure to present your observation tentatively, as a guess or hypothesis. For example, suppose you believe that your child's anger about an event is based on her feeling hurt, rejected, ignored, or devalued. If she is a youngster who does not readily acknowledge anger, you may want to share one of the following responses:

- "I'm not sure, but I would think that would leave you annoyed [or upset, irritated, or angry, depending on your child's capacity to acknowledge such feelings]. I know I would be angry in that kind of situation."
- "I know that when I'm hurt, I feel angry. I wonder if a part of you is angry."
- "Maybe you're a little angry about what happened."

If, in contrast, your child does express anger, the following responses may help to foster self-reflection:

- "I wonder if you're feeling somewhat disappointed and hurt besides being angry. I know in that type of situation, I would feel that way."
- "It sounds like a part of you is really hurting about how your friend treated you."
- "I would think it would be natural to feel frustrated in that kind of situation."

Such comments are best presented in a questioning tone that reflects curiosity. The goal of such comments is to arouse your child's self-questioning and curiosity. The purpose of presenting these reflections as hunches, guesses, or observations is to have your child focus on his internal experience. Present your comments as ideas for consideration and exploration rather than as a definitive evaluation of his internal experience. You want your child to ask a question of himself rather than experience you as having the right answer or as being able to somehow see into his internal experience. Presenting your views as definitive will, in many cases, lead a child or adolescent to shut down in communicating with you. A child or an adolescent on certain occasions may like you to read his mind but at other times will become quite resentful, puzzled, or intimidated if he experiences you as telling him how he feels. How often have you heard an adolescent say, "How do you know how I feel? You can't read my mind."

As stated previously, these types of comments can also be used to help children explore their expectations and conclusions regarding events that lead them to anger. Suppose your child is disappointed and angry about not being invited to a friend's house. You may want to review unrealistic expectations and conclusions to help you formulate hunches or observations in response to this scenario. For example, you may respond in any of the following ways.

- "Sometimes we think that if a best friend is really a best friend, he should behave exactly like we want him to behave."
- "I know you're disappointed and you think he doesn't like you. But could you think of other reasons to explain his not inviting you?"
- "When we are disappointed by a friend, we sometimes blame ourselves ... and yet we're not always to blame."

Only after self-reflection about an experience will your child be able to identify her major concern. If she does decide to candidly discuss her experience, she is then ready to identify the goal of his communication.

Help Your Child Identify the Goal of Communication

As I have emphasized throughout this book, anger provides us a signal that something is wrong. It helps us know when we need to address a need and desire. It can serve as a warning that unless we take some action, we may continue to feel threatened. As such, it is only after your child sorts through his thoughts and feelings that he can better know what he believes he needs. Only then can he decide what he hopes to achieve by his communication. As stated above, when we impulsively react to anger we may be motivated by a desire to vent, "win," prove we are right, or to inflict pain on those who lead us to become angry.

We may not always take time to clearly identify the goal in expressing our feelings. However, the more your child or teen practices this skill, the easier he will find it to trust himself and experience comfort when discussing his anger.

Help Your Child Decide How Candid to Be

Just as it may be inappropriate for you to express some of your feelings in your work setting, it may not be beneficial for a child or teen to be candid about her feelings with every adult or peer. However, there are a variety of ways in which she can still be assertive in addressing her needs related to her anger. She should be helped to carefully think through how much to share, especially in situations where others may not want to hear her feelings. For example, help her realize that she might want to be more cautious about being candid when she is communicating to others who have power or authority over her. They may not be concerned about her feelings or may be threatened by her anger. In such cases, encourage your child to share her expectations or her conclusions with others and ask for feedback about their accuracy.

For example, Brandon, a thirteen-year-old seventh grader, believed that his math teacher was annoyed with him. Lately she seemed to ignore Brandon when he raised his hand, and she spoke to him in a somewhat harsher tone than on previous occasions. Brandon concluded that she might have been frustrated with him because he had not performed well on recent tests. At the same time, he was very concerned about his grade and being an active participant in class. He realized he felt ignored, frustrated, and disappointed. As a result, he was becoming increasingly irritated with his teacher but knew that he did not want this reaction to escalate.

Through brainstorming, Brandon was helped to identify his expectations and conclusions regarding his interaction with his teacher. Based on observing the interaction of his peers with this teacher, he decided that he would not feel comfortable sharing all of his feelings, especially his anger. Instead, he focused on sharing with the teacher his expectations to do well and his realization that he had not put forth his best effort in preparing for the last few exams. In addition, he indicated that he was confused why he was not being called upon to answer questions even when his hand was raised. He did share his feeling that he was disappointed for not being chosen to answer. Rather than accuse her of speaking in an angry tone, state his anger, or accuse her of ignoring him, he focused on sharing his expectations and the feeling of disappointment. The teacher replied that she was not aware of purposely ignoring him but that she wanted everyone in class to have a chance to participate. Brandon reported that she seemed pleasantly surprised that he acknowledged not being well prepared for recent exams. The conversation ended with Brandon promising that he would let the teacher know sooner if he was having trouble with the assignments and the teacher telling him that she might select him to answer more often but was trying to engage others in class discussion. Her response to his assertive comments was proof to him that he had said just what he needed to say.

Help Your Child Select a Good Time for Communication

Your child is relaxed, and he knows what he hopes to achieve and what he wants to communicate. However, while he may be ready to speak, the person he wants to speak to may not be as ready. It is now time for your child to practice being empathic. Help him determine the best time to share his thoughts. Specifically, encourage him to be aware of the mood of the person with whom he wants to have a discussion. In addition, suggest he select an occasion when they will have sufficient time and there is little likelihood that others will interrupt them, as Brandon did when he addressed his concerns with his teacher.

Help Your Child Practice Assertive Communication

Assertive communication is the candid expression of how we think and feel without being aggressive toward others.[3] It includes communication that is not intended to hurt, punish, or intimidate others. Instead, it declares how we think and feel and includes the wish we may have for how things could be different in the future.

Assertive communication includes (1) objectively describing the events that led up to our reactions, (2) our specific feelings—for example, hurt, disappointment, rejection, and anger, and (3) a statement of how we want things to be in the future.

Whether your child is expressing anger toward you, describing her anger toward a friend or sibling, or expressing her reaction to a teacher, the more often you encourage her to assertively express her thoughts and emotions and offer positive reinforcement for doing so, the more comfortable she will be with managing her anger in this way.

Assertively communicating anger involves clearly sharing the other feelings that lead to anger as well as being specific about our experience of an event or interaction with another person. An extremely effective way of communicating anger to your child, and a way that he can practice, involves four components based on theories of assertiveness training.

1. *Positive statement.* Begin with a general positive statement about your interaction with your child.

   Examples:
   - "I love you a great deal."
   - "You give me so much pleasure."
   - "I really enjoy the time we spend together."

2. *"But" statement.* The second statement is about the exception to the first statement. Include a feeling you have in response to a specific action taken by your child.

Examples:
- "But when you don't listen to me, I feel frustrated [ignored, hurt, disappointed]."
- "But when you're late and don't call me, I feel fearful and also discounted [ignored, hurt, disappointed]."

3. *Statement of anger.* The third statement is one that communicates annoyance as a result of the first emotional reaction.

Example:
- "When I feel frustrated [ignored, discounted, hurt], I become annoyed [angry, irritated] with you for doing what you did."

4. *Statement of alternative behavior and reaction.* This statement should identify an alternative action that you want your child to take and how you would feel if she acted in that way.

Example:
- "Call me by nine-thirty if you think you'll be late. I'll feel much more assured that you are okay—and that you value my feelings."

This is a very structured format for communicating anger. You increase the likelihood of being heard by beginning with a positive statement instead of immediately addressing your anger. Similarly, you emphasize a positive quality of the relationship and, in doing so, highlight a specific behavior against the background of that positive relationship.

Beginning your discussion in this manner helps you, as well as your child, remember that no matter how angry you are, your anger is time-limited and focused on this particular behavior. Initiating the discussion by focusing on your anger is likely to lead your child to shut down and become minimally available for input. Prefaced in this manner, your communication is easier to listen to and is less likely to lead to a global negative assessment, either by you or by your child. The focus on your child's behavior reflects an especially important component in the expression of anger. It emphasizes your reaction to a specific behavior at a specific moment rather than a global response of anger that will lead your child to shut down.

The "but" statement is based on general principles of assertiveness and is consistent with the model of anger. Stating your underlying emotion first, before saying you are angry, leads to more effective communication for several reasons. First, by emphasizing that you have an emotional reaction that leads to anger, you model self-disclosure without venting your anger. Second, by expressing your underlying feelings first, you reduce the risk of having your expression of anger lead your child to shut down.

Try to recall any experience you have had as an adult or as a child when you were told that someone was angry with you. Very often we experience a knee-jerk reaction and become angry in return. Another response might be to tune out what the person is saying because it feels so uncomfortable, especially coming from a parent. And finally, by stating the underlying emotion first, you are being direct and clear in presenting the full complexity of your reactions. The actual phrasing— "When I feel hurt [disappointed, ignored], I end up feeling angry"— emphasizes the chain of reactions we have explored in this book.

Identifying a desired action provides a clear description of your expectation. Besides being told of your anger, your child needs direction and guidance in order to better know you and understand how you think and feel. Without the statement of alternative actions, your child will be left knowing only how you feel. You must also identify specific behaviors to address your expectations for the future, such as calling home or taking out the garbage.

This framework allows you to express anger in a verbal and direct manner. But you must use the wording that feels most comfortable for you and that you believe would be most easily understood by your child (that is, appropriate to his intellectual and emotional understanding). I am not suggesting that this will always get the results you want. But this type of communication represents the most honest and direct expression of anger. How your child responds to such directness is indicative of the underlying quality of the relationship your child has with you. If your child consistently states directly and in his behavior that he does not care how you feel, it is clear that he either does not experience empathy with you or does not want to be empathic toward you. This type of response also reflects a low motivation for self-reflection and understanding and may reflect the need for a behavioral reward program or special support from a professional.

Identify Anger as a Response to Inner Thoughts and Emotions

The more your child practices self-reflection with regard to anger, the more she will be connected to her experience of anger as a reaction to other emotions and to expectations and conclusions regarding how other people should behave. Communicating this awareness when sharing our anger emphasizes taking responsibility for our emotions.

Sharing our expectations and conclusions without blaming or shaming the other person invites them to share their thoughts and reflect rather than act.

Gary, a fifth grader, was really annoyed when, for the third time, his classmate Lisa didn't show up after school to help him with his homework, as she had promised. He could have responded by calling her a jerk, by refusing to speak to her, or by bad-mouthing her to her friends. Instead, he responded in the following way: "I was really disappointed and annoyed, especially after you promised me you would help me. I expected you to keep your word. I'm not sure what to make of it. You didn't want to help me? Maybe you had something more fun to do? I don't know."

Through this response, Gary simply stated out loud his expectations, conclusions, and emotions surrounding the event. While you may feel that this sounds awkward, I strongly recommend you think through what your reactions are to such comments. This response is perhaps the most honest and candid a person can be when sharing his anger. It may sound strange, especially if such candor was never a part of how you were taught to express anger. It may sound too intellectual if you believe that anger needs to be more emotional and focused on an expression of anger. You may even believe that this type of response somehow lets the other person get away with something. These ideas reflect the messages we receive about our emotions—messages that inhibit more constructive communication of anger. For example, such messages communicate that we should not expose our vulnerability, confusion, and self-doubts lest we appear weak, feel embarrassed, or be rejected.

Use Feeling Statements

Children and teens need a great deal of assistance in distinguishing "feeling" statements from "thinking" statements. If your child says, "I feel that Jason doesn't want to be my friend," he is really describing a thought. In contrast, he would be more directly stating his feelings if he states, "I feel sad or hurt because I think Jason does not want to be my friend." All too often we indicate we feel something when in fact we are simply saying that we believe or sense that a certain thought is true.[4]

Below are other examples of statements that reflect feelings about thoughts followed by statements about feelings that more accurately describe the emotional experience.

- "I feel like you shouldn't treat me that way." (*Thinking statement*)

- " I feel hurt when you treat me that way." (*Feeling statement*)
- "I feel that you have no respect for me when you do not follow the curfew." (*Thinking statement*)
- "I feel ignored when you do not follow the curfew, and I then feel hurt, disappointed, and irritated." (*Feeling statement*)
- "I feel that if you really were my friend, you would have helped me with the homework." (*Thinking statement*)
- "When you didn't help me with the homework, I was disappointed and hurt." (*Feeling statement*)

Making statements that actually describe our specific emotions leads to clear communication. In contrast, presenting a thought or attitude as a "feeling" leads to confusion, distraction, and miscommunication. Through honest communication your child remains genuine. Although he may be more vulnerable by not masking his emotions, true understanding in a relationship is based on candid sharing. Disguised or masked anger leads to confusion in the relationship and internal tension and confusion. All too often we mask our feelings in an attempt to avoid rejection or to appear invulnerable. When we mask our feelings, we will be misunderstood, feel more isolated, and become less hopeful about feeling connected with others.

Certainly there is no guarantee that our hopes or feelings will be recognized or that others will respond positively to us. But clear communication regarding anger and the emotions associated with anger will increase the likelihood that our needs will be heard.

Teaching Children and Teens the Right to Say No

At first you might react negatively to the idea that children, and especially teens, need to be taught to say no. But children or teens who have difficulty setting limits may become prone to experience anger. Saying no as a part of the "terrible twos" and saying no as a response by a teen preoccupied with taking control are both examples of setting boundaries. In fact, these are two developmental stages when children and teens may use anger to set boundaries in an effort to assert their individuality. In contrast, some children and teens may have extreme difficulty saying no to parents, while others can easily set limits with parents but are fearful of saying no to peers. But saying no may be very difficult for the child or teen who believes he must always avoid disappointing others so as not to arouse hurt, rejection, dislike, anger, or even abandonment. Those who have difficulty saying no often feel compelled to agree with others in order to avoid conflict. As a consequence, these children may experience anxiety with the slightest conflict and with their own anger.

They may turn their anger inward and be critical of themselves, which often predisposes them to feel unreasonable guilt and shame.

For such children, saying no is a tremendous challenge that can lead to an adulthood in which they lose track of their needs, become disconnected with themselves and others, and carry resentment. For all of us, the ability to set limits is an outgrowth of feeling comfortable with our needs and wants. Children and teens need help in being flexible about saying no.

While just a no might be all that is necessary in most situations, setting limits may be easier if your child is helped to respond in three ways. Specifically, suggest she (1) acknowledge the other person's needs, (2) clearly state her thoughts, feelings, or positions, and (3) say no.

For example, your child may be asked by another child to play a board game. If he is genuinely interested, he may acknowledge the other child's request by inquiring what game or when the other child wants to play. He may then tell the other child, "I really don't care for that game" or "I really want to watch a special television program tonight." If he isn't interested at all, he may say, "No, thanks, I'll pass on that." While there are times he may want to explain his feelings, he should be encouraged to believe that he does not need to justify them.

Encourage Your Child to Discuss Anger with Others

Friendships do not always come naturally. Children and teens need to be helped to develop relationships with others around their own age. It takes skills, time, effort, and cooperation to create lasting and meaningful friendships. Children and teens learn these skills from your modeling them as well as from their peers. And while they may have several or many friends, it is the especially close friendships that are most meaningful for your children. We share mutual support, connection, and enjoyable experiences with our friends. Sharing information about ourselves is one way of increasing the level of intimacy in a friendship. True friendship offers support and feedback for discussing our experiences. Your child or teen may prefer to discuss anger with one parent, a grandparent, or a friend. The more comfortable he feels in sharing his experiences, the more readily he will seek out others to discuss the full experience of anger. Whether he shares in order to vent or to help clarify options for managing his anger, discussing his feelings and thoughts with others should be encouraged, modeled, and valued.

Writing

While some children and teens can discuss their thoughts and feelings, others may feel more comfortable writing about them. Whether composing a letter, maintaining a journal, or using the creative form of a composition, poem, or short story, writing may be another way for your child or teen to express herself and to constructively make sense of and manage anger.

Writing a letter may be an easier way for older children and teens to express feelings when they feel uncomfortable being verbally direct. Writing a letter offers the opportunity to express themselves without being concerned about the immediate reactions of the other person. In this way, they can focus more on self-reflection and be less distracted by being preoccupied with the potential reactions of others. Similarly, writing letters provides time to try out a variety of approaches before finalizing one's thoughts. Letters may be used as practice for discussion, may actually be given to the person who is the target of your child's reactions, or may remain hidden. They may be shared for feedback and discussion, serve to prompt action, or allow for a healthy way to vent. In all of these ways, they encourage reflection and an emotional investment in words as a way of managing anger.

Maintaining a journal is another form of communication that helps a child or teen develop increased understanding of her anger. Whether or not she shares her thoughts with others, writing in a journal offers your child the opportunity to sort out her thoughts, express them without the fear of repercussions, and gain increased objectivity as she sees her concerns expressed in words. While we may not fully know ourselves until we express our thoughts out loud, maintaining a journal offers a similar opportunity to gain distance and objectivity in self-reflection. In addition, journal writing, especially with anger as its focus, is another way to value thinking and words over action.

Respecting the privacy of your child's journal is the only way to support and encourage its use. The only time when such privacy should be ignored is when, despite your best efforts, you have minimal communication with your child and truly suspect he or she is engaged in, or about to be engaged in, some activity that is threatening to himself or others.

Both boys and girls can be encouraged to engage in creative writing as a way to express the full range of anger, from slight annoyance to intense rage. While we may traditionally associate this format with girls, boys also experience tremendous satisfaction in creative writing, especially when they are supported, encouraged, and given permission to be honest. Read your child's writing the way you would use active listening when he talks to you. Empathy is just as important when you respond to your child's writing as when you are engaged in a conversation. Attend to the meaning of what is being said as well as the way it is being expressed. The content may be unsettling and cause you to become extremely critical or so anxious that you stifle further communication. At those moments, it will be helpful to look at your child's sharing as a means for engagement and connection. Use this moment as an opportunity to foster your relationship while at the same time learning more about how your child thinks and feels. Offering children and teens the freedom to creatively express themselves is a powerful way to potentially reduce the probability of acting on such feelings.

Creative Art

Children and teens can use a variety of creative art forms to express the full range of thoughts and emotions related to their anger. I have encouraged both young children and teens to paint or draw pictures as a way of expressing themselves. Others have channeled their energy and feelings into photography, music, or dance. These activities provide children and teens a form of expression that may actually resonate with, and more closely reflect, their internal feelings than the spoken or written word. These activities are often centering—that is, they reduce the internal tension created by having feelings that are challenging to express. As such, they promote self-soothing and foster reflection. They can be a means to vent negative feelings as well as express very specific ideas and emotions. At the same time, they can allow for spontaneity and even impulsivity that stands in stark contrast to the aggressive expression of anger.

It is no surprise that following the terrible events of September 11, 2001, children and teens (as well as adults) across the country began to express themselves in a wide range of ways involving the creative arts. These works were efforts to feel connected and to express a range of emotions, including anger. Such efforts contributed greatly toward healing, both for their authors and for those who saw or heard them.

As with writing, practicing empathy and the skills of active listening when discussing your child's work will greatly foster connection and further encourage her use of these activities as a way to express herself. As with every strategy so far discussed in this book, the more children and teens see you and others around them model these approaches in managing anger, the more they will value them and make them a part of their lives.

Becoming an Activist

The terrorist attacks against the World Trade Center and Pentagon in September 2001 led to a massive display of pride and activism throughout our country. Children, teens, and adults took action to communicate their support, sympathy, and genuine caring to the victims and surviving families of those horrific acts. Americans expressed themselves through music, letters, and pictures and by raising funds for the victims and families. Clearly, the first step in moving toward these actions was to express ourselves with each other. Whether in words or pictures, children and teens should be encouraged to express themselves and become involved in movements that support a good cause. The outpouring of children's donations and the creative ways they raised money were only another reminder that children and teens are very much aware of their emotions and need to channel them as much as adults do. It similarly emphasizes the value of activism as a way in which anger, fear, and sadness can be expressed and transformed into the most powerful form of caring, especially for those who are hurting and in need.

Children and teens should be encouraged to discuss and express themselves, whether in response to a national tragedy or in order to address grievances they may have regarding situations at home, in school, in the neighborhood, or in the larger community. They should be encouraged and supported in their discussions and helped to appropriately channel their views into action if this can be a realistic next step.

Fostering sharing regarding these grievances and helping children and teens identify and move toward appropriate actions further teaches them the value of thinking before taking action. At the same time, the process fosters a deeper and more lasting sense of empowerment.

Being "ready to talk about it" involves your child's reflection regarding her experience, what to share, how best to present it, and the most desirable time and place to do so. By teaching and modeling such reflection, active listening, and empathy, you provide your child skills for constructive self-expression that furthers healthy empowerment and her increased connection with self and others.

14

Acceptance and Forgiveness

Anytime you help your child reflect on anger, you help her practice acceptance and forgiveness. By helping your child increase awareness of her needs, hopes, expectations, and conclusions, and of the range of emotions surrounding anger, you assist her in moving past the provoking event, beyond anger and resentment. Similarly, you teach your child acceptance and forgiveness when you help her develop realistic expectations and appraisals. Finally, you teach her acceptance and forgiveness when you encourage her to identify and practice new ways to meet her needs.

Many people believe that acceptance and forgiveness involve condoning the actions of another. Some believe that acceptance and forgiveness involve ignoring or denying anger even when we have been abused or devalued. Others view forgiveness as merely understanding the rationale for why someone caused them pain. In actuality, true acceptance is the initial step toward forgiveness. Denial, minimizing our pain, or focusing only on intellectual understanding require much energy, are self-defeating, and ultimately interfere with genuine acceptance and forgiveness.

Acceptance

The Many Components of Acceptance

Acceptance takes many forms. All of the strategies that have so far been presented to help children and adolescents identify the components of anger are strategies that foster acceptance. Helping children and adolescents accept anger involves helping them to accept the entire experience—the feelings that lead up to anger, the expectations, the conclusions, and the needs or wants. Helping a child accept anger without recognizing the thoughts or feelings that lead up to it still leaves him hurt. Helping him to recognize and accept only his anger may lead him to maintain unrealistic expectations and conclusions and does little to help him increase awareness of his more basic wants and needs. Focusing only on acknowledging and accepting his anger without recognizing the complexity of that emotion is like trying to kill a weed by removing only the aboveground part of the plant, not its root.

Without fully accepting other components of his anger, a child is more vulnerable in several ways. Focusing only on anger leaves a child less aware of the complexity of his emotional life, less aware of the real precipitants of his anger, and, as a result, more vulnerable to anger. Focusing only on anger also leads him to blame others as a means of reducing the pain of hurt, rejection, shame, or embarrassment. At the same time, holding on to anger directed inward in the form of unjustified or excessive guilt and shame both wastes energy and is self-destructive.

Acceptance of the complexity of emotions. Acceptance includes recognizing and accepting the complexity of our emotions, including mixed or ambivalent emotions. For example, most children who experience their parents' divorce react with a wide variety of emotions. A child may be angry with his parents even though she deeply loves them. She may feel guilt regarding her anger or her unrealistic conclusion that she somehow contributed to their divorce. She may also experience loss, a sense of rejection, and feelings of abandonment at the prospect of seeing her parents end their marriage. Acknowledging and accepting all of these feelings is essential for making sense of and managing anger related to this type of family disruption. Identifying and acknowledging both realistic and unrealistic expectations and conclusions is another part of fully accepting the experience. Only by fully recognizing and acknowledging her thoughts and attitudes can a child or teen fully explore and clarify how unrealistic or realistic they are. Children and teens who are supported and encouraged to discuss these reactions will make a tremendous step forward toward acceptance and forgiveness, of others and themselves.

It is often difficult for a parent in this situation to help a child recognize and accept his emotions when the parent has difficulty acknowledging such reactions. As stated earlier, when a parent has difficulty acknowledging anger or other negative emotions, she may have a tendency to ignore, minimize, discount, or stifle a child's expression of such emotions. Another parent may be open only to recognizing and acknowledging anger. In doing so, he can unwittingly support his child's attention to anger while decreasing the child's awareness of other emotions. Another strategy that undermines acceptance is telling a child that he should not feel or think a certain way. I have worked with many parents who were in the process of divorce and, though well intentioned, suggested their child not be angry about the divorce or toward the other parent. Often, in an effort to minimize the full impact of the disruption, a parent may tell a child not to be too concerned because, after all, he will still get to see both parents and that many things will remain the same. These are all responses that interfere with full acceptance of the range of emotions that are typically aroused by a divorce.

A child or teen suffers in several ways when her feelings are stifled. She is not helped to move toward acceptance of the wider range of very natural reactions she may have to the divorce. She may also experience the burden of trying to protect her parents from experiencing negative and confusing emotions. In essence, she learns to avoid discussing with her parents those thoughts and feelings she believes will upset them. Subsequently, she feels less confirmed, understood, or supported and even more isolated as she is left to cope with her reactions on her own. By helping your child accept the complexity of her emotions, you will also help foster her ability to accept her own basic needs.

Acceptance of a child's basic needs. Acceptance involves recognizing and accepting our basic needs and not defensively masking them to avoid feeling hurt or vulnerable. Only when your child accepts his basic needs will he remain in touch with his genuine self. In contrast, when he denies, minimizes, or ignores his basic needs, he become less self-accepting and more disconnected from his feelings. In doing so, he becomes less open to his full humanity and to that of others. The child who lacks sensitivity to his own internal experiences, including his emotions, thoughts, and driving forces, is less able to be empathic with others or himself. This leads him to be even more vulnerable to anger and less able to move toward acceptance and forgiveness.

As described by William Pollack in his book *Real Boys,* many boys try to adapt to a "boy code," a way of being a boy or man that calls for masking or denying many feelings.[1] Boys are encouraged not to acknowledge or discuss real hurt or vulnerability in order to live up to an image of masculinity—an image maintained for themselves and others. And yet boys, just like girls, have real needs for connection, recognition, respect, and love. When children do not accept such needs, they are less able to progress toward acceptance and forgiveness of themselves or others. In fact, much of anger is based on these needs being ignored or denied. When children and adolescents do not acknowledge and accept these longings, they are more likely to experience isolation and the pain that leads to anger. In fact, boys who demonstrate aggression often do so as a vengeful reaction to their underlying pain. In doing so, they distract themselves from feeling emotionally weak about experiencing emotional pain.

The denial of basic needs is expressed by the angry child or teen who responds with "I don't care" as a way of dealing with disappointment or longing for connection. An adolescent or child may even convince himself that he really does not care, as a way of denying his needs and wants. At this point, he is telling himself and others, "You can't hurt me because I no longer have a need or want." When this happens, children and adolescents become stuck in a web of hurt and anger with little, if any, capacity for acceptance and forgiveness.

Distinguish between wants and needs. Acceptance necessitates distinguishing between and accepting the difference between wants and needs. For example, an eight-year-old boy may very much want to be accepted by a particular soccer team. His desire may be so strong that he experiences it as a need rather than a want. But while he strongly wants to be on the team, what are the real driving needs behind his desire? He may need connection to, as well as acceptance and recognition from, his peers, his parents, and himself.

Assume this team does not accept him. Clearly, rejection causes intense pain and anger. How could he deal with these feelings? He may continue to maintain the unrealistic expectation that he needs to be accepted by this specific team. Concluding that acceptance by this team will always ensure his future acceptance by others is unrealistic. Similarly, he would be unrealistic to conclude that his rejection implies that he is a failure or that he will never have his needs met.

There are times, when in spite of all his efforts, a child may not be accepted or recognized by those whom he wants most to accept him. Helping him accept this involves helping him distinguish between his wishes and his needs and assisting him to develop skills or strategies to help meet his desires. However, at some point he may need to be helped to realize that some of his needs or desires may be satisfied elsewhere. Acceptance in this situation involves acknowledging the reality of the situation and developing ways of moving on to increase the likelihood that his needs will be met. For example, if the soccer team does not accept him, you may help him problem-solve to determine what actions he can take to change the situation. He may decide to approach certain peers individually and share his reactions with them. He may seek them out in an effort to clarify what happened. He may channel his energies in ways that are nurturing for him, seeking out another team or improving his skills. Or he may seek out relationships with other people in groups that are more likely to accept him as he is.

Promoting acceptance. You can help children and adolescents move toward acceptance by doing the following:

1. Help your child identify the components of the model of anger as they apply to his own anger.
2. Model acceptance in your own life.
3. Model acceptance in managing your anger in your relationship with your child.

Modeling acceptance is the most powerful tool for helping your child learn it. This involves demonstrating acceptance of your emotions, wants, and needs, and acknowledgment of realistic and unrealistic conclusions and expectations. Children learn from what you say but, most significant, they learn by observing and modeling what you do. You especially model acceptance when you communicate support and permission for self-acceptance. In fact, your acceptance of your child serves as the foundation for his self-acceptance and, subsequently, fosters his ability to progress toward acceptance and forgiveness of himself and others.

When I was acting as assistant principal in an elementary school, two third graders, Chuck and Jeff, who were good friends, were referred to me following an intense argument that occurred between them while they were working on their respective art projects and escalated to a physical exchange. I asked each boy to describe his view of the incident. Both Chuck and Jeff reported how each had wanted to use the one pair of scissors, the one tube of glue, and the one roll of tape at the same time. I then asked them to share their thoughts and feelings regarding the event. Each boy described feeling treated unfairly, being bullied by the other, and feeling ignored and angry. I then helped each of them to clearly identify his expectations and conclusions regarding the event.

Both Chuck and Jeff shared the same expectation—being the first to use the supplies. In exploring their conclusions, each boy described the other as trying to control or take advantage of him. Each boy thought the other was self-centered and inconsiderate. They also talked about their impatience and competition to finish first. During further discussion, Chuck and Jeff discussed how the fight was a way of dealing with their disappointment and anger. While they were not prepared for a lengthy discussion, I helped them to fully recognize and acknowledge the event and identify their expectations and reactions to it. I also helped them to distinguish between unrealistic and realistic expectations and conclusions regarding their dispute, and eventually they both fully acknowledged that it would have been impossible to use the supplies at exactly the same time.

Following this discussion, we explored more constructive strategies for managing their anger. They arrived at several alternative solutions to the problem: rotating the use of the supplies, flipping a coin to see who would use them first, or asking the teacher for more supplies.

Before telling them to return to class, I made a suggestion that completely caught them off guard: I requested that they not shake hands at that moment. This response was very different from how other adults had responded to them following similar arguments. I told them, "Both of you still seem hurt and a little angry with each other right now. So, for right now, I'm not going to ask you to shake hands. Maybe you'll decide to make up in half an hour, maybe by the end of the day, maybe by the end of the week . . . or maybe you want to stay angry for some reason and will decide to no longer be friends. You get to choose how and when you want to let go of your hurt and anger."

Each boy left my office with an expression of surprise on his face—and they had their arms around each other's shoulders by the time they were halfway down the hall.

I was intent on helping Chuck and Jeff accept their thoughts and emotions and clarify their expectations, and I wanted to provide them with alternative ways for managing their anger. I was intent on helping them focus on acceptance. I was also intent on helping each boy realize that he could choose to hold on to his anger or to let go of it.

Forgiveness

Forgiveness, like acceptance, is a process that takes time and involves active self-reflection. Those who study forgiveness emphasize that it is a state of mind—an attitude that we can develop when dealing with hurt and anger.

Forgiveness, like acceptance, is blocked when anger is denied, minimized, ignored, or turned into chronic resentment. Such resentment is characterized by ongoing self-talk that is both conscious ("loud" self-talk) and unconscious ("quiet" self-talk). This dialogue may include statements beginning with "I could have ...," "I should have .... ," "He should have ...," and "If only ..." The self-talk, fueled by resentment, may include self-questioning or questioning why the other, the world, or God could have let such an event happen. Resentment destructively consumes time and energy and, in doing so, detracts from healthy living. The destructive aspect of resentment is well described by Robin Casarjian in her book *Forgiveness:* "Resentment has been compared to holding onto a burning ember with the intention of throwing it at another, all the while burning yourself."[2]

As emphasized throughout this book, holding on to anger can also have a physical impact on us. When we revisit anger in our thoughts and feelings, with and without our awareness, we also carry resentment in our bodies. Muscular tension that accompanies anger is reexperienced during periods of resentment. This can be most clearly seen by doing a part of the visual relaxation exercise described in Chapter 11.

Imagine a place that you have been to or would like to go to that is very peaceful, relaxing, and safe. Make the image in your mind as real as possible by attending to the colors, shapes, and textures of the objects in your scene. Again, imagine how the air feels in your scene, and the sounds or stillness that may be present. Shift your attention to your body and to how relaxed your breathing and muscles are as you imagine yourself in this very safe and peaceful setting. Do this for several minutes.

Now think about an event that led you to become angry in the recent past. Visualize the details of that event so that it is as real as possible in your mind's eye. Focus on the details of your scene for several minutes. Then shift your attention to your body. In most instances you will notice that your muscles are tenser and your breathing more rapid and shallow. This reveals the powerful influence of thoughts and images on your body tension. And research shows a correlation between chronic hostility and physical illness such as cardiac disease and hypertension.

Barriers to Forgiveness

Forgiveness is a difficult process for individuals of any age. Even when we want to commit ourselves to forgiveness, we may face obstacles to maintaining this commitment. One way to better understand how barriers inhibit forgiveness is to view them as motivations that compete with forgiveness. So although your child may be motivated to accept and forgive, he may have competing motivations that interfere with practicing forgiveness.

The need to feel in control. Some children and teens maintain their anger in an effort to experience a sense of control. They avoid acknowledging to themselves and others the intense underlying negative emotions that fuel their anger. It is more comfortable to experience anger and direct it outward than to acknowledge hurt, shame, or disappointment. This is especially the case for a child or adolescent who has experienced much hurt or even abuse and, as a result, has intense feelings of vulnerability. He may use anger to protect himself from revisiting such feelings.

While a child may experience some sense of control through his attempts to avoid feeling vulnerable, he really loses control by doing that. In actuality, he becomes unwittingly driven to avoid feeling hurt, disappointed, or helpless. At times, he may even begin to avoid situations that may provoke such emotions. Consequently, he becomes driven by and controlled by the need to avoid the discomfort of feeling vulnerable.

Anger may get people to do what we want them to do. Sometimes a child or teen believes that expressing only anger is the way to get things to happen or to control others. The high school student discussed earlier is a good example of this dynamic. When practicing with the other members of the basketball team, he typically expressed intense anger at his peers when they made mistakes. He had learned that when he expressed anger toward them, to some degree they would exert more effort. Anger is sometimes effective because others may respond out of fear and discomfort associated with being the target of anger. Children and adolescents who use anger this way are often children who have witnessed others do the same. They may have observed a parent, a peer, or another adult practicing this approach. They are often the targets of others' misdirected anger. While this strategy may occasionally achieve its intended results, it often leads to fear, resentment, and withdrawal by those who are on the receiving end of the anger.

Expressing anger may keep others away. Expressing anger verbally or through nonverbal means may actually be protective for many children and adolescents. Anger serves as a signal that others should back off. Certainly, there are times when such anger is helpful and protective. However, it interferes with more mature and assertive ways of setting limits and, ultimately, reduces the likelihood of increased intimacy.

Holding on to anger as a way of maintaining a sense of being "right." The need to be "right" is a very powerful force, especially for children who have self-doubts, who have difficulty dealing with a difference of opinion, or who tend to see things as black or white. Many children, teens, and adults expend a tremendous amount of energy in an effort to be right and to be seen as being right. This is often the price we pay in a culture that has so overly valued perfection. Harold Kushner states in *How Good Do We Have to Be?* that "a lot of misery could be traced to this one mistaken notion: we need to be perfect for people to love us and we forfeit that love if we ever fall short of perfection."[3]

Using anger to avoid being intimate. When we communicate anger *and* the feelings behind it, we are being open, candid, and vulnerable. This type of communication reflects a longing for understanding and connection. Some children may not move past anger because they fear intimacy or opening themselves up for potential hurt. Some may unwittingly hold on to anger to avoid experiencing caring.

Fifteen-year-old Justin struggled with conflicts regarding dependence and independence. He wanted closeness with his peers and his parents at the same time as he wanted to see himself as being independent. He had increasingly been spending more time with peers and communicating less candidly with his mother, and he was becoming more and more angry toward his father for not wanting to share in some of the activities they used to engage in together. At the same time, he felt childish and was self-critical about his wish to spend time with his father. Justin felt conflicted, and his anger served to distract him from his conflict. He was apprehensive about being honest with his father. On one hand, without being fully aware of it, he was somewhat fearful that his father might respond positively by offering to spend time with him. If his father did make himself available, Justin would be forced to acknowledge his own internal conflicts about closeness with his father. On the other hand, he was concerned that his father would reject his requests for time together. It was easier for Justin to remain angry toward his parents than to experience these conflicts.

Maintaining ties with others by remaining angry. Susan was nine years old when her parents divorced. She remained extremely angry toward her father because he did not make much time for her following the divorce. Six years later (and three years after her mother had remarried), Susan still remained bitter toward her father. Her emotions and thoughts focused on her wish for closeness with her dad. By remaining focused on what she did not have, she was not available to accept the genuine love and concern that were being offered by her stepfather. In spite of her stepfather's sincere efforts to reach out for closeness with her, Susan maintained her connection with her father. By holding on to her anger and thoughts regarding her father, she sabotaged all her stepfather's attempts at connection. She was unable to really give up her relationship with her father and make room for a new relationship. And yet, by holding on to her anger, she avoided mourning and fully acknowledging her hurt and sadness that her father was no longer available for the kind of relationship she most desired to have with him.

Holding on to anger as a way to avoid taking responsibility. When children and teens hold on to anger, they focus on others as being responsible for their feelings, thoughts, and actions. Remaining angry distracts them from accepting the fact that while another person may have a strong impact on them, they alone are responsible for their actions. While children and teens may not always seem able to be responsible and, in fact, may lack certain skills needed to take responsibility, they can learn these skills.

You can best teach your child this lesson by modeling the strategy of moving on. A father demonstrates moving on when in spite of having a distant or abusive relationship with his own father, he works at developing a nurturing and intimate relationship with his son. A mother demonstrates this in daily life when she shares experiences of anger and hurt, expresses the thoughts related to the experience, and addresses it and moves on.

Personality factors predisposing us to quickly become angry. Recent research regarding forgiveness suggests that individuals with certain types of personality are more likely to experience anger.[4] Specifically, people who are quick to feel personally slighted have a low tolerance for frustration and have less ability to soothe themselves when experiencing negative emotions. As a result, they are more likely to become angry and remain angry when their needs are not satisfied. People who are prone to feel that life is unfair may experience an immediate loss of self-esteem. In contrast, a relatively mature capacity for being objective and regulating our impulses and emotions is a prerequisite for forgiveness. Some individuals, perhaps because of early and severe hurt, lack such objectivity and capacity for self-regulation. As a result, they may be paralyzed with anger and pain that interferes with movement toward forgiveness.

Some individuals have such a fragile (or overly inflated) sense of self that they have a diminished capacity for being empathic with others. They are only minimally able to recognize and identify with the emotions or motivations of others. However, because the capacity for being empathic is another component of forgiveness, individuals who are less empathic are more likely to feel slighted and are less sensitive to the needs of others and themselves. Their diminished capacity to be empathic leaves them more vulnerable to becoming angry and less open to forgiveness.

Components of Forgiveness

The following characteristics define forgiveness.

When we forgive, we do not condone another's behavior. Helping your child practice forgiveness does not mean encouraging her to ignore her feelings when her best friend disappoints her. In fact, as emphasized in the discussion of acceptance, a child needs to recognize and accept the range of her emotional reactions and thoughts related to her disappointment. Helping a child forgive means helping her explore options for dealing with her reactions so that she does not become stuck in her anger.

We are not weak when we practice forgiveness. Children and teens can more readily learn forgiveness when they are helped to realize that forgiveness does not reflect weakness. In reality, forgiveness fosters strength. When a child or teen practices forgiveness, he increases control over his life. Through forgiveness he is able to direct his energies toward meeting his needs and wants rather than focusing them on the object of his anger. In spite of hurt, disappointment, and anger, forgiveness helps him become less dependent on another person to satisfy his needs or wants. Similarly, through forgiveness, he is no longer held hostage by the belief that he must seek revenge to make his life better.

For example, the child whose best friend disappoints him can remain focused on his anger or choose to do something about it. If he stays focused on his anger, his intense disappointment may lead him to conclude that he could never trust his friend again. In contrast, he may decide to give his best friend another chance, or he may discuss his disappointment and anger with his friend to determine if his friend is understanding or remorseful. Through acceptance, he can clarify which of his expectations or conclusions are realistic or unrealistic. He may decide that his unrealistic conclusions led to his disappointment and anger. Or he may conclude that he needs to develop more realistic expectations of his friend. At that point he can decide if he wants to redefine the friendship. He may act in one of a variety of ways to make himself less vulnerable to disappointment by his friend. He may share less, expect less from the friendship, or resume the friendship with reduced trust and observe how it develops. A child or teen who is helped to accept his reactions and identify this repertoire of strategies will experience increased control and a sense of competency in managing hurt and anger. Helping him move toward forgiveness involves helping him realize that he can choose to maintain his anger or take actions to move beyond it.

Forgiveness takes time. As stated previously, forgiveness is a process that takes time. Each child has her own timeline in working toward forgiveness. Katie, age fifteen, told me she often became angry when her older sister, Beth, violated her privacy. In part this was related to the fact that Beth frequently went into Katie's room and took her CDs and clothes without first asking Katie for permission to do so. Katie indicated that when she was angry, she usually got over it in a couple of hours. In contrast, when Beth became angry with Katie, she remained angry for an entire day.

The only way to determine where your child is in the process of forgiveness is to maintain ongoing and open communication with him. You may conclude that your child has moved beyond anger if his actions or conversations do not reflect anger regarding the event that triggered anger for him. However, it is only through genuine communication and a trusting relationship that includes the kind of sharing advocated throughout this book that you will be more certain to what degree your child is forgiving.

Specific Steps to Promote Forgiveness

Forgiveness, like anger management, depends on learning a variety of skills. The following guidelines will help your child make progress in practicing the process of forgiveness.

Identify what it is that has hurt your child. By helping your child or teen discuss her anger and the feelings that lead to it, you will be helping her to specifically recognize and articulate her emotional reactions, her expectations, and her conclusions. Through further discussion you will help her identify needs or wants that have been disappointed. With each clarification of the components of anger, you will be helping your child or teen move toward forgiveness.

Determine what your child really needs to move past the hurt. Help your child clearly distinguish between what he wants and what he genuinely needs. Explain that needs are very different from wants. Your child needs food, shelter, clothing, and love. His desire to be accepted by a particular friend or group of friends is a hope or wish rather than a need. Certainly he needs friendship, acceptance, and connection with others. But no matter how strong his desire is to be accepted by a particular individual or group, it is not a need. A child is similarly expressing a wish and not a genuine need when he emphatically states that he needs a certain toy or to attend a certain event. This is a very difficult challenge for any parent. However, the best way to help a child manage his reactions in this situation is to allow him to express his feelings, provide support for his anger and disappointment, and, most important, help him realize that even though he feels his desire is a need, it is not.

Helping a child distinguish between a want and a need becomes more complicated when a child is convinced that his entire future is dependent on one single event. For example, a high school senior may believe that her entire success in life depends on getting an A in one class, gaining admission to a certain school, or winning a certain competition. While not succeeding at such challenges may result in extreme disappointment and hurt over the loss of genuine opportunities, life can go on and other actions can be taken to satisfy the basic need behind these desires. It may be especially difficult for you to help your child make this distinction if you are also convinced that the desire is a need. The difficulty in making this distinction is often related to all-or-nothing thinking: "If I don't succeed at this challenge, I am a failure." It is difficult to mourn the loss of opportunities. However, such mourning is an essential component of forgiveness of others and oneself.

Identify what you can realistically expect from yourself and others. Forgiveness very much involves clarifying whether we have realistic or unrealistic expectations for ourselves and for others. When a child can make this distinction, she can more readily decide whether she should work on a relationship, adjust her expectations regarding this relationship, or terminate the relationship. When an adolescent can answer this question, she can be more forgiving of herself and others when her expectations are not satisfied. This does not imply that she has to condone the actions of others when they disappoint her. Similarly, forgiveness does not mean she should stop trying to meet the expectations she has for herself.

Identify the advantages and disadvantages of communicating your anger. Helping children and teens move toward forgiveness involves helping them identify the advantages and disadvantages of expressing their thoughts and feelings related to their anger.

Recall Russell, the twelve-year-old who was referred to me because of increased conflicts at home and disruptive behavior at school. Although at first hesitant to share his feelings, he soon revealed much disappointment and anger over the fact that although the entire family shared many enjoyable activities together, Russell never had special time alone with his father. Russell was helped to clarify his expectations, his conclusions, and the range of his emotions, including his anger regarding his disappointment with his father.

Russell was encouraged to role-play various ways of expressing himself to his father in order to determine the best and most comfortable way to communicate that he wanted more one-on-one time. He then role-played his father in an effort to better understand and predict how his father might feel and how he might react. Once he had rehearsed a conversation with which he was comfortable, Russell decided to take a chance and speak to his dad. I had met only briefly with his father but was fairly optimistic that he would respond positively to Russell.

However, Russell appeared quite sullen the next time we met. He told me that his father had become agitated in reaction to his request for time together and criticized him for being selfish. Subsequently, I met with both Russell and his father, separately and together.

Through discussion, Russell's father was able to further explore and understand his reaction. He reported that he was the second oldest child in a family with six children. As he discussed his family experience, he acknowledged that he too had experienced hurt and disappointment about wanting some special time with his own dad. Russell's grandfather had always worked very hard, and he had communicated to his children both directly and indirectly that any free time he had would be spent with the entire family.

Russell's father realized that his negative response to his son's request came from this background. Further discussion revealed that when he thought about spending time with his son, he would also revisit some of the pain he experienced as a child when his own wishes for one-on-one time with his father were rejected. By revisiting these feelings and working on his forgiveness, Russell's father was more able to spend time with his son.

Forgiveness is an ongoing process. Forgiveness is a complex process in which your child repeatedly makes the commitment to forgive even though she may, at times, reexperience hurt and anger. At those times, she will need to make a conscious decision to forgive. As the process of forgiveness unfolds, the intensity of these emotions will diminish. Similarly, the duration of time between reexperiencing such reactions will increase. To some degree, this process is very much like mourning.

Forgiveness and Mourning

Forgiveness shares many similarities with mourning. Like mourning, forgiveness is a process that may involve self-talk beginning with "If only ... ," "What if ...," "I should have ...," "He should have ...," or "She could have ..." During forgiveness and mourning, we initially focus our thoughts and emotions on the person being forgiven or mourned. During the process of forgiveness, especially at the beginning of the process, we may picture in our minds, over and over again, different scenarios about what could have been, or relive our past experiences with the other person.

Forgiveness, like mourning, involves grieving the loss of hopes as well as realistic and unrealistic expectations. Forgiveness may also include giving up unrealistic conclusions—the characteristic meaning one gives to events. A child who is quick to feel slighted may characteristically conclude that people do not like him, that he is not lovable, or that he has done something wrong. These conclusions become a part of one's self-image when they are repeatedly made. For these reasons, when a child learns forgiveness, he entertains new self-images as he gives up a part of his identity. He may feel scared and anxious in making this change.

Forgiveness, like mourning, is a process that requires healing. Forgiveness, like mourning, consists of a person gradually investing more thoughts and emotions in the present, including relationships, activities, and the excitement and challenge of daily living.

Healing, as a part of forgiveness, implies letting go of the need to blame or find fault with ourselves or others. Real forgiveness involves moving beyond globally viewing the other (or ourselves) as all bad. In contrast, maintaining resentment involves focusing mostly on the negative aspect of the other or ourselves. To the degree that we can look beyond the negative behavior and consider the person as a whole, we practice forgiveness that reflects compassion.

Forgiveness, Empathy, and Compassion

In *Forgiveness*, Robin Casarjian suggests that when we forgive, we are genuinely more loving and able to consider the greater humanity of another person. As such, forgiveness depends on and includes practicing empathy and compassion.

We are empathic when we recognize and are sensitive to the emotions, thoughts, and experiences of another person. We are empathic with someone who has upset us when we are able to understand, intellectually and emotionally, how a person could act the way she does. Being empathic, we focus on more fully understanding the other person instead of focusing only on how we are impacted. Instead of selectively attending only to our immediate and personal conclusions, we consider alternative motivations from the other person's perspective.

Similarly, our ability to empathize with others allows us to be more tolerant of their differences. The capacity to be tolerant very rapidly diminishes anger. As emphasized by Redford Williams and Virginia Williams in *Anger Kills*, "All you have to do to practice tolerance is to accept other people as they are, not as you would like them to be."[5]

When we are compassionate we are more able to experience another person in a way that recognizes his pain and vulnerabilities. When we practice compassion we think and act in ways that recognize the whole person and do not see a specific behavior as reflecting her "essence." Being compassionate involves viewing the other person, in all of her humanity, as imperfect and as doing her best with what she has.

In contrast, by remaining angry toward someone who has led to my pain, I maintain a global image of that person as "one who gives pain." I am less open to his humanity when maintaining this view. "Looking beyond his behavior" does not mean ignoring his behavior. Rather, it means that I acknowledge his behavior but experience him as more than his action. Through compassion I experience the other person as someone who is capable of causing pain, not as someone who only causes pain.

By recognizing another person's greater humanity, I become more open to viewing his action as reflecting just a part of a more complex person. If he failed to meet my expectations, perhaps he was not available to do so. If he failed to meet an expectation, perhaps his personal pain, lack of awareness, lack of sensitivity, lack of skills, or other barrier contributed to his failure to meet my expectation. As I look at another person with a more open mind, I begin to see him as human: possessing both strengths and weaknesses, and imperfect.

The essence of maintaining a compassionate view allows us to empathize with another's weakness, and compassion helps foster forgiveness. While this state of mind is not easy to achieve, the process of forgiveness includes a commitment to strive to maintain this perspective. It is a perspective that recognizes that each of us is imperfect. It emphasizes equality in our common struggles to meet life's complex challenges. We see others as having motivations, expectations, and conclusions that may be realistic or unrealistic. We see them as having goals, hopes, and the range of human emotions. Most important, we can see them as having vulnerabilities.

It is a part of human nature to want to avoid the inner tension that accompanies ambivalence in our thoughts and feelings. The tension related to these contradictory or mixed thoughts and feelings is easily reduced when we view things in all-or-nothing or black-and-white terms. The more anger a child or teen experiences, the more quickly she may develop and maintain this too-simple perspective. When a child is angry, it is difficult for her to be aware of caring for the whole person, and it is a challenge to feel compassion. As described in previous chapters, her conclusions or assessment about her disappointment may, at that moment, be overly influenced by child logic. At such a moment, she experiences too much pain or anger to consider a more comprehensive view of the other person.

Your five-year-old may find it much easier to be angry and say "I hate you" than to acknowledge both his love and his anger. An adolescent may be quicker to feel slighted and experience just negative feelings toward a disappointing friend than to consider the motivations and feelings that influenced her friend's behavior. For these reasons, it is unrealistic to expect children and teens to experience compassion at the moment when they are experiencing their most intense anger. Dealing with anger is a process that takes time. Compassion, as a part of forgiveness, helps children and adolescents move beyond holding on to anger.

Forgiveness: Moving Beyond Guilt and Shame

Just as we may hold on to anger with others, we may have difficulty letting go of anger with ourselves. Such anger, in the form of guilt and shame, interferes with forgiveness of ourselves and of others. For this reason, being compassionate with oneself is an essential component of forgiveness when dealing with anger directed at oneself.

Certainly, some guilt is justified. When we have caused harm or acted unjustly to others, guilt serves as a signal and often provides direction for changing our behavior. In contrast, guilt is destructive when we hold on to it unduly and let it dominate our sense of self. At some point, holding on to guilt leaves us with a narrowed view of ourselves and interferes with moving on. Letting guilt dominate us leaves little room for developing positive self-esteem based on true growth and change. Compassion, as an element of forgiveness, allows us to move beyond a prolonged focus on our inability to measure up to a particular self-expectation. Again, such compassion does not deny the behavior, nor does it deny responsibility or guilt when either of those is justified. But being compassionate with ourselves allows us to accept our full humanity—that our needs are complex, that we have needs and expectations that are realistic and unrealistic, that we have hopes, and, most significant, that we have vulnerabilities. Forgiveness does not excuse such events or make attempts to deny them. Instead, the process of forgiveness involves committing ourselves to move toward accepting our humanity.

Forgiveness also involves moving beyond shame. This is often a difficult challenge because, as described in Chapter 7, while guilt is painful, it is not all-encompassing and it often leads to defining an action that can be taken to rectify a situation. In contrast, shame is much more profound and involves an all-embracing negative self-evaluation.

When we commit to forgiveness and to move beyond shame, we commit ourselves to the statement "I did something wrong" as opposed to "I am wrong." John Bradshaw, in his book *Healing the Shame That Binds You*, distinguishes between "passing shame" and "toxic shame."[6] Passing shame is a temporary experience. In contrast, toxic shame becomes a core component of our identity as a response to rejection, abuse, and abandonment. This leaves the child with a sense of being flawed and with an increased vulnerability to experience shame. Ironically, difficulties surrounding shame lead us to be more vulnerable to anger and to have difficulty letting go of it. It leads to self-talk and expectations that foster the experience of shame and related anger toward ourselves and others. As emphasized throughout the model of anger, it is only when we can become increasingly aware of these expectations and conclusions that we can be helped to move forward with forgiveness.

Strategies to Foster Forgiveness

While general strategies to foster forgiveness have been described above, the remainder of this chapter will focus on describing specific skills and strategies to help children and adolescents move toward forgiveness as a way of managing anger.

Using the model of anger to foster forgiveness. As discussed throughout this book, using the model of anger helps children and teens develop increased awareness of their needs, hopes, expectations, conclusions, and the range of emotions surrounding anger. Helping children work through any component of the model of anger moves them forward with an increased capacity for forgiveness. Helping children recognize the emotions that lead to anger assists them in recognizing the complexity of emotional life and increases self-acceptance, which translates into sensitivity to others. Helping children identify and develop more realistic expectations and conclusions further fosters the identification of ways to satisfy wants and needs and recognition of those that cannot be satisfied. In this way, children are helped to realize that, as Mick Jagger said, "You can't always get what you want, but if you try real hard, you may find, you get what you need."[7]

As an example, seven-year-old Billy can be helped to move toward forgiveness regarding anger when his friend Vince refuses to play with him. Specifically, he can be helped to recognize the disappointment and hurt that underlie his annoyance. In addition, he could be helped to recognize realistic and unrealistic conclusions he forms about himself or Vince.

As described in Chapter 8, Billy can be helped to identify possible conclusions such as "This must mean he does not like me," "Other children will no longer want to play with me," "He's an absolute jerk," or "Vince is so selfish." By helping him challenge himself with self-talk that considers alternative explanations, he will become less prone to personalize the rejection, see himself as flawed, or see his friend as just a mean and rejecting person. He may conclude that Vince's interests have changed, that his friend wants to spend time with others, that Vince is fickle, or that the other boy is annoyed as the result of a misunderstanding. Similarly, Billy may be helped to realistically appraise his contribution to the situation. Developing and practicing these alternative explanations are powerful steps that foster forgiveness.

As Billy recognizes his needs for companionship, he may decide to share his concerns with Vince, recognize the limitations of the friendship, or seek out the friendship of others. As he identifies alternative ways of meeting his needs, he will also learn how to move beyond his anger and disappointment. Billy will learn that forgiveness involves recognizing what he can control, what he cannot control, and knowing the difference.

The more you discuss the components of anger, the more your child will learn how to move toward forgiveness. However, it is by modeling forgiveness in your relationship with your child that you will have the most impact in teaching her acceptance and forgiveness as ways of dealing with anger. The more you accept and promote acceptance of her feelings, the more you encourage her to discuss and identify her expectations and conclusions in regard to her relationship with you. At the same time, the more you give her permission to brainstorm when problem solving, the more she will be able to accept and forgive in dealing with anger.

Finally, the more you give your child permission to move beyond unjustified guilt and shame, the more you will teach her forgiveness. This is a very complex challenge because it requires you to be sensitive to your own unjustified guilt and shame, to realize how such reactions have been motivators in your life, and to move beyond them. As you do this, you will be practicing compassion toward yourself and, as a result, be more able to help your child do the same.

Promoting and practicing compassion. Being compassionate with your child can enhance forgiveness. In part, this involves praising and nurturing your child for his attempts to improve himself, rather than focusing only on his failure to be perfect. It involves acknowledging his feelings whether you agree with them or not. It consists of recognizing that he may have unrealistic expectations and conclusions and helping him identify them. Practicing compassion involves letting your child know that you accept his anger but may disagree with how he expresses it. Compassion involves expressing your anger toward him in a way that focuses on a very specific behavior rather than devalues his whole being and leads to unnecessary guilt or shame. Compassion is further communicated when you are able to keep your child's humanity in your awareness. Compassion is similarly expressed when you maintain your awareness of your love for his essence even while you are frustrated, disappointed, or angry with him.

Your child experiences compassion when she experiences being taken seriously by you. The years that have passed since your own childhood or adolescence may make it difficult to really identify with, take seriously, or make sense of your child's emotions, expectations, and conclusions. Similarly, the lack of sufficient empathy and compassion from those who parented you may also interfere with your being available to be empathic and compassionate with your child. Taking time to listen to her in order to better understand her perspective truly communicates that you take her seriously. This does not mean you have to agree with her or feel compelled to satisfy her expectations. Your expression of empathy for her hurt, disappointment, or anger, while not necessarily satisfying an expectation or need, is another component of compassion.

The ability to be empathic and compassionate is especially difficult for a parent who does not want to disappoint a child. Parents who overly identify with the hurt or disappointment of a child have difficulty setting limits, saying no, and even being empathic. As stated earlier, if you are uncomfortable with emotional pain, you may avoid acknowledging when your child is in pain, protect your child from experiencing it, and not recognize it as a part of his experience. But children actually gain strength in being helped to sit with the disappointment and frustration of not having certain needs satisfied. These are children who learn a tolerance for frustration and the reality that not all wants and hopes are satisfied. These are children who are also helped to be sensitive and compassionate with the pain of others.

Acknowledging vulnerability. When children are openly encouraged to identify and evaluate expectations and conclusions, they are also helped to identify vulnerabilities. Children are helped to accept their vulnerabilities when they are nurtured and supported for trying their best and not just for perfection. Yet we live in a highly competitive time that reflects and fosters expectations for perfection, making it especially challenging to maintain this compassionate perspective.

Even for adults, any performance short of perfection is frequently devalued. These high expectations are so ingrained in many of us that we feel weak and inadequate when we do not achieve such lofty goals. In our roles as parents, discomfort associated with feeling weak or vulnerable interferes with our capacity to recognize or discuss our children's experience of vulnerability. Too, if we maintain such overly elevated expectations for ourselves, we very often model them for our children to learn.

Yet, in spite of intense pressure to compete, children and teens best develop forgiveness when they are rewarded and praised for effort and not just for perfection. They need to be supported and encouraged when they put forth their best efforts, not praised only for perfection. They also need support in expressing their vulnerabilities, especially those that relate to self-expectations for perfection. When a child is not allowed to discuss her vulnerability, she ends up feeling even more emotionally isolated from others and from herself. When a child receives the message that feeling vulnerable is a weakness, she directs a great amount of emotional energy toward minimizing or denying such emotions. When her vulnerability is denied, she is more likely to develop unrealistic expectations for others and for herself. Such denial leads to a greater predisposition to experience anger with others and herself. Consequently, she becomes less able to move on to acceptance and forgiveness.

Another outcome of a child's not being allowed to acknowledge and recognize his vulnerability might be a complete withdrawal from the pursuit of any new activity or challenge. This was reflected by Tim, an eighth grader, who decided to take guitar lessons after thinking about it for several years. Three months later he very abruptly discontinued his lessons. Tim initially claimed that he just lost interest in playing the guitar. When questioned further, he responded, "Well, my fingers hurt after practice. And even though I practiced about an hour every few days, after three months I still couldn't play a song as well as one I heard on the radio!" Tim indirectly communicated that he felt inadequate and that his expectations did not acknowledge the reality that learning to play a guitar takes effort. He had difficulty recognizing how unrealistic he was in his expectation that he sound like a professional after just three months of practice. Most important, by quitting, Tim avoided the feeling of vulnerability that is a natural part of taking on any new skill. It is the vulnerability that accompanies feeling inadequate. So instead of acknowledging that he felt inadequate, the feeling became a global self-assessment. In that situation, "I feel inadequate" becomes an unrealistic conclusion that "I am inadequate." For many teens like Tim, choosing to give up playing the guitar may seem like the most reasonable way to avoid the uncomfortable feelings that result from this conclusion.

Being compassionate involves being empathic with a child's sense of vulnerability. It involves helping him feel all right about himself while he also feels vulnerable. Being compassionate involves helping him be okay with feeling vulnerable and helping him move beyond it by developing realistic expectations and conclusions about himself and about others. When he can acknowledge feeling vulnerable, he is more likely to be compassionate. With compassion comes an increased potential for forgiveness when dealing with others and with himself.

Specific Exercises

Understanding other people's motivations. One strategy that helps a child move beyond anger toward forgiveness is to help him answer the following questions. This exercise should be performed at a time when he is calm and able to think clearly. He may initially need support in brainstorming as he tries to answer these questions.

1. What might have interfered with the other person doing what I hoped he would do?
2. What are five possible reasons that led him to do what he did—reasons that have absolutely nothing to do with me?
3. Realistically, is there anything I could have done to increase the likelihood that he would have done what I wanted?
4. What weakness or vulnerability might he have that led him to do what he did?
5. Realistically, is there anything I can do in the future to improve the situation?

6. Is my expectation based on a genuine need or a want?

Answering each of these questions helps promote a reality check regarding both the other person's behavior and the child's own behavior. The last question emphasizes the view that when someone hurts or disappoints us, it is helpful to look beyond our immediate reaction and try to identify the vulnerability that may have led the other person to his or her action.

Understanding what I really need. Another effective strategy to help children and teens move toward forgiveness is to help them differentiate between what they want and what they think they need.

Brian's grades began to drop gradually when he started seventh grade in a new school. Now, in eighth grade, though his reading skills were above grade level and he did not have any learning disabilities, his grades had fallen from A's and B's to C's and D's. He barely spoke during our first meetings. I sensed his silence reflected depression and anger. His mother had remarried two years ago, after being divorced from his father for three years. Although his stepfather was emotionally distant, he tried to take on a very active disciplinary role with Brian. Until this time, Brian had always been a well-behaved boy who tried to please both his mother and father. Only since his mother's remarriage had he begun to challenge attempts to discipline him. In time, Brian was able to discuss his anger about his parents' divorce, his strong feelings of loss regarding his dad, and his lack of closeness with his stepfather.

When asked directly what he was angry about, Brian indicated that he was hurt that his parents could not get along, that his dad had become increasingly self-absorbed, and that his stepfather was verbally abusive. When asked what he wished for, Brian replied that he had hoped to have a dad with whom he could do things and who loved him. I then asked him what would be different about his life if he had such a dad now. He thought about this for a while and responded, "I would just like to feel that my father loves me!" He cried and shared his anger about not feeling loved by his natural father or his stepfather. I agreed that all of us need love and that it hurts when the people we most want to love us are not available to provide that love. We spent several sessions exploring his hurt and disappointment. At one point, I asked him how he would feel about himself if he felt loved. With minimal hesitation, he responded, "I guess I would like myself better." Not all children or teens are as self-aware as Brian.

This was the starting point in helping Brian to better understand what he needed. While he needed love, he also needed to feel better about himself. Certainly he was justified in feeling hurt and angry toward both his father and stepfather. However, I helped him to understand that the conclusions he had made about not getting their love—that he himself was not lovable—were distorted. He was caught in a cycle of negative thinking that ran this way: "If they don't love me, I'm not lovable. I'll show them. Why please anyone? Why do well in school? They don't care." Brian's reduced academic performance was an expression of his anger.

Brian needed to acknowledge that he wanted love as well as his need to love himself. Through trusting himself and increasing his self-confidence, he was more able to take a risk and be candid about his wishes for an improved relationship with both his father and stepfather. While his attempts to improve these relationships were not always met with success, he made progress in meeting some of his expectations. Many sessions focused on helping Brian to feel more positive about himself and increase his ability to distinguish between his needs and wants. His progress involved learning to recognize his needs, developing realistic expectations about them, and his repeated experiences of anger and mourning as he continued to redefine his expectations of both men. He was also helped to nurture himself while accepting the caring that was available from his mother, relatives, and friends.

He did not deny his pain or anger. He made attempts to change the situation but did not remain embedded in resentment or paralyzed by his hurt and disappointment. While his relationships with his father and stepfather improved, neither was as emotionally available as Brian had hoped for. Brian went through a period of mourning—grieving related to hopes and desires that could not be satisfied. This is acceptance and forgiveness.

Letter writing. One strategy that is extremely effective in furthering the process of forgiveness is to encourage a child to compose a letter to the person with whom they experience anger. This is especially useful with an older child or teen, but it can be adapted to use with a younger child by having her dictate a message on a tape recorder. Emphasize that writing or dictating the letter is a separate and distinct activity from sending it. Encourage her to express the range of her emotions, including anger, and her expectations and conclusions surrounding the event(s) that led to her reaction. Suggest she also express her hope for how things should be in the future—how she wishes the other person will behave. Suggest she take time in composing the letter, put it aside for several days, and then reread and correct it.

After she has finished the letter, suggest she take time to write a letter that represents, based on her best insights, the other person's response.

This is a very powerful exercise for helping children and adolescents clarify their thoughts and emotions and what it is they hope the other person will say or do. Most important, it helps them explore how likely it is that the other person will meet their expectations. You can then explore with your child the differences between what she hopes for and how she really believes the other person will react. Even without sending the letter, a child or teen can, through her own statements, be helped to better identify expectations that may be unrealistic. Through discussion of the model of anger, you can help your child explore the range of emotions and thoughts regarding her experience. You can also help her better determine the potential benefits and potential harm related to actually sending the letter. Help her address the range of consequences that may occur if she is honest.

Emphasize that sending the letter involves taking a risk, and help your child explore how she might react if the other person does not respond favorably. This discussion is especially important for helping a child or teen realize that directing anger and pain toward another may, in fact, not be useful. Under some circumstances it may lead to further anger, fear, and tension for both individuals.

Many of the children and adolescents (and adults) I have worked with have done this exercise. Some have sent the letter, and others have not. What is most important is that by doing this exercise, they were helped to clarify their needs, wants, and expectations and were helped to move toward forgiveness.

Sitting with pain. Much of anger management and forgiveness related to anger depend on our ability to acknowledge and accept emotional pain. Extreme and impulsive anger, difficulties with letting go of resentment, and distracting ourselves from genuine emotions are often the result of not being able to genuinely sit with pain. In fact, many of the expressions of anger of children and teens are ways of shifting attention from their pain and attempts to distract themselves from this uncomfortable emotion. Helping a child sit with his pain involves being there for him to explore his experience in a very focused way. This calls for you to be empathic in a way that may be very challenging. To the degree that you tend to flee from your own emotional pain, you may be less available to engage your child in this exercise.

Engage your child in a discussion about his anger. Apply the model of anger and help him explore the many components related to his experience. When discussing his hurt or pain, take time to really communicate to him, directly and indirectly, that:

1. It is natural to experience pain even if his expectations or conclusions were unrealistic.
2. Pain needs to be experienced and expressed to help heal.

3. Pain needs to be labeled.
4. The intensity of pain reduces over time.
5. Pain is a part of life.
6. You are there to help him when he needs it.

The fact that your child's pain is based on unrealistic expectations or conclusions does not make the pain any less real or unjustifiable. It may lead to being more realistic in the future and should influence how he decides to manage his anger. But it does not mean that he is less entitled to feel pain or that his pain is silly or unimportant. Helping a child discuss his feelings offers him validation of his feelings. This helps him to experience your empathy and encourages him to be better connected with his true emotions. Clearly your validation of his emotions is not the same as validating how he manages his anger.

By labeling pain, I mean having a discussion with your child or teen in which he is helped to express the many aspects of his pain. Ask him what it feels like. Inquire whether he experiences his pain in any part of his body. Suggest he identify an image that best reflects his pain. Then use imagery to help him identify ways to help reduce that pain.

One child I worked with indicated that his emotional pain felt like a critter inside him slowly eating him. I encouraged him to identify ways of dealing with this critter—picturing it getting smaller, reminding himself that he was bigger than this critter and that he was not being physically harmed, and having him tell the critter that he will take care of it.

Reminding a child that pain takes time to manage is essential to helping her cope with pain as a process. Forecasting the course of her pain is a helpful strategy to emphasize this process. Remind her that she will experience the pain for a while, especially if it is over something very meaningful to her. Similarly, help her recognize that the intensity of the pain gradually reduces. Making the analogy to a physical hurt is another approach that helps children understand the course of pain. A physical injury is initially very painful, but the pain gradually subsides, with occasional flare-ups, as the healing progresses.

While we seek to lead lives without pain and do our best to protect our children from pain, there are times when each of us has moments of disappointment and emotional pain. Some of these are more severe than others. And some people have a greater share of pain. Helping children and teens recognize that pain is a part of life does not mean you emphasize the pain of life or forecast that they will invariably experience much pain. It does mean that when we have expectations that are not satisfied, when things happen that we do not want to happen, when we experience hurt or disappointment, when we experience loss, we will experience pain. Sharing this discussion also emphasizes that it is unrealistic to expect that everything will always go well.

Perhaps the most meaningful way to help your child with her pain is to emphasize that you are there for her. Your being available to discuss her emotions, thoughts, or experiences related to her pain communicates your empathy, your connection, and your love. In your presence your child will experience nurturance and develop a sense of self-soothing that is an essential component in dealing with her pain—and in learning to forgive.

All of the strategies described in this chapter can be related to other people in his life or to characters in videos, books, or other media in an effort to help your child better understand forgiveness. You will often find that he is more comfortable thinking about and discussing the experiences of these other people or characters rather than more directly address experiences in his life. Any strategy you use to help your child make sense of and manage anger will help him in the process of forgiveness. For it is by constructively responding to anger and finding ways to genuinely let go of it that we learn to forgive others and ourselves.

III

Special Considerations

15

Rewarding Behaviors

Behavior management programs have been used to help children and adolescents in a variety of settings. In this chapter, I discuss the application of this approach for helping children and adolescents manage anger. As the term implies, the focus of this approach is on behavior rather than on the self-reflection needed to make sense of anger. A behavior management program involves the use of rewards, privileges, and consequences. These are presented to the child in such a way as to help increase desirable behaviors and reduce undesirable behaviors.

For example, a child or adolescent may be rewarded with money or extra television viewing time for practicing relaxation exercises. Similarly, he may be rewarded for reducing aggressive behavior or for more constructively expressing anger.

In contrast, inappropriate behaviors may be punished. For example, a child may have to forfeit television viewing time after hitting her younger brother. An adolescent may be grounded for striking his fist against a door while arguing with a parent.

When to Use a Reward Program for Anger Management

A behavior management program can be a very powerful means of helping children and adolescents develop and maintain certain behaviors. However, it is recommended only under very specific circumstances.[1]

A reward program should be reserved for working with children and teens who resist making efforts to make sense of and manage their anger and for those who refuse to take part in learning the strategies described in this book. These children may resist because they are rebellious, need more structure, are impulsive, or for other reasons lack internal motivations for making sense of and managing anger. Their anger, hurt, lack of ability, or other factors may lead them to be minimally motivated to reflect on their thoughts and emotions. They may refuse to practice relaxation techniques, use foul language instead of feeling words, or act aggressively instead of exploring their anger. In contrast, they may deny or minimize any anger and so feel no need to discuss it.

Determine if your child's refusal to engage in such discussion is based on fear, has to do with a lack of skills in self-reflection, or is related to some trauma that may underlie her resistance. A behavior reward program may not be necessary if these concerns are identified as the basis for her resistance and addressed appropriately.

Using a formal reward program is not necessary if your child is already motivated to engage in the strategies and exercises presented throughout the book. He does not need to be rewarded for behaviors that are already a part of his repertoire. Clearly, if he engages with you in discussing his feelings and cooperates in working on the strategies presented, he may already possess the internal motivation to make sense of and manage anger. Similarly, engaging in such discussions demonstrate that he experiences a level of comfort and trust in himself that allows for self-disclosure. His capacity to discuss his thoughts and emotions with you also demonstrates that your relationship has fostered comfort and trust. He is already experiencing positive rewards for his efforts and behaviors.

Do not use a reward program if your child is even minimally cooperative. Progress takes time, effort, and commitment. You may be tempted to use a behavior reward program in an effort to hasten his progress. However, when used in this way, the behavior management program may only distract him from furthering intrinsic motivation for self-reflection and change in general.

The Need for Addressing Behavior and Self-Reflection

When a behavioral reward program for anger management focuses only on behavior, a child or adolescent gains little self-awareness regarding the emotions, motivations, expectations, or conclusions that influence his arousal of anger. As a result, the reward program may lead to self-monitoring of behavior, but it does not directly promote self-reflection unless self-reflective behaviors and discussions of self-reflection are rewarded. These behaviors need to be specifically identified and rewarded in order to help your child genuinely make sense of and manage anger.

A behavioral reward program can help a child or teen learn constructive ways to manage anger. But if he is to make sense of anger, he needs to be rewarded for self-reflection regarding his motivations, related emotions, expectations, and conclusions regarding situations that arouse his anger. A behavioral reward program does not provide an understanding of anger management but offers techniques to help promote specific behaviors that foster constructive anger management. It is not a replacement for your modeling constructive ways of managing anger. Similarly, it is not a replacement for teaching children and adolescents to reflect on their internal experiences related to anger management.

General Guidelines

Identifying the Target Behavior

A target behavior is an identified behavior that you want to help your child increase or decrease. A key issue to keep in mind when developing a reward program regarding anger management is that you are rewarding more-constructive ways of managing anger and punishing less-constructive ways of managing anger. You will need to clearly identify for yourself and for your child those behaviors that you target. They should involve actions that are clearly observable and can be recorded. Descriptions of such behavior should be defined so clearly that there is no disagreement about whether the specific behavior did or did not occur.

Make sure you are punishing a specific way of expressing anger rather than the general expression of anger. The punishment should be a consequence for the way anger was expressed. The goal is to reward a child for a more constructive expression of anger rather than for not expressing anger at all.

Below is a list of sample target behaviors that you may wish to reward.

- Discussing anger
- Discussing the emotions related to anger
- Exploring expectations regarding anger
- Exploring conclusions regarding anger
- Exploring motivations related to anger
- Practicing relaxation exercises
- Engaging in physical ways of managing anger that are constructive
- Discussing physical reactions to anger
- Writing a letter to express feelings
- Keeping a journal to express feelings
- Learning new words to describe emotions
- Discussing examples of anger from the media
- Discussing how characters from books or movies manage anger
- Communicating assertively rather than aggressively (i.e., using "I" statements)
- Being candid in communications

This list identifies very specific behaviors that should be encouraged as constructive ways for making sense of and managing anger. In contrast, when you punish undesirable behaviors, you clearly help a child to recognize what he should not be doing but give little direction for new and alternative behaviors. This is a major reason for emphasizing the use of positive rewards to increase desired behavior (and not negative outcomes to decrease undesired behaviors). Here is a list of target behaviors that you may wish to reduce or eliminate.

- Tantrums
- Yelling
- The use of foul language
- Hitting oneself or others
- Breaking things
- Being disruptive as a way of expressing anger
- Devaluing others

A comprehensive behavior management program consists of rewarding both the demonstration of more constructive behaviors and the absence of negative behaviors. For example, you could reward your eight-year-old both for reduced use of foul language when he is angered and for being able to discuss his feelings regarding the event that provoked his anger. Similarly, your adolescent daughter could be rewarded both for candidly sharing her anger with her sister and for not devaluing her. Rewards should be based mostly on how your child constructively manages anger.

Be Realistic

Target behaviors that your child can realistically master. Factors to be considered in making these choices are age, intelligence, vocabulary, and emotional maturity, including the capacity to self-reflect, identify emotions, and manage anxiety.

Be realistic when identifying target behaviors. For example, if your nine-year-old is able to identify unrealistic conclusions or expectations, you may want to encourage him to reflect on these components of his anger. In contrast, your five-year-old may need to be taught words that describe his emotions before he can realistically be ready to receive rewards for discussing them. When working with some adolescents you may have to start by targeting relaxation techniques long before they can be helped to really identify other emotions surrounding anger.

Once you complete your lists of behaviors to be increased and those to be eliminated, discuss them with your child so that she understands exactly what you mean and expect of her. These behaviors, as well as any part of the reward program, should be presented in a written format in order to promote clear expectations for both you and your child. A sample chart will be provided later in this chapter.

Identifying a Baseline of Behavior

Identifying a baseline of behavior is an essential first step when using a behavior management program. The baseline is a record of the frequency of how often a particular behavior is demonstrated within a specified period of time. In order to develop a baseline, observe your child over a period of days and record the number of times that behavior is evidenced during that time frame. A baseline may involve keeping a record of the frequency with which a desired behavior occurs and how often the child demonstrates behaviors you want to reduce or eliminate. For example, you may want to develop a baseline of how often your adolescent practices relaxation techniques or how frequently your seven-year-old appropriately discusses anger related to a genuinely anger-provoking event. Similarly, you may want your child to replace tantrum behavior by more constructive behaviors when he becomes angry. Observing him over a week, you may find that his baseline for tantrums is four occurrences in that one week. The baseline provides you a starting point for assessing progress toward the target behavior.

Use Positive Rewards

Overall, positive rewards are more powerful than punishment in encouraging positive behavior. A positive reward is a reward that is given after the desired behavior is demonstrated. In contrast, punishment is a negative consequence that occurs when an unwanted behavior arises. This might include taking something away or denying a privilege. While punishment may be necessary, as discussed shortly, it should be used minimally, since positive reinforcement has a greater potential for helping children learn new behaviors, in part because it rewards clearly defined and appropriate behaviors.

Token Rewards

A token reward is a reward in the form of chips, stars, coupons, points, or even play money that a child can later "cash in" to obtain rewards. There are several benefits to token rewards in a behavior reward program. Primarily, the use of tokens allows for greater consistency—the same behavior leads to obtaining a specific number of points. The use of tokens allows for greater mobility, since you and your child can carry the token rewards more easily. The rewards can be presented in a timely manner immediately after the behavior is demonstrated. It is important that your child understands the process and is capable of calculating the addition of points. Since the process parallels the use of money and allows for greater flexibility in choosing rewards, using a token program will increase your child's motivation to make changes in her behavior.

By using tokens, you can also occasionally reward your child with a bonus—a greater number of points than originally assigned to the behavior. Doing this periodically has been found to be highly effective in strengthening the motivation for behavioral change.

Assign the behaviors a certain value, with a more challenging behavior deserving a greater number of points. For example:

- Performing relaxation exercises = 3 points
- Discussing the emotions related to anger = 3 points
- Discussing the expectations related to anger = 3 points
- Discussing the conclusions related to anger = 3 points
- Showing how an incident from the media exemplifies part of the model of anger = 2 points
- Writing a letter to express anger = 2 points
- Keeping a journal = 2 points

Similarly, you may give a child a greater number of points for not demonstrating (for a period of time, such as an hour, an afternoon, or an entire day—the specific interval will be determined by the baseline) the behaviors you most strongly want to see reduced. For example:

- Reducing tantrums = 5 points
- Reducing yelling = 3 points

- Not breaking anything = 5 points
- Not hitting others = 7 points

Determine the number of points needed to redeem a specific reward. Examples of rewards and their redemption values might be:

- Thirty minutes of extra TV time = 15 points
- Thirty minutes of video game time = 15 points
- Action figure = 10 points
- Fifteen minutes on the telephone = 20 points
- Choice of a restaurant = 12 points
- Permission to have a friend sleep over = 30 points
- Permission to stay up an extra half hour = 15 points
- Getting to see a specific movie = 10 points
- Permission to use the car = 25 points
- Extra allowance = 25 points

Your child is then allowed to choose from the rewards based on how many points he has accumulated. Try to discourage him from saving the tokens for more than a few days. Postponing the reward often leads to reduced motivation, especially for younger children, who have little frustration tolerance.

It is advisable to reward young children with tangible tokens (star stickers, paper coupons, or chips), while older children and adolescents can easily accept points that are recorded on a chart.

Negative Consequences

The major focus of an effective behavior management program should be providing positive rewards for desired behaviors. A child or teen knows exactly what is expected of him when the desired behavior is clearly described. In contrast, punishing an undesirable behavior, while emphasizing what behavior to reduce or eliminate, does not clearly identify the specific behavior that should be practiced instead.

But there are times when negative consequences follow undesirable behavior. Some advocates of behavior management programs suggest subtracting points or tokens from the child's total when he has demonstrated an undesirable behavior. For example, a child who throws tantrums or an adolescent who uses profanity may lose points. The difficulty with this practice is that a major infraction may lead to losing points that have taken several hours or days to accumulate. Similarly, subtracting points communicates the message that an undesirable behavior negates a desired behavior. If your child's points are taken away, he receives the indirect message "I do not care how much progress you made in other behaviors. Your undesirable behavior shows me that you have not made any progress." When this happens, a child or teen who may already be resistant may lose motivation to improve his behavior. Remember, changing behavior takes time—for example, eliminating tantrum behaviors involves gradual learning, just like the development of any skill—and so while he may be making progress in some areas, he may still evidence certain problematic behaviors.

There are a variety of alternative strategies that can be used as negative consequences rather than taking away points. These include discussion, a time-out, logical consequences, removing a privilege that was not on the list of rewards, or eliminating some of the choices of reward.

Through discussion, you may help your child better understand the factors that contributed to his undesirable behavior and more effectively manage his reactions the next time. However, a brief time-out—between ten and fifteen minutes—can sometimes be useful, not as a punishment but as a way for a child to calm down and reflect. Preferably the time-out should take place in full view of the parent—for example, sitting in a chair in the kitchen or living room. Your child should be told to spend the time-out identifying alternative ways of handling the situation. These can be written or recorded on tape, and both of you can discuss their merits after the time-out.

A time-out for any extended period serves as a punishment but provides no new experience to help a child correct his behavior. Similarly, a time-out that involves sending a child to her room adds the complicated factor of rejection and isolation to what she may already be experiencing. When presented with this form of punishment, a child may conclude that she should never be angry, that she should just hide her anger, or that she does not deserve to experience anger. Such conclusions go against the focus of the program, which is to help children better understand and manage their anger rather than deny or minimize it or express it inappropriately.

This form of appropriate time-out, by contrast, is an example of a logical consequence—a consequence that directly relates to an offense and contributes toward rectifying the offense or improving the behavior.[2] For example, an adolescent may be told he has to pay to replace a dish he broke when angry rather than being told he is grounded from going out with his friends. A child may be required to identify five ways of appropriately expressing her anger to her sister rather than directing vulgar language toward her.

Another possibility is to identify certain enjoyable activities that are not listed as rewards but may be eliminated as a punishment. In this way, all positive experiences are not based entirely on accumulated points.

At this point I want to emphasize my belief that physical punishment should never be used. I stress this point for a variety of reasons. Any form of physical punishment used to address a child's anger models aggression and, typically, a loss of control. While some parents may say they can maintain control, such behavior can very quickly lead to an escalation of aggression. Similarly, when physical punishment is used as a consequence for a child's anger, it is often experienced as an act of revenge. It may also convince the child that all forms of anger should be stifled. Physical punishment usually communicates the message that anger is not acceptable rather than the message that inappropriate expressions of anger are unacceptable.

Physical punishment also creates an emotional atmosphere that is antagonistic to trust and candid sharing. I have worked with many adults who report that in their own childhoods, being physically punished was an effective means of discipline. While some of these adults say they did and do feel much love for their parents, they also often report a lack of genuine trust and open communication with them. They may say that they deserved the punishment because they behaved inappropriately, but all too often they indicate they were toughened by the experience. In effect, they learned to squelch pain, hurt, and anger. In turn, through such suppression, they are more likely to forget these earlier reactions when they decide to use physical punishment with their own children.

Identifying Rewards

A key point to remember when creating a behavior management program is that the reward must in fact be rewarding for your child. This means it must genuinely be rewarding—not that you believe it should be rewarding, not that your child was motivated by it several months ago, not that his brother is motivated by it. Be sure that he genuinely has the motivation to obtain the reward. For example, your son may like bowling, but your teenage daughter may have a preference for tennis lessons. Similarly, you may think your twelve-year-old son loves to play golf, and he may even tell you that he really enjoys the game when asked directly, but he may tense up when you give him advice in a serious and competitive tone about how to improve his swing. In this case, playing golf with you may not be as rewarding as you believe it to be.

One of the best ways to identify what is rewarding is to observe your child and assess those activities that he most enjoys. In addition, try to identify those activities that have been most motivating for your child in the recent past. Pinpoint the activities and interests that most excite him. For example, your middle child may like playing with clay, collecting baseball cards, or playing video games. Your youngest child may readily become excited about playing with action figures, being read to, or watching Disney videos. In contrast, your adolescent may be most motivated to have increased telephone time, obtain computer time, go skating, obtain CDs, or be allowed to spend more time with her friends.

After creating your list, discuss with your child your intention to use a reward program and ask her to make a list of things and privileges she would find rewarding. Her involvement in the planning of a reward program will further support her willingness to cooperate.

Be realistic in what you identify as a reward. Think about your resources in deciding what you will use as a reward. Specifically, be clear about the amount of time, energy, and money you can invest, as well as the interest and ability of other adults to participate in these rewards. For example, you may know that your child likes model airplanes, but giving him one each night may be too costly. Instead, you may want to place a value on the parts of the model so he could redeem points for a few parts each night.

Carefully consider using concert tickets or CDs as a reward for your adolescent. The cost of these rewards can add up very quickly. However, you may want to offer these rewards as a kind of "grand" reward. For example, while you may present a choice of daily rewards for certain behaviors, you may give the grand reward if the targeted behavior is demonstrated daily for an entire week.

Make sure you really do have the time if you schedule an activity in which you both will take part. Similarly, do not promise time together as a reward. Relaxed, enjoyable time together is essential to a relationship that invites discussion about anger and other topics. A child should not be rewarded with time with you or be punished by having time together reduced. Instead, you may want to offer as a reward a specific way of spending time together. Going to a particular restaurant or a sporting event, playing a particular board game or a video game, or just going for a car ride to a favorite location may be specific ways of spending time together that can serve as rewards.

Also remember that, in general, adolescents tend to be more independent and consequently more resistant and less motivated by rewards or privileges. I have often suggested to parents that the only motivators for teens age sixteen and seventeen are money, tickets for concerts, or use of the family car. While you may have a great deal of difficulty identifying a reward for the very resistant child or adolescent, be creative and you will identify a reward that truly is motivating for your child.

Variety of Rewards

The need to use a variety of rewards is another key issue to consider when developing a behavior management program. While the interests of some children may be very narrow, other children have a wide variety of interests. This should be considered when identifying the rewards, since offering an assortment of rewards will help to maintain motivation and interest in the reward program. Even when a child expresses extreme interest in only one type of reward, try to present a variety of rewards related to that area of interest.

Timeliness

Points must be received in a timely manner for them to be experienced as a meaningful reward. Receiving the points immediately after the behavior has been demonstrated will most strengthen the likelihood of the behavior being learned and repeated. Similarly, the rewards or privileges need to be received in a timely manner. While once a day may be good for some children and adolescents, children and adolescents who have a low tolerance for frustration (such as children with attention deficit disorder) need to be rewarded more frequently, perhaps two or three times a day.

I recall helping a mother develop a reward program for her six-year-old son, who was disruptive whenever she took him grocery shopping. We discussed the program, but I did not emphasize the need for immediate rewards for her son, who also suffered from attention deficit disorder. When she returned the following week, she indicated that the reward program had not worked—she had promised points toward a toy if he successfully behaved through all ten aisles, and he had behaved well when strolling down the first aisle but became disruptive in the middle of the second aisle. I then presented a more detailed discussion of how he needed to be rewarded immediately after demonstrating good behavior through each aisle, one at a time.

Know your child. It takes much sensitivity to know what is timely for a particular child. A child who is impulsive, is experiencing temporary stress, or has a low tolerance for frustration may need to be rewarded more immediately than a child who can be more patient.

Consistency in Giving the Reward

Consistency in giving a reward for desired behaviors is essential for a behavioral reward program to be effective. Desired behaviors need to be consistently rewarded and undesirable behaviors consistently punished if your child's motivation is to be maintained. A major reason for the failure of reward programs is often the lack of such consistency. For example, inclement weather may force you to cancel a promised visit to the zoo, or you promise to take your child to a movie but have to postpone it to attend to other activities, or you simply forget about the reward. Ironically, this often happens especially when a child seems to show improvement in more consistently demonstrating the desired behavior.

Make Sense of and Manage Anger: Rewards Program

Increase these behaviors	Pts	Su	Mo	Tu	We	Th	Fr	Sa
Discusses anger								
Practices relaxation exercises								
Identifies emotions related to anger								
Explores expectations								
Explores conclusions								
Discusses anger in the media								
Explores motivations								
Writes a letter regarding anger								
Maintains a journal								
Total points for the day								

Figure 15.1: Chart for monitoring rewards for increasing behaviors

Consistency in the way the program is practiced is also essential for an effective behavioral reward program. A lack of consistency may also occur when differing amount of points are rewarded by both parents for the same behavior, or one parent does not reward certain behaviors while the other parent does. In order to foster consistency, both parents should agree to all terms of the program, be consistent with each other's implementation of the program, and model the behaviors that are rewarded.

Monitoring the Program

Maintaining a chart for the reward program is another essential element in developing a comprehensive program. An example of a chart is presented in Figure 15.1. The chart is used to list rewards that are available, the number of points required for them, and the accumulated points. In addition, a chart should include a calendar that identifies the days and the weeks, displays a log of the child's achievement, and lists the rewards obtained to date. Providing a concrete visual representation of the program is valuable for children of all ages. It provides a written record of progress as well as leads to reduced misunderstanding. Have your child make entries so that she experiences being a more active participant in the program.

Figure 15.2 presents a model of a chart that can be used to monitor progress in reducing targeted behaviors.

Make Sense of and Manage Anger: Rewards Program

Decrease these behaviors	Pts	Su	Mo	Tu	We	Th	Fr	Sa
Has tantrums								
Yells								
Hits self								
Hits others								
Breaks things								
Is disruptive								
Devalues others								
Uses inappropriate language								
Total points for the day								

Figure 15.2: Chart for monitoring rewards for increasing behaviors

Troubleshooting

A behavioral reward program demands a commitment to planning, rewarding, and monitoring a child's progress. There are a number of potential difficulties with each of these components that can undermine progress.

Not Determining the Right Value of Points Needed for Rewards

A child may quickly lose motivation to change his behavior if the reward requires too many points and, consequently, too much time or effort to obtain them. In contrast, the reward may be too easy to obtain if it requires too few points. As a result, you may experience pressure on your resources to provide the reward, and your child will not have to demonstrate much change in his behavior to be rewarded.

The Target Behaviors Are Not Described in Clear Terms

Both desirable and undesirable behaviors may be described in vague terms that lead to misunderstanding and conflict related to your differing expectations regarding the reward program. For example, when you state that your child needs to discuss his emotions surrounding anger, you may want to specify that he engage with you in discussion for ten minutes. Similarly, if you require that your child not have a tantrum, clearly define behaviors that you associate with a tantrum.

Selecting Rewards That Are Not Really Motivating or Very Quickly Lose Their Appeal

It may take several weeks to recognize that a particular reward is not very exciting to your child. In addition, since reward programs may last several months, it is important to remember to update the choices of rewards so that they correspond to your child's most recent areas of interest and motivation.

A Delay or Neglect in Providing a Reward to a Child

A reward program requires consistency to be effective. Neglecting to provide the points or reward in a timely manner introduces uncertainty and disappointment and reduces trust. As emphasized previously, the children and teens who most need a behavioral reward program likely are those who lack a sense of trust. For this reason, a failure to give the points or reward as scheduled may lead to resentment and reduced motivation to change the targeted behavior.

Making Mistakes in Monitoring

Mistakes made in monitoring will have a similar impact on trust and dependability that is the foundation of trust. When made frequently, mistakes may also communicate a lack of real commitment and concern to monitor progress. Clearly this conclusion interferes with a child's progress in attaining more appropriate behaviors.

Prematurely Terminating the Program

It is not unusual for parents to stop practicing the reward program before the child has fully integrated the new behavior as part of his repertoire. Because a reward program is demanding in terms of commitment and organization, you may be tempted to stop giving rewards shortly after your child has begun to demonstrate the target behaviors most of the time. However, it is advisable to continue the program for at least a month (and sometimes longer for adolescents) for the target behaviors to become second nature for your child.

Modeling Undesirable Behaviors While Rewarding Appropriate Ones

A behavioral reward program can be extremely successful in helping a child learn certain behaviors. However, to the degree that your child is rewarded for behaviors that you and other family members do not model, she will be getting inconsistent messages from you. For example, if you or your spouse or a sibling is allowed to express anger inappropriately, your child will be getting mixed messages about how to manage anger. Most important, if a child sees that inappropriate behaviors succeed in having certain needs met, she will continue to behave inappropriately.

William was a fourteen-year-old whose parents developed a behavior reward program to help him decrease his use of inappropriate language. However, William frequently observed his father using such language. He very much admired his father, wanted to be like him, and, most important, saw that such language allowed his dad to exert power through intimidation. Consequently, William continued to use the same language when expressing his anger toward peers and his siblings.

A reward program can be very powerful, but if it is to be effective, it takes a great amount of preparation, monitoring, and evaluation. However, it can be an effective means of helping the more resistant child or adolescent incorporate certain attitudes and behaviors.

As already indicated, reward programs are often most useful for children and teens who are minimally motivated or less emotionally available to learn anger management through modeling and discussion. But some children and teens have more severe anger management difficulties that interfere even with their ability and motivation to take part in a behavioral reward program. These youth may need professional help that might include a reward program in addition to other forms of therapy. These children and teens are described in Chapter 17.

16

Responding to Escalating Anger

This chapter focuses on strategies to help diffuse your child's anger, especially when it begins to physically escalate out of control. Perhaps the most challenging aspect of anger management for most parents is responding to these more severe expressions of anger.

It is extremely uncomfortable to witness any child expressing anger through tantrums or physical aggression. His raised voice, angry facial expression, or aggression toward people or objects may very quickly activate your own child logic, invoking your automatic thoughts and feelings surrounding anger and the expression of anger. You may experience a range of emotions and thoughts that include hurt, frustration, rejection, a sense of inadequacy, self-doubt, and anger. This is a moment when you will feel tested. The more thoroughly you have learned the strategies discussed so far, the more prepared you will be to constructively respond to this form of anger. There are, however, very specific skills and strategies that can be implemented to help you and your child gain self-control in such situations.

Model Physical Control

How do you react to a child when his anger is escalating? Do you become tense or agitated when he raises his voice, turns red, or becomes verbally abusive? Do you feel inadequate as a parent and out of control when responding to this intensity of anger? Or are you able to remain calm and in control in the face of his escalating anger? You are probably in the minority if you can fully maintain your composure. This ability requires a great degree of self-assuredness, confidence, and practice in remaining calm in the presence of someone whose anger is escalating. It requires security within yourself to tolerate being the target of your child's anger. It requires the ability to accept your own anger and that of your child even when such anger does not appear justified.

Do the following exercise to highlight your own experience of how it feels to be in the presence of someone who is escalating his or her anger. Recall a time when someone spoke to you in an angry tone—a parent, a spouse, a friend, a colleague, your supervisor, or even your child. Try to recall your reactions and the self-talk with which you reacted while being the target of such anger. You may recall a quickness to develop your own angry dialogue, turn inward, or try to tune out the experience. We often react with anger when anger is directed toward us. It is this reaction that needs to be minimized when your child begins to escalate his physical expression of anger. Below are eight guidelines to consider when confronted by your child's escalating anger. These guidelines are relevant for dealing with children and teens whose anger is escalating but not yet at the point of a tantrum or being out of control.

Maintain Your Composure

The first step to help your child gain self-control is for you to maintain your own composure. As emphasized throughout this book, we lose our ability to think clearly when our physical reactions to anger escalate. Practice visualization, breathing, muscle relaxation, or visual imagery (see Chapter 11).

Your ability to remain and appear calm will greatly impact your child's reactions to anger and her ability to be self-soothing. Anger and physical reactions to anger are contagious. When you are physically calm, your child will experience you as providing structure and vicariously experience the stability that will foster her increased capacity for self-control. She will similarly be reassured that her anger will not chase you away and will not cause you to lose control. Through repeated experiences of this type, your child will gain increased internal comfort with her anger and an increased capacity to moderate her expressions of anger.

I should emphasize that when I suggest you remain calm, I am not advocating that you be aloof or unemotional. Maintaining composure without communicating your sensitivity to your child's pain and anger may increase her sense of isolation and being discounted, which in turn may only further escalate her anger in order to get a reaction. Instead, remain calm but firmly set limits and clearly define your expectations of her.

Focus Your Verbal Communication on Helping Your Child Become Calm

When your child's anger is escalating, you may be tempted to reason with him, believing you need to make just one more comment in order to convince him of your position or help him feel less anger or hurt. Or your child may try to engage you in a logical discussion of the situation. But the immediate intensity of strong negative emotion interferes with his capacity for clear expression as well as with his ability to genuinely listen to your perspective at this time. His level of anger makes him unavailable to effectively use his cognitive skills to cope with the specific source of his anger. At this point, directly state, "Right now I want to help you gain control. When you are calm, we will talk about this." Focus your attention on helping him become calm. Suggest, "You're okay. Calm down. Relax. You're angry, and that's all right for now, but you need to calm down."[1]

Focus Your Nonverbal Communication on Helping Your Child Become Calm

Maintain close physical proximity with a firm stance and a facial expression that communicates you are in control of yourself and that you are going to help your child maintain self-control. Try to communicate in your posture and appearance that you are interested in your child, that you are relaxed, that your child is special to you, and that you will help her regain control.

Speak in a low tone and in a relaxed manner. As stated previously, if you are trying to be empathic but speak in an angry, impatient, anxious, or critical tone, your child will hear anger, impatience, anxiety, or criticism. These nonverbal aspects of your communication will distract him from your message and from experiencing empathy. Certainly your facial expression, like your tone of voice, can convey genuine concern for your child's experience or a negative message that undermines the impact of what you are trying to communicate.

Good eye contact really communicates genuine presence and concern. I am not suggesting that you maintain a fixed stare, but rather a more relaxed gaze. Such connection also competes for attention with your child's thoughts or emotions. We take in most information visually. Your eye contact and close physical proximity help capture her attention and encourage her to be more receptive to you than if you were to talk to her from across the room.

Place your hand on your child's shoulder as you talk with him. This will further enhance his experience of you as someone who can be caring and soothing. Clearly, use your judgment and first determine if his anger is at such a level that even this gesture will lead him to increased anger. However, this may be especially important in helping a young child to calm himself. Your touch should be confirming, nurturing, redirecting, and even restrictive if necessary, but not punitive.

This approach has the greatest impact when a child is just beginning to escalate in her anger, a time when the bond between you may feel tentative and threatened. Responding in this manner will help increase your child's sense of attachment and alliance between you.

Practicing these strategies may not always be easy. But maintaining your self-control is essential if you are to be available to model more constructive ways of handling and expressing anger. This is very important when responding to any angry child, but especially so when your child is experiencing little or no control of the physical side of his anger, as in a tantrum.

Avoid Criticizing Your Child's Bodily Reactions to Anger

Avoid being critical of your child's flushed face, curled lip, or flared nostrils. Belittling these reactions often leads to an escalation of a child's anger. Children and especially teens are already self-conscious, and so they are often quick to feel criticized about their behavior or physical appearance. But these physiological reactions are aspects of anger over which your child may have little control.

Focusing on the physiological reactions may also be experienced as being insensitive to the core hurt as well as anger experienced at the moment. Criticism of these reactions may also be experienced as shaming. As described in previous chapters, shame can be used to influence a child, but it leads to very destructive consequences in terms of self-esteem as well as in the management of anger.

Pointing out physiological reactions may actually be helpful when you are trying to encourage your child to become calm. Comments such as "You're slowing down your breathing ... that's good ... now breathe deeply ... take your time ... that will help you relax" are useful when a child is escalating his anger.

Communicate Acceptance of Your Child's Anger But Rejection of the Inappropriate Expression of Anger

Providing reassurance and acceptance of your child's anger is a major aspect of anger management. At the same time, such acceptance should not include tolerance of behavior that is disrespectful or threatening to you, your child, or the safety of others. Offer an empathic comment such as "I can tell you are angry and hurt [in pain, feeling ignored, feeling discounted], but I am not going to let you hurt me or yourself." Tell her that you recognize she is angry and that her anger is a natural reaction to being hurt, disappointed, or frustrated.

Allow Venting

If your child's expression of anger is within the boundaries of what you deem to be acceptable behavior, allow him to vent and state his feelings for a while. Much of the energy aroused by anger usually dissipates within fifteen or twenty minutes. However, I do not mean to imply that you should tolerate name-calling or physical aggression.

Avoid Being Critical, Sarcastic, or Threatening

Any message that appears critical, sarcastic, or threatening will foster the escalation of your child's anger. You may feel angry yourself, but if you vent your frustration in this way, be prepared for further escalation or prolonged expression of anger. Realize too that your inappropriate expressions of anger further model the use of anger to gain control.

Clearly Define Your Expectations

Clearly state your expectations with specific guidelines for how your child can gain self-control. For example, remind her to relax her body. Direct her to slowly take a deep breath and then slowly let it out, or to remember a visual image she has used to practice relaxation. Similarly, when giving your child permission to vent, be specific about helping her to appropriately express her anger.

Managing a Tantrum

A tantrum is a state of increased agitation (most often based on anger or anxiety) that communicates to you that your child is not in control of himself. While some children have tantrums in early childhood, many children never do. Some throw tantrums only when facing perceived trauma, and others seem to immediately have a tantrum as a reaction to the slightest experience of frustration. Some youngsters may continue to throw tantrums well into middle childhood.

Tantrums are demonstrated in a variety of ways. When I was teaching, there was a girl in my fourth-grade class who had a tantrum whenever she perceived other children as being against her. She was predisposed to perceive their interactions with her in this negative light and was quick to feel slighted when her peers did not immediately respond positively to all of her expectations. At those times she would stop whatever she was doing, throw all of her belongings around the room or down the hall, and yell in a piercing voice how much she hated everybody and how she thought they were against her.

I have worked with numerous adolescents who have described breaking objects or punching a wall or door as a final step in the escalation of their anger. Some children and even adolescents have tantrums during which they become physically aggressive toward themselves or others. They may throw objects, hit others, or destroy things while they are screaming. Certain children escalate to the point that they physically threaten anyone who appears to be in their way.

While your child may use tantrums to express anger, a tantrum also shows you that he has little or no control over his anger. He is showing a lack of frustration tolerance, a weak ability to be self-soothing, and a lack of flexibility in being able to manage his anger. Answer the following questions when deciding how to respond to your child's tantrums.

1. Is your child truly out of control, or is he purposely trying to appear out of control?
2. Is he escalating to the degree that he appears to be losing self-control even though he still seems to have some control?
3. Is your child placing himself in a potentially dangerous situation while exhibiting his tantrum?
4. What is the best way to respond to him so that he increases his capacity for self-control?
5. How can you provide sufficient support to communicate that you are available to help and protect him?

Most likely you will not be able to answer each of these questions each time your child has a tantrum. However, if you can form some general answers based on assessing your child, you will be much better prepared to decide how to react to your child's next display of tantrum behavior. By answering these questions, you will be more aware of the personal meaning tantrums have for your child. You will be able to better decide how intrusive to be and how much control you will need to exert.

Some children have the ability to be self-soothing when coping with disappointment, frustration, confusion, hurt, and other emotions that precipitate anger. However, children who temporarily experience an unusual amount of stress may regress, behaving as they did when they were younger. Your three- or four-year-old may be experiencing real anxiety about a visit to a doctor or an anticipated separation, and so may throw a tantrum. A seven-year-old may have a tantrum because he knows that when he does, you become guilty or embarrassed and he will ultimately get his way. For these reasons, it is helpful to know the answers to the questions presented above.

When asking yourself how much control your child really has, consider her age, past experiences in similar situations, and whether she has experienced any unusually stressful situations recently. Very young children may have very little self-control. Other children, such as those who tantrum in a shopping mall, may have quickly learned that tantrums will stop you from walking away or convince you to give in to their desires.

If your child has had few tantrums in the past and if he has shown fairly good self-control, a tantrum may indicate that he is especially frustrated by something. If he has a past history of tantrums and seems to have the self-control to stop himself, remind him that you will listen to him when he becomes calm. At this level of intensity, a tantrum in a public place such as a mall is often handled very well by firmly reassuring your child that you love him very much and know he can calm himself. If your child has a good history of self-control, he will, at this point, become calm when you indicate in words and action that you are going to continue with your activity.

When confronted with a tantrum, determine if there is real potential for injury. Similarly, determine if your child in fact has the judgment and skills essential for self-calming. If you decide to ignore the tantrum, reassure her that you know something is bothering her and that your are concerned about her feelings, but explain that you will not discuss the situation until she has ended the tantrum. Move physically close and gently hold her shoulder to orient her so you can establish good eye contact. At this point, you can say something like the following in a relaxed and calm voice: "I can tell that you are hurt [disappointed, frustrated], and so now you are angry." Indicate if you need to move on and when you will discuss his feelings with him—in a half hour, when she calms down, or when you get home. Request feedback from her to determine if she has really heard you. Assess whether she is reacting to your comments by showing less agitation, increasing eye contact, slowing her breathing, giving you longer replies, or reducing the muscle tension in her face and in her body.

Do not call attention to her self-calming yet. Continue to provide reassurance that you know what she is feeling, that she is safe, and that you are here for her.

Once she has calmed down, casually praise her with "Wow—you calmed yourself" or "Now that you are calm, help me understand what was bothering you."

Present the comments in a calm, firm voice to help your child feel that you are in control. Calmness is contagious. If you speak calmly and appear in control, this will help your child to experience safety, security, and a sense of being protected. All of these elements contribute to foster the development of increased internal self-control.

This is an ideal intervention. However, to the degree that you can show some of these reactions, you will communicate your own sense of control and consistency, which is essential for your child's self-calming.

Responding to Escalating Anger

There may be times when your child is completely out of control. Do not ignore him at these times; instead, determine if you can manage him or if you need assistance. You may need help on occasion. Try the following strategies if you determine you can manage him on your own. (Note that they may not be as effective with an adolescent.)

When reacting to a young child who is out of control, position yourself so that you can hold him in your arms just as you would an infant. In addition to holding him, wrap your arms around him so that both of his arms are restrained from striking out and hurting you or himself. Similarly, if necessary, hold his feet between your legs so that he is physically restrained from kicking out and hurting you or himself. In the ideal position, you will be able to maintain eye contact with him. Your physical restraint should communicate protective restriction and concerned limit setting rather than punitive, hurtful, or threatening restraint. This type of limit setting is not intended to be threatening or a display of power. Rather, it is intended to communicate to your child that you are supporting him to help him regain self-control. Through such physical interaction, you are communicating that while he may not be fully in control of himself, you will help him gain such control.

As you restrain him, state in a relaxed tone, "You are okay. You are safe. I am not going to hurt you. I do not want to see you hurt yourself. Just calm down." At this time, focus all of your attention and communications on the task of helping him to become calm. Any attempts at this time to discuss the precipitating events, to reason, or to explore his feelings will distract him from self-soothing. He may try to engage you in discussion about the event and try to reason with you. Reassure him that you very much want to discuss his thoughts and feelings about the event but that he needs to focus on becoming calm at this moment.

Depending on the age of your child, you may want to further communicate statements that encourage and praise his attempts to calm himself—for example, "I know you're upset, but I can feel you becoming more relaxed. ... Calm down, it's okay, you're okay ... just relax."

As you notice your child beginning to feel the effects of self-soothing, you may want to remind him of methods that he has used in the past to help him relax. These may include the visual imagery, muscle relaxation exercises, or breathing techniques described in Chapter 11. It may appear that his self-calming is achieved more by exhaustion than by his own efforts at self-control, initiative, and judgment. This intervention may feel very uncomfortable for you if you experience discomfort in exerting such control and limit setting, as many parents do. Providing this type of physical support and restraint may seem like punitive discipline to some parents. You may feel you are being too restrictive or controlling. However, if you do this while you are able to remain calm, you communicate acceptance and you support your child's capacity to gain self-control.

Using this strategy with a child can be both emotionally and physically challenging. It is a physically assertive intervention that should not be used if you genuinely believe your child is already calming himself. Similarly, do not engage in this strategy if you sense that you will not really be able to control him or that the situation may be dangerous for either one of you. Respond in a firm, soft voice and indicate your availability to talk after he has become calm. If possible, try to encourage him to sit in a very comfortable chair to further foster his relaxation. Similarly, try to have him move to an area of the room where there are no objects to throw or hit. If he still is expressing anger in his tone of voice and in his words but is not really acting on his anger and does not appear dangerous, remember that such venting usually dissipates within half an hour.

Seek immediate support if you believe your child's aggression may escalate to a dangerous point or if you fear he may overpower you. Similarly, remove yourself physically if you believe that you might lose self-control.

You may decide to withdraw from the situation as another way of responding to his anger. This should be considered if you genuinely believe that he will deescalate in his anger as you withdraw. Or you may withdraw only to get help. Your withdrawal may be an attempt to avoid aggression, and you may feel like you have "lost face" or power in your relationship. However, once physical fighting has occurred, it may become a precedent for conflict resolution and continue to escalate as each family member experiences diminished self-control. If you react to your child's anger by becoming aggressive, you have modeled aggression as a strategy to deal with anger, demonstrated that you have little capacity for control, and communicated that you cannot be trusted. In addition, resorting to physical aggression may leave you feeling guilty, frustrated, and with a sense of having lost self-control. This may then increase the likelihood of your responding in a similar way the next time.

I strongly recommend that you seek counseling if you frequently withdraw from such interactions or if you resort to being physically aggressive in dealing with your child's anger. Such strategies work only temporarily and have great potential to foster destructive outbursts and serve as the foundation for further domestic violence.

The controversy over spanking children is one that has supporters on both sides. There are many reasons parents offer in support of such discipline. Some believe that a gentle slap on the hand, arm, or buttocks is harmless. This strategy often works, especially to get a child's attention. Other parents justify spanking a child by emphasizing that their parents spanked them. As a part of this belief, they point to the fact that they are not the worse for it.

However, striking a child may be the easy way to exert discipline when parents have not more fully thought through alternative strategies. Whether the punishment is light-handed or heavy-handed, being hit by a parent reflects physical aggression as a way of exerting one's will over another person. It is a demonstration of power rather than respect, control rather than empathy, and it creates fear rather than an emotional connection.

The child or teen who demonstrates chronic anger or aggression may be experiencing a variety of difficulties. While this chapter has focused on children who rarely, if ever, lose control, the next chapter offers understanding and recommendations for helping children and teens with chronic problems in managing their anger.

17

Anger, Hostility, and Aggression: The Need for Special Support

When does anger become so problematic that special help is indicated for your child? Is there always a clear indication when such support is necessary? What are the specific signals that your child or teen is increasingly having difficulty with anger? Should you wait until your child or teen is physically aggressive before seeking help? Could children or teens have severe difficulty with anger even though they never express any form of anger? These are just a few of the questions that will be answered in this chapter.

As previously indicated, the strategies in this book are primarily intended for teaching healthy anger management to children and teens who do not experience severe difficulties with anger. However, those with more acute difficulties with anger can benefit from learning these skills when they are used in conjunction with special support.

In addition, special help may be needed for teens who experience minimal connection with their parents. Even healthy teens increasingly value the feedback and modeling of peers as they struggle with their needs to be independent and yet feel connected. For this reason, they may be more open to develop understanding and skills related to anger management when they are in a group with their peers.

Some children and teens with severe anger need to be assessed to determine if there is a medical problem involving a chemical disorder (such as a hormonal imbalance or drug reaction), an organic problem (such as neurological damage related to certain forms of brain injury), or a psychological disorder. These children and teens may need medication; individual, family, or group therapy; behavior management programs; or the structure of a residential group home or a psychiatric inpatient setting.

As emphasized throughout this book, anger is an emotion and is distinct from aggression, the behavioral expression of anger. While in recent years much attention has focused on aggression and violence by children and teens, it should again be stated that aggression is just one way of managing and expressing anger. In fact, as reported by psychologist James Averill, in a study of a large population of individuals who reported being angry within a certain period of time, only 10 percent actually resorted to aggression.[1]

Characteristics of Severely Problematic Anger

Anger that is severely problematic is distinguishable from other forms of anger in three distinct ways: intensity, frequency, and duration.[2]

Intensity

Excessive intensity in anger expression is perhaps the most noticeable sign that your child needs special assistance. Even verbally expressed anger can be reflective of more serious difficulties when it is intense. Yelling, cursing, raging, or other forms of verbally abusive language, while evidenced by many children and teens at one time or another, may indicate more serious problems with anger. It is also important to be alert to severe intensity of anger even when the acceptable norms for such behavior may vary by family and culture.

More problematic is anger that is expressed in violence, with intensity that progresses from destroying things to physically hurting people. Whether expressed through vandalism or in physical aggression toward others, such behavior indicates a loss of control that ignores and endangers the rights of others and calls for some form of intervention. While intensity, frequency, and duration should usually be considered together when deciding if special help is needed, severe intensity alone should warrant the need for help even if there is no history of similar anger. An older child who beats and injures another in anything beyond a minor scuffle, a young child who tortures animals, teens who destroy property, or a teen who threatens suicide or purposely injures himself—all of these are examples of severe anger that necessitates special help.

Frequency

Any one-time occurrence of the abovementioned behaviors may suggest more serious problems with anger. However, the urgency for special help increases the more frequently your child demonstrates such behaviors. The high frequency of even less intense expressions of anger, such as chronic cynicism, sarcasm, or verbally abusive behavior, also signals a more serious difficulty with anger. Similarly, consider how pervasive your child's anger is. Does she become irritated mostly with a sibling or a peer, or is she easily angered in many interactions with most people?

Duration

Silent treatment by a child or teen that lasts for more than several days, tantrums that last for hours, and chronic anger in the form of resentment or hostility that lasts for months are just a few examples of more severe problems that warrant special help.

Lack of Empathy

In addition to the three general considerations of intensity, frequency, and duration, lack of empathy is another characteristic that may also be associated with more severe anger and require special assistance.[3] Children and teens who lack empathy are unable to identify with the feelings of others. As such, they are more self-focused in their attention and behavior and lack sensitivity to the pain of others. Being empathic involves not only an ability to share the emotions of another person but a genuine interest in experiencing the thoughts and emotions of that person—a desire to better understand the perspective of another. The ability to be empathic reflects a quality of compassion and understanding for another's behavior or attitudes.

   Children and teens who lack empathy fail to notice or ignore cues regarding how others feel. As a result, when interpersonal conflict arises, they are more likely to express anger without consideration for the feelings of others. Being empathic can serve as a deterrent when they experience anger. A child or teen who can be empathic is more likely to monitor how he expresses anger. In the absence of sufficient empathy, a teen may slap his brother for interrupting his viewing of a favorite television program. Similarly, a seven-year-old may quickly become verbally abusive when her friend excitedly grabs her doll without asking her permission.

   At a more severe level, a child or teen may become physically aggressive or violent with little consideration for the well-being or life of others. These are often the children and teens who make headlines for behaviors that reflect their gross inhumanity toward others.

A Deficiency in Guilt or Conscience Regarding Aggression

Some children and teens experience little or no guilt or conscience regarding aggression or violence. In part, this is very much related to their lack of empathy. These children and teens may be diagnosed with conduct disorder, as described in the DSM-IV-TR (*Diagnostic and Statistical Manual of Mental Disorders,* fourth edition).[4] These children or teens are especially challenging to help because they tend to externalize the causes of their pain. They blame others and exhibit minimal motivation to look inward or alter their behavior. Antisocial personality disorder is another diagnosis used for some teens and adults when the expression of anger and lack of conscience appear to be even more severe. This diagnosis is reserved for those over eighteen years of age whose symptoms have been in evidence since they were fifteen years old. These disorders will be described in greater detail later in this chapter.

An Attitude of Entitlement and Distorted Beliefs of Wrongdoing

Aaron Beck, a world-renowned psychologist, offers useful insights into how an attitude of entitlement and distorted beliefs of wrongdoing predispose us toward anger.[5] Specifically, individuals prone to anger maintain rigid beliefs regarding how others should behave toward them. These thoughts are based on child logic and form the basis of these individuals' automatic thoughts about their relationships with others. Such beliefs are beyond a longing or desire for how others should behave. Instead, individuals with these fixed beliefs feel entitled to be treated in a way that always fulfills their wishes and needs. Here are examples of these beliefs.

- People must show respect for me at all times.
- People should be sensitive to my needs.
- People should do what I ask of them.

Those who maintain these beliefs are quick to feel wronged when they are not satisfied. As a result, they may impulsively form the following conclusions.

- The other person wronged me in some way and is responsible for my hurt feelings.
- The injury was deliberate and unjustified.
- The offender should be punished or eliminated.

The degree to which children or teens maintain thoughts of entitlement will influence the intensity and quality of their anger. Children and teens develop these thoughts based on child logic. And indeed, much anger results from feeling wronged. But it is the degree to which these thoughts dominate their view of others that will determine whether they feel irritated, enraged, and hateful or act aggressively. Children and teens who strongly maintain these beliefs are often diagnosed with conduct disorder.

Some youths maintain extremely powerful feelings of entitlement coupled with a fragile self-esteem. Much of their energy is channeled toward trying to maintain positive self-esteem and defending against feeling low self-worth. They experience little flexibility in their ability to perceive others in a more favorable light or with greater complexity. They feel extremely devalued when they perceive they have been wronged. Consequently, their anger may lead to hatred and viewing others in a dehumanized way. Others may be experienced as adversaries when this severe level of distortion occurs. They may then be viewed as threatening to one's overall self-esteem. Children or teens who experience this level of distortion in their beliefs may assault those who they perceive as being a threat to their self-worth. These teens are often diagnosed with conduct disorder and later with antisocial personality disorder (described below).

Recognizing distortions in reasoning may help us to better understand the actions of those children and teens involved in shootings. While they may in fact experience depression or alienation, their rigid thoughts of entitlement and wrongdoing may convince them that others need to be punished or even eliminated. The teen who maintains such beliefs is quick to react to his perceptions of others, to overly exaggerate the intensity of his victimization, and to respond with extreme behavior.

Impulsivity

Children and teens who have difficulties with impulse control are likely to experience more severe difficulties with anger. They are quick to act without taking time to think about the actions. As with the other characteristics described so far, this behavior becomes more problematic to the degree that it is pervasive and severe. Some children are simply more impulsive and excitable than others. It is more serious when a child is very frequently impulsive in a range of areas, and when it interferes with academic progress. Similarly, special support is indicated for a child or teen who exhibits impulsivity accompanied by difficulties in concentration and distractibility. These three areas of behavior are most often evidenced together in children with attention deficit hyperactivity disorder (ADHD), described in more detail later.

Demonstrations of Anger That Appear Unusual or Bizarre

Children and teens occasionally behave in ways that are inconsistent with their usual behavior. A typically outgoing child may at times become quiet and withdrawn; a teen may seem emotionally all over the map within a few days or even within a few hours. Certainly, adolescents try out new behaviors in the process of developing their unique identity. However, it is a more serious concern when a child or teen demonstrates unusual or out-of-character anger that leaves you puzzled, confused, and anxious.

A five-year-old hitting her otherwise favorite teddy bear might capture your attention. Doing the same to her three-year-old brother and making serious threats to harm him should be viewed with much concern. Every effort should be made to determine the level of anger she is experiencing, her capacity to control her anger, and how well she understands the impact of her actions. Often parents are quick to assess such anger as just typical sibling rivalry when in fact it may be symptomatic of more serious underlying jealousies, insecurities, hurt, and related anger.

Examples of bizarre anger include a seven-year-old who locks himself in the bathroom and threatens to cut his wrists when he is angry with his parents, a ten-year-old who smears feces across a wall following a conflict with his parents, and a teen who, never having acted aggressively in the past, suddenly becomes verbally explosive or slashes someone's tires.

Anger that is expressed in an aggressive manner that is out of character needs to be further explored, and special help should be considered.

An Absence of Anger

Anger is a very natural part of our human condition. Children and teens who never express anger may easily go unnoticed, especially if they are well behaved in school and at home. They may be praised by parents, teachers, and other adults, and even by certain peers. However, the complete absence of anger may be just as significant a reason to seek professional help as a violent display of aggression. There are many situations in life that cause even the healthiest child or teen to experience anger. Those who do not recognize or acknowledge such feelings pay a high price in terms of emotional energy. As described previously, children who deny, minimize, or ignore anger gradually lose touch with feelings in general. As a result, they may experience alienation, become withdrawn or depressed, avoid expressing themselves, or develop other symptoms.

In addition to knowing the general characteristics of severe anger, you will be more alert to the need for special help for your child when you can recognize the warning signs that suggest anger may turn to violence.

Warning Signs of Teen Violence

Child and teen violence that involves purposely hurting someone, in particular other children and teens, has increased in the last decade. Some children and teens are violent as an act of retaliation for feeling wronged, while others are aggressive in order to control others. The school shootings that have made the headlines in recent years have summoned our attention and spurred efforts to prevent such violence. One response to this need was the development of "Warning Signs of Teen Violence," a brochure and program created by the American Psychological Association and MTV in 1999.[6] (See the Appendix for more information.)

While developing and maintaining a stable and supportive connection with your child or teen may be the best defense against his becoming violent, other factors may also contribute to violent behavior. These include:

- Peer pressure
- Need for attention or respect
- Feelings of low self-worth
- Witnessing violence at home, in the community, or in the media
- Easy access to weapons

The following behaviors have been identified as *immediate warning signs that violence is a serious possibility:*

- Frequent loss of temper
- Frequent fighting
- Significant vandalism or property damage
- Increase in the use of drugs or alcohol
- Increase in risk-taking behavior
- Detailed plans to commit acts of violence
- Announcements of threats or plans for hurting others
- Enjoying hurting animals
- Carrying a weapon

In addition, other warning signs of violence that may be observed over time include the following:

- A history of violent or aggressive behavior
- Serious drug or alcohol use

- Gang membership or a strong desire to be in a gang
- Access to or fascination with weapons, especially guns
- Threatening others regularly
- Trouble controlling feelings such as anger
- Withdrawal from friends and usual activities
- Feeling rejected or alone
- Having been a victim of bullying
- Poor school performance
- History of discipline problems or frequent run-ins with authority
- Feeling constantly disrespected
- Failing to acknowledge the feelings or rights of others

While no single behavior is clearly predictive of violence, each deserves further attention and exploration. In combination, the more behaviors your child demonstrates, the more she may be prone to act violently. Because of their high risk for violence, these children and teens do require special help. If your child is open to discussing her feelings with you, a sibling, a peer, or another adult, teaching her strategies to reduce her physical arousal to anger should be a priority. Breathing techniques, visual relaxation exercises, and directed self-talk are just a few strategies that can be used initially while you are seeking professional assistance.

Self-Directed Violence

As discussed earlier, some children and teens direct anger inward and toward themselves rather than at others. Self-directed violence may include suicide or self-injury. Both require recognizing warning signs and seeking help.

Suicide. Suicide is the third leading cause of death in youth ages fifteen to nineteen.[7] While the frequency is much lower for younger children, they do make attempts, and some succeed. Suicidal thoughts are based on a wish to end emotional pain. The suicidal child or teen is distorted in her thinking that suicide is the only way to escape his turmoil. Warning signs of potential suicide include:

- Previous suicide attempts
- Significant alcohol or drug use
- Threatening suicide or communicating thoughts of suicide, death, dying, or the afterlife
- Sudden increase in moodiness, withdrawal, or isolation
- Major changes in eating or sleeping habits
- Feelings of hopelessness, guilt, or worthlessness
- Poor control over behavior

- Impulsive, aggressive behavior
- Drop in quality of school performance or interest
- Lack of interest in usual activities
- Getting into trouble with authority figures
- Perfectionism
- Giving away important possessions
- Hinting at not being around in the future or saying goodbye

These warning signs are even more meaningful when a child or teen has experienced the recent death or suicide of a friend or family member, when there has been a breakup with a boyfriend or girlfriend or a conflict with parents, or when other children or teens in the community have committed suicide. While severely depressed children or teens often make suicidal attempts, it is often a "final-straw" anger-provoking event that triggers a suicide attempt. The best way to be of help to your child or teen who appears suicidal is to:

1. *Take it seriously.* Talk with your child about your concerns and seek professional help. Remember that most teens who make suicide attempts have discussed suicide with others.

2. *Listen empathically.* Be available to express your concern with a focus on listening to his or her pain and suicidal ideation without being judgmental.

3. *Ask questions.* Inquire both about your child's feelings and if he has a specific plan for suicide.

4. *Reassure.* Remind your child that suicide is a permanent solution to a temporary problem. Emphasize that while right now she may not believe or feel as though she will ever overcome her pain, she should not trust her feelings or beliefs at this moment. Strongly make the point that she can be helped.

5. *Do not leave your child alone.* Suicidal children often act impulsively when making suicide attempts. Some do so even though they appear calm. Not until you have both met with a professional should you leave your child unattended. If necessary, elicit the help of friends or other family members to help monitor your child.

Self-Injury.   Children and teens may injure themselves in various ways—cutting, burning, or otherwise hurting themselves—without having suicidal intentions. Engaging in these activities is a reaction to a variety of intense emotions that may include anger, depression, and anxiety. Their self-injury may serve as a way of distracting themselves from their emotional pain and, for some, as a way of focusing on the here and now rather than on their thoughts or emotional tension. Factors that contribute to depression and suicide may similarly contribute to self-injury. In addition to warning signs regarding suicide, signs of self-injury include:

1. Periods of increased isolation or withdrawal
2. Wearing long-sleeved shirts or blouses or long skirts or pants even in warm weather
3. Reports of injuries as accidents
4. Sudden refusal to engage in physical education (since doing so might expose their injuries)

Emotional Disorders

Anger that is chronic and pervasive can also be a symptom of a serious emotional disorder. Specifically, this degree of anger has been associated with depression, ADHD, bipolar disorder, conduct disorder, oppositional disorder, and substance abuse.

Depression

As indicated in the discussion of suicide, anger is often one of the symptoms of severe depression in children and teens. Just as we may wish to overlook anger in children and teens, we may desire to believe that they do not become depressed. In fact, only in the past three decades have mental health professionals more fully recognized that children and teens do in fact get depressed. Studies indicate that 2.5 percent of children and 8 percent of teens in the United States experience depression.[8] While some children and teens with depression are aggressive in their behavior, most exhibit a lower level of intensity, but their depression seriously impacts them in many ways.

Jason, fifteen, was referred primarily because of a gradual drop in his grades over a period of a year and a half. Although his academic performance in the past had been superior, he no longer studied for tests or handed in assignments. His parents were mostly concerned about his deteriorating academic performance. Only after specifically being asked did they indicate that Jason seemed increasingly "lazy," fatigued, and irritable.

I met with Jason shortly after he began his summer break. A thorough assessment was conducted to better determine what factors might have contributed to his underachievement. As part of that assessment, Jason revealed in his interview that he had become increasingly bored and irritable, and he lacked interest in doing any of the activities he had engaged in the previous summer. He reported that in the last few weeks he slept ten to twelve hours daily and awoke close to noon each day. Upon awakening, he was unable to decide how to spend his time and had little interest in contacting his friends. This behavior was in sharp contrast to the previous summer, during which he had been excited about having time off, awoke early so he could get together with friends, and could easily plan how to spend the day.

Through discussion, he gradually revealed that he had tremendous anger regarding expectations to do well in school. While he felt he had always been a "good boy," he was tired of feeling obligated to do what others expected of him. He increasingly resented studying and his parents' expectations that he do well in school.

While he was not suicidal, Jason evidenced many of the following symptoms of children and teens diagnosed with depression (as described in the DSM-IV-TR):

1. Depressed mood most of the day, nearly every day, as indicated by either subjective report (e.g., feels sad or empty) or observation made by others (e.g., appears tearful). Note: in children and adolescents, can be irritable mood.
2. Markedly diminished interest or pleasure in all, or almost all, activities most of the day, nearly every day (as indicated by either subjective account or observation made by others.
3. Significant weight loss when not dieting or weight gain or decrease in appetite nearly every day.
4. Insomnia or hypersomnia nearly every day.
5. Psychomotor agitation or retardation nearly everey day (observable by others, not merely subjective feelings of restlessness or being slowed down).
6. Fatigue or loss of energy nearly all day.
7. Feelings of worthlessness or excessive or inapprpriate guilt (which may be delusional) nearly every day (not merely self-reproach or guilt about being sick).
8. Diminished ability to think or concentrate, or indecisiveness, nearly every day (either by subjective account or as observed by others).
9. Recurrent thoughts of death (not just fear of dying), recurrent suicidal ideation without a specific plan for committing suicide.

A child or teen must display five or more of these symptoms for two or more weeks to be diagnosed with depression. The National Institute of Mental Health identifies several additional symptoms that may also be evidenced by children and teens who experience depression.[9]

1. Frequent vague physical complaints
2. Excessive absences from school or poor school performance
3. Talk of running away from home

4. Outburst of shouting, complaining, or frequent periods of un-
explained irritability
5. Being bored
6. Lack of interest in being with friends
7. Alcohol or substance abuse
8. Social isolation
9. Increased irritability, anger, or hostility
10. Reckless behavior
11. Difficulty with relationships

As described earlier, depression is also associated with thinking that
is pessimistic and fosters a sense of helplessness and hopelessness.
Children and teens suffering from depression feel they have little impact in their own lives and in the lives of friends and family.

Even infants can experience forms of depression. They may be irritable, display extreme agitation, or appear emotionally withdrawn. Depression in infants and young children is often related to prolonged
separations from their parents. But such depression may also be a reaction to a parent's emotional unavailability. A mother's postpartum
depression, the death of a loved one, a marital conflict, or other difficulties may compete with a parent's being available to form a nurturing
connection with a child.

More specifically, however, depression in children and teens is often
related to trauma, a biological predisposition, learned helplessness (a
learned pattern of giving up when faced with challenge—maintaining
the belief that whatever one does cannot have an impact), or a combination of these factors.[10] Children or teens who experience physical or
emotional abuse, the death of a parent or other close family member, a
physical injury, chronic illness, or other major changes may become
more vulnerable to depression.

Some children and adolescents become depressed following what
others describe as a minor event or change. I have worked with young
children whose experience of mild depression was triggered by a change
in a parent's work schedule, the loss of a pet, or the anticipated or actual
birth of a sibling. I have also counseled many teens who on the surface
indicated positive excitement about graduating from high school but
began experiencing depression in their senior year as they anticipated the
challenge of leaving friends, going to college, or starting a job.

Some children and teens may be more vulnerable to depression because of a genetic history. A tendency toward depression may be inherited from parents who have serious depression. Even if there is no
family history of depression, the trauma of stressful events may trigger
certain chemical changes in the nervous system that lead to depression.

Regardless of the individual or combination of causes, depressed children and teens are more prone to experience anger. While Jason passively expressed his anger by not completing his assignments, he also expressed his anger in his irritability. In contrast, some depressed teens also act out their anger in more serious ways that may involve breaking the law, vandalism, or driving recklessly.

At the same time, it is helpful to remember that adolescence is a period of great challenge and change. Teens are confronted with the tasks of developing a personal identity, mourning the end of childhood, seeking acceptance by peers, and recognizing the weaknesses of their parents and other adults. Add to this mix the influence of hormonal changes and it becomes easier to understand how some teens may periodically feel down and angry. While some have the coping skills, support, and confidence to successfully meet these challenges, others may experience depression and related anger that require special help.

Another consideration that needs clarification is the distinction between sadness and depression. Sadness is associated with a gloomy or down mood and is relatively short-lived and more specific in focus. In contrast, depression more often involves a decreased sense of self-confidence and general esteem that is related to self-critical self-talk. The best way to know whether your child is depressed or is merely sad is to remain connected with her and directly inquire about her feelings.

A thorough assessment is necessary to determine the need for medication or for individual, family, or group treatment. Medication may be essential for some children and teens with more severe depression. It can help a child or teen think more clearly and, as a result, be more able to manage the challenges of school and relationships. In addition, psychotherapy may be indicated, as it can be extremely effective in treating depression in children and teens.

Attention Deficit Hyperactivity Disorder

ADHD is another disorder that may influence the degree to which a child or teen experiences difficulties with anger management. However, diagnosing ADHD is a major challenge since certain symptoms of this disorder are often associated with other difficulties or disorders. Children and teens with learning disabilities, anxiety disorders, medical problems, and stress reactions to trauma, including physical and sexual abuse, may exhibit one or more of the same symptoms.

According to the DSM-IV-TR, to be diagnosed with ADHD children must have six or more of the symptoms present in either of two categories: inattention and hyperactivity-impulsivity.

1. Inattention

- Often fails to give close attention to details or makes careless mistakes in schoolwork, work, or other activities.
- Often has difficulty sustaining attention in tasks or play activities.
- Often does not seem to listen when spoken to directly.
- Often does not follow through on instructions and fails to finish schoolwork, chores, or duties in the workplace (not due to oppositional behavior or failure to understand instructions).
- Often has difficulty organizing tasks and activities.
- Often avoids, dislikes, or is reluctant to engage in tasks that require sustained mental effort (such as schoolwork or homework).
- Often loses things necessary for tasks or activites (e.g., toys, school assignments, pencils, books, or tools).
- Is often easily distracted by extraneous stimuli.
- Is often forgetful in daily activities.

2. Hyperactivity—Impulsivity

Hyperactivity

- Often fidgets with hands or feet or squirms in seat.
- Often leaves seat in classroom or in other situations in which remaining seated is expected.
- Often runs about or climbs excessively in situations in which it is inappropriate (in adolescents or adults, may be limited to subjective feelings of restlessness).
- Often has difficulty playing or engaging in leisure activities quietly.
- Is often "on the go" or often acts as if "driven by a motor."
- Often talks excessively.

Impulsivity

- Often blurts out answers before questions have been completed.
- Often has difficulty awaiting turn.
- Often interrupts or intrudes on others (e.g., butts into conversations or games).

In addition, a diagnosis of ADHD requires that the symptoms persist for at least six months to a degree that is maladaptive and inconsistent with the child's developmental level. Furthermore, in May 2000 the American Academy of Pediatrics issued guidelines for the diagnosis of

ADHD requiring that a child must exhibit symptoms in at least two settings (e.g., in the home and at school) and that the symptoms interfere with a child's academic or social functioning for at least six months.

Some children and teens (as well as adults) with this diagnosis do not evidence physical hyperactivity. They may instead experience feelings of restlessness or excessive shifting of thoughts. They may be physically still in the classroom but distracted by the whirlwind of their thoughts.

A diagnosis of ADHD requires that these characteristics are chronic, not short-lived reactions to a particularly stressful event. Most important, chronic anger is not a defining characteristic of ADHD, but it is often seen in children and teens with this disorder. They may be quick to experience frustration when learning new information or skills in class. They are similarly challenged in learning motor coordination skills that are essential for other activities such as engaging in sports or playing musical instruments. Their difficulty is related not to an inability to perform these tasks but to the concentration, attention, and organization needed to learn them.

Children and teens with ADHD are also challenged in their social interactions. Keith, seven, loved his sister and often demonstrated his affection by hugging her. However, he had difficulty attending to cues regarding his sister's reaction to his caring gesture. In his enthusiasm he failed to notice that while she enjoyed his initial hug, she soon experienced his embrace as increasingly painful. Children and teens with this disorder have difficulty assessing cues and attending to feedback from others. Consequently, they may become targets for criticism by others as well as experience frustration and anger related to their feeling out of sync with peers.

Whether faced by academic or social challenges, children and teens with ADHD are quick to experience frustration. Their impulsivity in thinking, difficulty concentrating, and short attention span cause them to quickly act rather than thoughtfully evaluate ways of responding to their anger.

Diagnosis requires a thorough assessment that includes an evaluation of the child and observations reported by those who interact with the child on a daily basis, including teachers, parents, day care workers, coaches, or others. Early diagnosis is essential, as children with this disorder often develop a range of emotional difficulties secondary to the symptoms of ADHD. In time, without proper treatment, such children may experience challenges to their self-worth based on the impact of this disorder on their daily functioning.

Children and teens with ADHD can benefit from a variety of therapies that may include medication, psychotherapy, parent guidance, and behavioral reward programs. Several points should be kept in mind when teaching anger management to children and teens with ADHD: (1) present instructions in steps, providing small amounts of information at a time, (2) emphasize self-monitoring and arousal control, (3) present the information in several different ways—for example, instead of just discussing relevant theory and skills, write it down or present it on posters or flash cards, and (4) be aware of your own unrealistic expectations and how they may impact your attitudes and interactions with your child, especially as it may relate to your frustration with his behavior. Fortunately, there are extensive resources available for helping children with this disorder. (See the Appendix.)

Bipolar Disorder

Bipolar disorder, also referred to as manic-depression, is marked by changes in mood from mania (characterized by high energy, excitability, and elation) to depression. It is a diagnosis that was formerly reserved primarily for adults but in the last twenty years has been more frequently applied to children and adolescents.[11] Mental health professionals have been hesitant to apply the diagnosis to children primarily because the symptoms in childhood do not match those of adults diagnosed with the disorder.[12]

Extreme irritability and emotional lability (changeability) are the most characteristic symptoms of depression and mania in childhood. Children with bipolar disorder are reported to cycle from depression to mania over a period of several days or even several times in one day. Similarly, young children diagnosed with bipolar disorder may have tantrums that last for hours or that subside after several hours only to resume again later that day and again in the following few days.

Children and adolescents with bipolar disorder may demonstrate intense rage that is verbally and physically directed toward peers, siblings, parents, teachers, and even themselves. Such children may appear precocious in the language they use to express their anger. Their rage may seem to have no identifiable precipitant. This behavior reflects the extreme impulsivity and hyperactivity associated with bipolar disorder.

Children with bipolar disorder may experience sleep disorders and may display increased activity such as playing with toys, rearranging furniture, or working on several craft projects simultaneously. They may also experience night terrors. Children normally have nightmares, but those diagnosed with bipolar disorder have intense night terrors involving blood and gore. In contrast, teens with this disorder may use nighttime to experiment with drugs, party with peers, and drive recklessly.[13]

Children with this disorder may use language or behave in ways that reflect a sexual preoccupation even when they have not been the victims of sexual abuse or exposed to sexual activity. Adolescents with this diagnosis may exhibit symptoms that are more like those of adults diagnosed with this disorder. They may be extremely sexually active, with multiple partners.

Children and adolescents with this disorder are extremely anxious. Children and infants, especially, tremendously fear even short separations. Children and teens may be preoccupied with death, separation, and abandonment.

Some children and teens with bipolar illness may hallucinate, typically hearing voices or having imaginary conversations with another person who they report is really present. Most significant, children and teens with bipolar disorder may experience suicidal ideation and act on these thoughts. Their suicidal thoughts may be a part of their depression about having the disorder.

The major challenge in diagnosing bipolar disorder in children and teens is assessing whether the child has another disorder with similar symptoms, only bipolar disorder, or a combination of diagnoses including bipolar disorder. Making this determination may require numerous consultations.

While the child with ADHD may consistently exhibit hyperactivity and impulsivity, these two characteristics are much more erratic and intense in children diagnosed with bipolar disorder. In addition, risk-taking behavior by children and teens with this disorder is much more bizarre and dangerous than that of children with ADHD. The child who is hyperactive may jump around in a room or race down the stairs several steps at a time. In contrast, the child or teen with bipolar disorder may jump from a tree, walk the ledges of a roof, or engage in other activities that reflect a combination of grandiosity, impulsiveness, hyperactivity, and suicidal ideation.

Children and teens with bipolar disorder or conduct disorder (described below) often exhibit rage or aggression. However, those diagnosed with bipolar disorder evidence intense shame or guilt immediately after their transgressions, in contrast to those with conduct disorder. The difficulty in distinguishing between these two disorders occurs because up to 69 percent of children and teens diagnosed with bipolar disorder may at some time also be diagnosed with conduct disorder.[14]

Early diagnosis and prompt treatment of children and teens with mood disorder is essential to reduce the tremendous impact of this illness on their developing years. Bipolar disorder can lead to periods of tremendous instability in basic functioning that seriously impair a child's life.

While no single treatment regimen has been clearly identified, a combination of treatments can help children and teens manage the symptoms of bipolar disorder. The most effective treatment is medication in combination with other therapies such as individual and family therapy and psychoeducation (education about the illness and specific skills for coping with it).

Conduct Disorder

Children and teens diagnosed with conduct disorder exhibit a repetitive and persistent pattern of problematic behavior that may include aggression directed against people or animals, destruction of property, deceitfulness, theft, or serious violations of rules. The diagnosis requires that the symptoms be present for a period of at least twelve months and that the disturbance in behavior causes clinically significant impairment in social, academic, or occupational functioning.[15] These children and teens demonstrate severe difficulties with anger and aggression. They may exhibit any of the following:

Aggression to people and animals
- Often bullies, threatens, or intimidates others.
- Often initiates physical fights.
- Has used a weapon that can cause serious physical harm to others (e.g., a bat, brick, broken bottle, knife, gun).
- Has been physically cruel to people.
- Has been physically cruel to animals.
- Has stolen while confronting a victim (e.g., mugging, purse snatching, extortion, armed robbery).
- Has forced someone into sexual activity.

Destruction of property
- Has deliberately engaged in fire setting with the intention of causing serious damage.
- Has deliberately destroyed others' property (other than by fire setting).

Deceitfulness or theft
- Has broken into someone else's house, building, or car.
- Often lies to obtain goods or favors to avoid obligations (e.g., "cons" others).
- Has stolen items of nontrivial value without confronting a victim (e.g., shoplifting, but without breaking or entering; forgery).

Violation of rules
- Serious violation of rules.
- Often stays out at night despite parental prohibitions, beginning before age 13 years.

- Has run away from home overnight at least twice while living in parental or parental surrogate home (or once without returning for a lengthy period).
- Is often truant from school, beginning before age 13 years.

These children and teens are greatly in need of skills and understanding regarding anger management. At the same time, those diagnosed with conduct disorder have little or no motivation for such learning. While they could benefit from all of the strategies presented in this book, they rarely are amenable to this kind of help. More typically, they may be required to learn these skills while living in a structured environment such as a group home, a residential facility, or a youth correctional facility. Because these youth are often simultaneously diagnosed with depression, they may receive anger management training in a psychiatric inpatient setting. Behavioral reward programs, group therapy, individual treatment, and family therapy or psychoeducation may also be a part of the treatment approach for youth in these settings.

Antisocial Personality Disorder

Teens may be diagnosed with antisocial personality disorder if they are eighteen or older and have exhibited many of the behaviors described above since age fifteen. However, their behaviors reflect a greater intensity in symptoms. Specifically, they have to exhibit three or more of the following behaviors to be diagnosed with antisocial personality disorder.[16]

1. Failure to conform to social norms with respect to lawful behaviors as indicated by repeatedly performing acts that are grounds for arrest.
2. Deceitfulness, as indicated by repeated lying, use of aliases, or conning others for personal profit or pleasure.
3. Impulsivity or failure to plan ahead.
4. Irritability and aggressiveness, as indicated by repeated physical fights or assaults.
5. Reckless disregard for safety of self or others.
6. Consistent irresponsibility, indicated by repeated failure to sustain consistent work behavior or honor financial obligations.
7. Lack of remorse, as indicated by being indifferent to or rationalizing having hurt, mistreated, or stolen from another.

Those with this diagnosis need a variety of special services that may include the structure of a correctional facility. While their anger is extremely difficult to manage, those diagnosed with antisocial personality disorder often experience their anger as essential for maintaining control and preserving their safety. However, there are new programs, including those based on the work of Aaron Beck, that are proving increasingly successful even with this very challenging population.

Oppositional Defiant Disorder

Oppositional defiant disorder is another disorder very much defined by difficulties related to anger. Whereas children and teens with conduct disorder exhibit highly aggressive behavior and directly violate the rights of others, those with oppositional defiant disorder are defined by a pattern of negativistic, hostile, and defiant behavior. This disorder is defined by attitudes and expressions of anger that are much less severe than those with conduct disorder. The diagnosis is made when four or more of the following behaviors have lasted for a period of at least six months:[17]

1. Often loses temper.
2. Often argues with adults.
3. Often actively defies or refuses to comply with adults' requests or rules.
4. Often deliberately annoys people.
5. Often blames others for his or her mistakes or misbehavior.
6. Is often touchy or easily annoyed by others.
7. Is often angry and resentful.
8. Is often spiteful and vindictive.

The symptoms must reflect a level of severity that causes significant impairment in social, academic, or occupational functioning.

These children clearly need help in understanding and managing anger. Special help in the form of treatment and parent guidance is indicated to help such children and teens gain both self-understanding and the motivation to learn and practice the skills presented throughout this book. The initial focus of effective treatment is on shared exploration and understanding of factors that contribute to such negativism. Such children need individual work to increase their connections with themselves while they are helped to improve relationships in the family.

Substance Abuse

Children and teens abuse drugs or alcohol for a variety of reasons. Such abuse may reflect experimentation, a strong desire for peer acceptance, an escape from intensely uncomfortable emotions, or the influence of genetic vulnerability. Some youth use drugs to escape depression, while others self-medicate to decrease their anxiety. Changing sleep patterns, irritability, a sudden drop in grades, evidence of reduced responsibility in completing chores or caring for siblings, reduced eye contact, increased evasiveness, and deceitfulness are just a few of the signs of substance abuse.

Some children and teens decrease expressions of anger when intoxicated, while others become more aggressive. Although anger may not be the key issue motivating the abuse, it is very much influenced by patterns of substance abuse. While some youth who use drugs may seem relaxed when high, they may be irritable without them. It should also be noted that some of the most severe expressions of anger might occur under the influence of certain types of drugs or alcohol.

∾ ∾ ∾

The purpose of this chapter is to help you better identify conditions that may underlie more severe forms of anger and when you should seek help from mental health professionals. At the same time, it is intended to offer you reassurance that help is available for these children and teens. Locating the right professional to help you with your specific concerns can be a challenge. When you believe there is a need for special support, speak to your family physician, teachers, other parents, religious leaders in your community, or anyone else you trust to help you find the professional guidance you need. A variety of resources is presented in the Appendix.

If your child is involved in psychotherapy, remember that some children and teens really do work better with one therapist than with another. However, those whose anger is severe and intense may resist every effort you make as well as those made by the best mental health professional. It took children and teens who exhibit severe difficulties with anger time to develop their habits, and they will need time, support, structure, limit setting, and connection if they are to actively take a part in their treatment.

Recognizing the signs of severe anger will prepare you for a more timely response to your child's needs. Trust yourself when you believe special help is necessary. Listen to your own fear or anxiety regarding your child's aggression. Just as anger is a signal that a problem needs to be addressed, trust that your reaction may be an indication that further action is necessary.

Be alert to any tendency you may have to overlook, minimize, or ignore your own fear. As emphasized earlier, our own experiences with anger may lead to our being oversensitive or undersensitive to expressions of anger. If necessary, seek guidance to help you clarify your reactions, what you can do to help feel more secure, and determine if your child needs professional assessment. Share your experiences with your spouse or others who are close with your child. Try to continue to maintain open communication and discuss your concerns with your child, but only if he is emotionally available to engage in such sharing. However, at some point you may need to act even without the approval of your child. Make sure you obtain support for yourself as you respond to this complex and difficult challenge.

Conclusion

This book has been part of a long journey that had its roots in my childhood. It was then that I recognized my own difficulties with anger and also a sense of isolation in making sense of and managing it. It took one final incident to prompt me in the direction of more constructively managing anger—an event that clearly demonstrated the interaction of emotions, thoughts, and physical reactions highlighted throughout this book. However, my anger did not end with that event. Dealing with this complex and challenging emotion has been a lifelong process. At the same time, it has been a driving force in much of my work. And it has increasingly become a subject of great concern for many people in a variety of settings.

In the past few years we have heard more and more media accounts of rage in schools, on the road, in the air, and in the workplace. As emphasized throughout this book, these behaviors reflect the most extreme form of anger. However, the mismanagement of anger is destructive to the human spirit, whether expressed in these severe forms or experienced at a less intense level. Individuals in all walks of life at every socioeconomic level—regardless of formal education, and regardless of racial or ethnic background—are faced with the challenge to constructively understand and manage anger. For this reason, teaching children and teens how to make sense of and manage anger should be a top priority for parents, caretakers, and teachers.

We can no longer say that we do not know enough about anger to teach how to manage it. Similarly, we do not need to choose between two equally ineffective alternatives—to stifle anger or to let it all hang out. Instead, as reflected in *Healthy Anger,* we can feel confident to return to the classics in looking for guidance.

> Anyone can become angry—that is easy. But to be angry with the right person, to the right degree, at the right time, for the right purpose, and in the right way—that is not easy.
>
> —Aristotle, *Nicomachean Ethics*

Anger is clearly a highly charged and complex emotion. However, as Aristotle implies, it is an emotion that requires thought and reflection if we are to effectively understand and manage it in everyday life.

Notes

Chapter 1

1. Elliot Aronson, *Nobody Left to Hate* (New York: Worth Publishers, 2000).
2. William Pollack, "Preventing Violence Through Family Connection," *Brown University Child and Adolescent Behavior Letter* 17, 12 (2001): 1, 3–4.
3. William Pollack, *Real Boys* (New York: Henry Holt, 1998).
4. Carol Stearns and Peter Stearns, *Anger: The Struggle for Emotional Control in America's History* (Chicago: University of Chicago Press, 1986).
5. Harriet Lerner, *The Dance of Anger* (New York: Harper & Row, 1985).
6. Mary Pipher, *Reviving Ophelia* (New York: Ballantine, 1994).

Chapter 3

1. Hans Selye, *The Stress of Life* (New York: McGraw-Hill, 1978).
2. Linnus Pecaut, *Understanding and Influencing Student Motivation* (Lombard, IL: Institute for Motivational Development, 1986).

Chapter 4

1. Aaron Beck, *Prisoners of Hate: The Cognitive Basis of Anger, Hostility, and Violence* (New York: Harper Collins, 1999).
2. Ibid.
3. Aaron Beck, *Love Is Not Enough* (New York: Haworth Press, 1988).

Chapter 7

1. Carolyn Saarni, *The Development of Emotional Competence* (New York: Guilford Press, 1999).
2. Martin Seligman, *The Optimistic Child* (New York: Harper Perennial, 1995), 53.
3. Michael Lewis, *Shame: The Exposed Self* (New York: Free Press, 1995).
4. William Pollack, *Real Boys* (New York: Henry Holt, 1998).

Chapter 8

1. Aaron Beck, *Cognitive Therapy and the Emotional Disorders* (New York: International Universities Press, 1976).
2. David Burns, *Feeling Good: The New Mood Therapy* (New York: William Morrow, 1980).

Chapter 9

1. Daniel Goleman, *Emotional Intelligence* (New York: Bantam Books, 1995).
2. Carolyn Saarni, *The Development of Emotional Competence* (New York: Guilford Press, 1999).

Chapter 10

1. Martin Seligman, *The Optimistic Child* (New York: Harper Perennial, 1995).
2. Lawrence Shapiro, *How to Raise a Child With a High EQ* (New York:

Harper Collins, 1997).

3. William F. White, "What Every Teacher Should Know About the Functions of Emotions in Children and Adolescents," *Education* 119, 1 (1998): 120–26.

Chapter 11

1. Herbert Benson, *The Relaxation Response* (New York: Avon, 1975).

2. Ann Jernberg, *Theraplay: A New Treatment Using Structured Play for Problem Children and Their Families* (San Francisco: Jossey-Bass, 1979).

3. Beata Jencks, *Your Body: Biofeedback at Its Best* (Chicago: Nelson Hall, 1977).

4. Lawrence LeShan, *How to Meditate* (New York: Bantam, 1988).

Chapter 12

1. Eva Feindler and Randolph Ecton, *Adolescent Anger Control* (New York: Pergamon Press, 1986).

2. Richard Gardner, *The Psychotherapeutic Techniques of Richard A. Gardner* (Crosskill, NJ: Creative Therapeutics, 1986).

3. Myrna Shure, *Raising a Thinking Child* (New York: Henry Holt, 1994).

4. Feindler and Ecton, *Adolescent Anger Control.*

5. Martin Seligman, *The Optimistic Child* (New York: Harper Perennial, 1995).

6. Ibid.

7. James Adams, *Conceptual Blockbusting* (Menlo Park, CA: Addison-Wesley, 1986).

Chapter 13

1. David Johnson, *Reaching Out: Interpersonal Effectiveness and Self-Actualization,* 7th ed. (Englewood, NJ: Prentice Hall, 1999).

2. Carolyn Saarni, *The Development of Emotional Competence* (New York: Guilford Press, 1999).

3. Johnson, *Reaching Out.*

4. Hendrie Weisinger, *Dr. Weisinger's Anger Workout Book* (New York: Quill, 1985).

Chapter 14

1. William Pollack, *Real Boys* (New York: Henry Holt, 1998).

2. Robin Casarjian, *Forgiveness: A Bold Choice for a Peaceful Heart* (New York: Bantam, 1992), 16.

3. Harold S. Kushner, *How Good Do We Have to Be?* (Boston: Little, Brown, 1997), 9.

4. Michael McCullough et al., *Forgiveness: Theory, Practice and Research* (New York: Guilford Press, 2000).

5. Redford Williams and Virginia Williams, *Anger Kills* (New York: Random House, 1993), 149.

6. John Bradshaw, *Healing the Shame That Binds You* (Deerfield Beach, FL: Health Communications, 1998).

7. Mick Jagger, "You Can't Always Get What You Want," in *The Rolling*

Stones: Hot Rocks 1964–71 (New York: Abkco Music, 1986).

Chapter 15

1. Harvey Parker, *Behavior Management at Home* (Plantation, FL: Specialty Press, 1995).

2. R. Dreikurs and L. Grey, *A Parent's Guide to Child Discipline* (New York: Hawthorne/Dutton, 1970).

Chapter 16

1. Ann Jernberg, *Theraplay: A New Treatment Using Structured Play for Problem Children and Their Families* (San Francisco, CA: Jossey-Bass, 1979).

Chapter 17

1. James Averill, "Studies on Anger and Aggression: Implications for Theories of Emotion," *American Psychologist* 38 (1983): 1145–60.

2. Raymond Novaco, "The Function and Regulation of the Arousal of Anger," *American Journal of Psychiatry* 133 (1976): 1124–28.

3. Aaron Beck, *Prisoners of Hate: The Cognitive Basis of Anger, Hostility, and Violence* (New York: HarperCollins, 1999).

4. American Psychiatric Association, *Diagnostic and Statistical Manual of Mental Disorders*, 4th ed. (DSM-IV-TR) (Washington, DC: American Psychiatric Association, 2000).

5. Beck, *Prisoners of Hate.*

6. American Psychological Association, *Warning Signs of Teen Violence* (Washington, DC: American Psychological Association, 1999).

7. Richard Hall et al., "Suicide Risk Assessment: A Review of Risk Factors for Suicide in 100 Patients Who Made Severe Suicide Attempts," *Psychosomatics* 40 (1999): 18–27.

8. D. Birmaher et al., "Childhood and Adolescent Depression," *Journal of American Academy of Child and Adolescent Psychiatry* 35 (1996): 1427–39.

9. "Depression in Children and Adolescents: A Fact Sheet for Physicians," National Institutes of Health publication no. 00-744, September 2000.

10. Martin Seligman, *Learned Optimism* (New York: Pocket Books, 1998).

11. Jan Fawcett et al., *New Hope for People with People with Bipolar Disorder* (Roseville, CA: Prima Publishing, 2000).

12. M. Bowring and M. Kovacs, "Difficulties in Diagnosing Manic Disorders in Children and Adolescents," *Journal of the American Academy of Child and Adolescent Psychiatry* 31 (1992): 611–14.

13. Demitri Papolos and Janice Papolos, *The Bipolar Child* (New York: Broadway Books, 1999).

14. M. Kovacs and M. Pollack, "Bipolar Disorder and Co-morbid Conduct Disorder in Childhood and Adolescence," *Journal of the American Academy of Child and Adolescent Psychiatry* 34 (1995): 715–23.

15. American Psychiatric Association, *Diagnostic and Statistical Manual of Mental Disorders*, 4th ed.

16. Ibid.

17. Ibid.

Resources

Anger Management Education
Bernard Golden, Ph.D.
Website: www.angermanagementeducation.com

American Association of Child and Adolescent Psychiatry
3615 Wisconsin Avenue, NW
Washington, DC 20016
Phone: 1-202-966-7300
Web site: www.aacap.org

American Foundation for Suicide Prevention
120 Wall Street, 22nd floor
New York, NY 10005
Phone: 1-888-333-2377
Website: www.afsp.org

American Psychological Association
750 First Street, NW
Washington, DC 20002
Phone: 1-202-336-5700 or 1-800-374-3120
Website: www.helping.apq.org/warningsigns

Child and Adolescent Bipolar Foundation
Website: www.cabf.org

National Mental Health Association
1201 Prince Street
Alexandria, VA 22314
Phone: 1-800-969-6642
Fax: 1-703-684-5968
Website: www.nmha.org

Children of Violence
Website: www.erickson.edu
A program to prevent violence and help children who have been exposed to violence.

Safe Havens Training Project
Website: www.misterrogers.org
A program to assist parents and teachers in helping children who have witnessed violence.

Movies

For Teens

The Breakfast Club / Director: John Hughes / Universal, 1985
Portrays a group of students forced to serve detention together. Each student describes a variety of factors that have contributed to his or her anger and the underlying pain and hurt. Their discussions and behavior reflects the range of constructive and destructive strategies for managing anger.

Anne of Green Gables / Director: Kevin Sullivan / Sullivan Films, 1985
A coming-of-age movie that depicts the emotional growth of a young girl from her early adoption through her beginning career in teaching. It is a lesson about developing confidence and love in relationships and includes examples of managing resentment and conflict.

Rudy / Director: David Anspaugh / Coliseum/Tristar Video, 1993
A young man's struggle to overcome hardships faced in his challenge to be accepted on a college football team. In part, the movie depicts how he channels his energy in constructive ways to overcome frustration and anger related to his quest.

Ordinary People / Director: Robert Redford / Universal, 1980
An emotionally intense movie about a young man who experiences survivor's guilt related to his brother's death. In exploring his reactions, he is helped to recognize, understand, and better manage conflicts and anger related to his parents.

What's Eating Gilbert Grape / Director: Casse Hallstrom / Paramount, 1994
This movie portrays the range of emotions, including anger, in a family challenged by a mother who is depressed, overweight, and withdrawn. It presents an extremely moving portrayal of how the children and teens deal with this situation and its impact on their lives.

American X / Director: Tony Kaye / New Line Cinema, 1997
An extremely intense and graphic movie depicting violence related to racism and hatred. At the same time, it offers understanding into how the experience with violence can shape violence and racist attitudes.

October Sky / Director: Joe Johnston / Universal, 2000
A delightful story of a boy who follows his dreams to be involved in space exploration. This movie, based on a true story, depicts how he managed his anger and frustration related to failures and a lack of support in his endeavors.

Publications

For Younger Children

Agassi, Martine. *Hands Are Not for Hitting*. Minneapolis: Free Spirit, 2000.

Bang, Molly Garrett. *When Sophie Gets Angry—Really, Really, Angry ...* New York: Scholastic Trade, 1999.

Crary, Elizabeth. *I'm Furious*. Seattle, WA: Parenting Press, 1996

Whiteouse, Eliane, and Warwick Pudney. *A Volcano in My Tummy: Helping Children to Handle Anger*. Gabriola Island, BC, Canada: New Society Publishers, 1996.

Attention Deficit Disorder

Amen, Daniel. *Healing ADD: The Breakthrough Program That Allows You to See and Heal the Six Types of ADD*. New York: G. P. Putnam's Sons, 2001.

Flick, L. *ADD/ADHD Behavioral Change Resource Kit*. West Nyack, NY: The Center for Applied Research in Education, 1998.

Hallowell, E. and J. Ratey. *Driven to Distraction: Recognizing and Coping with Attention Deficit Disorder from Childhood Through Adulthood*. Bethesda, MD: Touchstone, 1995.

Wender, P. *Attention Deficit Disorder in Children, Adolescents and Adults*. New York: Oxford University Press, 2000.

Distributors of Resources for Parents, Teachers and Therapists

Courage to Change
P.O. Box 1268
Newburgh, NY 12551-1268
Phone: 1-800-772-6499

Play2Grow
4 Berkeley Street
Norwalk, CT 06850
Phone: 1-800.238-2702
Website: www.Play2Grow.com

Bibliography

Adams, James. *Conceptual Blockbusting*. Menlo Park, CA: Addison-Wesley, 1986.

American Psychological Association. *Warning Signs of Teen Violence*. Washington, DC: 1999.

Aronson, Elliot. *Nobody Left to Hate*. New York: Worth, 2000.

Averill, James. "Studies on Anger and Aggression: Implications for theories of emotion." *American Psychologist* 38 (1983): 1145–60.

Beck, Aaron. *Cognitive Therapy and the Emotional Disorders*. New York: International Universities Press, 1976.

———. *Love Is Not Enough*. New York: Haworth Press, 1988.

———. *Prisoners of Hate: The Cognitive Basis of Anger, Hostility, and Violence*. New York: HarperCollins, 1999.

Benson, Herbert. *The Relaxation Response*. New York: Avon, 1975.

Bowring, M., and M. Kovacs. "Difficulties in Diagnosing Manic Disorders in Children and Adolescents." *Journal of the American Academy of Child and Adolescent Psychiatry* 31 (1992): 611–14.

Bradshaw, John. *Healing the Shame That Binds You*. Deerfield Beach, FL: Health Communications, 1998.

Burns, David. *Feeling Good: The New Mood Therapy*. New York: William Morrow, 1980.

Casarjian, Robin. *Forgiveness: A Bold Choice for a Peaceful Heart*. New York: Bantam, 1992.

Dowrick, Stephanie. *Forgiveness and Other Acts of Love*. New York: W. W. Norton, 1998.

Enright, Robert. *Forgiveness Is a Choice*. Washington, DC: American Psychological Association, 2001.

Fawcett, Jan, et al. *New Hope for People with People with Bipolar Disorder*. Roseville, CA: Prima Publishing, 2000.

Fein, Melvyn L. *I.A.M.: A Common Sense Guide to Coping with Anger*. Westport, CT: Praeger, 1993.

Feindler, Eva, and Randolph Ecton. *Adolescent Anger Control*. New York: Pergamon Press, 1986.

Garbarino, James. *Lost Boys*. New York: Free Press, 1999.

Gardner, Richard. *The Psychotherapeutic Techniques of Richard A. Gardner*. Crosskill, NJ: Creative Therapeutics, 1986.

Gentry, W. Doyle. *Anger-Free*. New York: William Morrow, 1999.

Goldestein, Arnold, and Harold Keller. *Aggressive Behavior: Assessment and Intervention*. New York: Pergamon Press, 1989.

Goleman, Daniel. *Emotional Intelligence*. New York: Bantam, 1995.

Hall, Richard, et al. "Suicide Risk Assessment: A Review of Risk Factors for Suicide in 100 Patients Who Made Severe Suicide Attempts." *Psychosomatics* 40 (1999): 18–27.

Jencks, Beata. *Your Body: Biofeedback at Its Best*. Chicago: Nelson Hall, 1977.

Jernberg, Ann, and Phyllis Rubin. *Theraplay: Helping Parents and Children Build Better Relationships through Attachment-Based Play.* 2nd ed.. San Francisco, CA: Jossey-Bass, 1999.

Johnson, David. *Reaching Out: Interpersonal Effectiveness and Self-Actualization.* 7th ed. Englewood, NJ: Prentice Hall, 1999.

Kassinove, Howard. *Anger Disorders: Definition, Diagnosis, and Treatment.* Washington, DC: Taylor and Francis, 1995.

Kindlon, D., and M. Thompson. *Raising Cain: Protecting the Emotional Life of Boys.* New York: Ballantine, 1999.

Kovacs, M., and M. Pollock. "Bipolar Disorder and Co-morbid Conduct Disorder in Childhood and Adolescence." *Journal of the American Academy of Child and Adolescent Psychiatry* 34 (1995): 715–23.

Kushner, Harold S. *How Good Do We Have to Be?* New York: Little, Brown, 1997.

LeShan, Lawrence. *How to Meditate.* New York: Bantam, 1988.

Lewis, Michael. *Shame: The Exposed Self.* New York: Free Press, 1995.

McCullough, Michael, et al. *Forgiveness: Theory, Practice and Research.* New York: Guilford Press, 2000.

Novaco, Raymond. "The Function and Regulation of the Arousal of Anger." *American Journal of Psychiatry* 133 (1976): 1124–28.

Papolos, Demitri, and Janice Papolos. *The Bipolar Child.* New York: Broadway Books, 1999.

Parker, Harvey. *Behavior Management at Home.* Plantation, FL: Specialty Press, 1995.

Pecaut, Linnus. *Understanding and Influencing Student Motivation.* Lombard, IL: Institute for Motivational Development, 1986.

Pollack, William. *Real Boys.* New York: Henry Holt, 1998.

Saarni, Carolyn. *The Development of Emotional Competence.* New York: Guilford Press, 1999.

Seligman, Martin. *The Optimistic Child.* New York: Harper Perennial, 1995.

Selye, Hans. *The Stress of Life.* New York: McGraw-Hill, 1978.

Shapiro, Lawrence. *How to Raise a Child with a High EQ.* New York: HarperCollins, 1997.

Shure, Myrna. *Raising a Thinking Child.* New York: Henry Holt, 1994.

Weisinger, Hendrie. *Dr. Weisinger's Anger Workout Book.* New York: Quill, 1985.

Wexler, David B. *The Adolescent Self.* New York: W. W. Norton, 1991.

White, William F. "What Every Teacher Should Know About the Functions of Emotions in Children and Adolescents." *Education* 119, 1 (1998): 120–26.

Williams, Redford, and Virginia Williams. *Anger Kills.* New York: Random House, 1993.

Index

A

absence of anger, 285

abuse and neglect
  aggression and, 4
  depression and, 291–92
  expectations affected by, 44
  forgiveness and, 233–34
  runaway behavior, 90

acceptance
  acknowledging anger, 273–74
  condoning compared to, 227
  modeling, 231
  mourning and forgiveness, 249
  as response to anger, 60–61, 228–32

acknowledging anger, 60–61, 152, 273–74

actions in response to anger, 103

activism, 225–26

adolescents
  anger scenarios in movies, 168
  communication with, 207
  modeling the use of challenges, 142–44
  relaxation strategies, 187, 190
  struggling with control, 18

adults
  children seeking company of, 76
  as children's confidants, 116–17, 154–56, 223–24
  in couples, 49–50
  learning anger management, 19, 26

adverse effects of anger, 29–36

affective development programs, 173

affirmations, positive, 141

age appropriate skills, 26

aggression
  absence of anger, 285
  abuse and neglect and, 4
  anger and, 5, 167
  anxiety and, 125
  assertiveness compared to, 79
  communication and, 206
  conduct disorder, 297
  danger levels, 278
  discussing anger scenarios, 168, 170–71
  incidence of, 281, 303
  lack of empathy, 282

  lack of guilt or conscience, 283
  in news reports, 171
  physical activity as relaxation strategy, 191–92
  physical aggression, 24–25, 58–59, 74, 297, 298
  physical punishment, 263, 279
  problematic anger, 281, 282, 283, 285
  responding to escalating anger, 272, 274
  shame and, 127–30
  substance abuse, 300
  tantrums, 275 (*see also main entry*)
  tension and, 58
  vandalism, 91
  verbal aggression, 24–25, 72–73
  video games, 172–73

alienation, 54
  See also isolation

alliance formation
  managing anger through, 79–80, 101
  promiscuity and, 92
  relational anger and, 84

alternative strategies for anger management, 165, 194–97

American Academy of Pediatrics, 293–94

American Psychological Association, 286, 308

Anger: The Struggle for Emotional Control in America's History (Stearns and Stearns), 14

Anger Kills (Williams and Williams), 241

animal cruelty, 286, 297

annoying others purposely, 299

antisocial personality disorder, 283, 284, 298–99

anxiety
  about anger, 163
  associated with anger, 79, 123–25
  limit setting behaviors, 222–23
  reward programs and, 259
  substance abuse, 299
  tantrums, 275